Corsham Revealed

C000284975

This book 'Corsham Revealed' is dedicated to the memory of all those poor souls who died in the making of the great Corsham to Box railway tunnel (see Chapter 4.)

571

The cover shows the Dry Arch's west side Key stone.

ISBN 978-1-5272-2022-5

9 781527 220225 >

Corsham Revealed

First edition published 2018.

Printed by
Corsham Print Ltd.
Unit 4, Leafield Way,
Leafield Industrial Estate,
Corsham,
Wiltshire
SN13 9SW

ISBN 978-1-5272-2022-5

Please do not venture on private land in Corsham without the proper permission.

© Copyright 2018 Giuliano (Julian) Carosi. All rights reserved.

No part of this book may be reproduced in any written, electronic, recording, or photocopying without written permission of the printer or author. The exception would be in the case of brief quotations embodied in the critical articles or reviews and pages where permission is specifically granted by the printer or author.

Although every precaution has been taken to verify the accuracy of the information contained herein, the author and printer assume no responsibility for any errors or omissions.

No offence is intended towards anyone or towards any family, as most of the information in this book is already available (and has been for many years) in some form in the public domain.

As the author of this book, I have made every effort to ensure that the information was correct at the time of publication, I do not assume and hereby disclaim any liability to any party for any loss, damage, or disruption caused by errors or omissions, whether such errors or omissions result from my negligence, accident, or any other cause. No liability is therefore assumed for damages that may result from the use of any of information contained within.

Giuliano (Julian) Carosi.

Corsham Revealed

Preface: The idea for this book came to me forty years ago, when I surprisingly *beat* my Regis Primary School teacher Mr. Williams in a *'Know Your Corsham'* history competition organised by the Britannia Building Society, who were then based in the High Street. The prize was a small amount of cash placed in one of their Savings Accounts. As a child growing up in Corsham, there were no technical contraptions to keep me indoors. We children created our own adventures by delving into every corner (above and below ground) of Corsham that we could - and even some corners that we shouldn't have! Much later (and sadly much older), after family and work responsibilities had diminished, I renewed my childhood *wanderlust* for re-exploring every square inch of Corsham once again, and in doing so, I found some *even more* interesting places and some more startling facts.

In *Corsham Revealed*, my aim is to share with you what I have found. You don't necessarily have to read this book from cover to cover; you can dip your toe in from time to time into any chapter that catches your fancy. Inside, you will find the hidden, long-forgotten and sometimes mysterious history of Corsham. You *will not* find much on Corsham's usual subjects, such as Corsham Court or the Alms Houses; information on these can be found in many other books. Instead, in this book you will learn about our Roman skeleton, Ice-Houses, the Post Office, the *Rising Sun* explosion, the Poor House, the Whore's Pond, the Corsham Bandstand, a history of Corsham F.C and the Cricket Club, the Regal Cinema, the Dry Arch, the Turnpike Road, the history of the town's Urinals, the Fire Brigade, the death in one of our fields of a famous explorer who discovered the source of the Nile, the great flood of 1935, the Castle Mound at Hartham, twenty seven Corsham Ghost Stories, a Highwayman, the old Libraries, Murders and gruesome deaths aplenty over the years - and much more; in fact, the book contains *55* individual chapters - about Corsham!

Gathering this information required years of research. Many hours were spent *head down* in the brilliant Chippenham and Swindon History Centre in Chippenham trawling though their newspaper archives; interrogation of the internet, purchasing historical books, postcards and maps, and even more hours walking around our beautiful Corsham. The last effort in putting this book together, required six months of sifting through the huge amount of material collected over the past ten or more years, and piecing it all together; to rewrite and produce something that I hope you will enjoy.

Near the end of this book, you will find a chapter on acknowledgements to the many sources used.

When I started this project, it was my intention to dedicate this book to the young girl found in the Roman coffin unearthed at Hudswell in 1942 *(see Chapter 41)*, but it was not until I started researching the building of the Great Corsham to Box Tunnel *(see Chapter 4)*, that I was stunned (and still am) by the number of preventable deaths that occurred here on Corsham's doorstep. Some of those names are long forgotten - but they are now remembered here.

'This book is dedicated to all those who perished in the building of the Great Box Tunnel. R.I.P.'

Now, please let me take you on a journey that will hopefully change your perception of Corsham; but I make no apologies for some of the remarkable and sometimes gruesome findings. Enjoy.

Julian Carosi

Giuliano (Julian) Carosi.

Contents in alphabetical order:

Chapter 1. Accident - Fatal accident in Monks Lane 1787.

Set in the wall in front of the old cottage in Monks Lane (known as Cock Street in 1570) at the edge of Gastard just before you get to Monks Chapel, there is an old stone plaque embedded into the dry stone cottage wall inscribed with the following:

'J.A. Porter killed March the 22 1787. His head was crushed when falling from a cart whilst the horse was bolting.'

The writing on the plaque is slowly disappearing more and more each year.

This is the place where the poor J.A. Porter was tumbled out of his cart and dashed his head open.

J.A. Porter was driving his cart down Monks Lane. As he approached Monks Chapel, the horse was spooked and started bolting down the hill, with Porter hanging on tightly.

He eventually lost control and just before the nearby houses on his left, he tumbled out of the cart, crushing his head. Another hidden secret of Corsham's past.

Gastard seems to be fated with horse and cart accidents, such as on Whit-Monday of 1850 when a young man named Daniel Sawyer in the employment of Mr. Dunsdon of Gastard had a sad mischance. He fell off a heavy wagon loaded with tiles and before he could escape, both wheels passed over his stomach. After lingering for a few hours he sadly passed away.

A Jury returned a verdict of 'Accidental Death'.

Chapter 2. Bandstand - in the Recreation Ground.

Corsham Bandstand 1956

There are still a few of us left who can just about remember the Corsham Bandstand that stood at the very top centre of the Recreation Ground in Meriton Avenue. It was a large square structure with a pointed roof, built of large pillars, stone and wood. Originally, the Corsham Band used it regularly to entertain the crowds sitting on the grass during the sunny summer days. There was an area under the bandstand which children used as a toilet.

The sour urine smell in the latter days was something never to be forgotten!

The photo was taken at a charity football match in 1956.

Below is a short history of the Corsham Bandstand.

1925: The Corsham Parish Council decided that they wanted to build a bandstand in the Recreation Ground adjacent to Meriton Avenue. The Corsham Town Band agreed to pay the costs. With the help of the Parish Council, the £250 building costs were kept down to just £70 by use of local voluntary labour.

1926: The bandstand *(even though it still lacked a roof and stairs to the platform)* was first used on Wednesday 14th July 1926, as a focal point, during the *'Children's Fourth Annual Sports Day'* at the Recreation Field. An article covering the event appeared in the Saturday July 20th, 1926 Wiltshire News but sadly, no photographs of the event appeared.

1927: The roof was finally added onto the bandstand in November. Proper steps at the side, leading up to the bandstand platform, had yet to be added!

1928: The bandstand *'build'* is finally completed. The Corsham Band, had its first practice session there on the 11th July. Afterwards, the Corsham Band *played* alongside twenty-two charabancs of Sunday School excursionists, as they travelled into town via Pickwick Road. This must have been a magnificent festive and a happy occasion for the residents of our *(then very)* small town of Corsham.

This was followed a few days later by the *official* opening of the *completed* bandstand at 5 o'clock, during the 'Corsham Sports Day', on Wednesday 18th July, by Col. A.C. Nicholson from Hartham Park. It was a very hot day.

Following the official opening, the Corsham Parish Council expressed concerns about the illegal use of the bandstand, i.e., that it should not be used as a playground, a toilet, a gymnasium, or for a free-view of the popular Corsham Town football matches taking place on Saturday afternoons in the adjacent field *(now the top of Arnolds Mead),* over the top of the nearby dry-stone wall.

The bandstand was now regularly being used for music, including regular Sunday Concerts.

1931: The Parish Council tried to recoup costs, by hiring out the bandstand to other town local brass bands. But it was uneconomical for bands to travel to Corsham to play on the bandstand.

1939: During WWI as a precaution against enemy bombing, the Parish Council considered using the bandstand as an air-raid shelter. Repeated appeals for voluntary help for this got little response from the residents of Corsham. The County Council started work on the conversion, but this proved unpractical and the idea was quickly abandoned.

1940: The conversion of the bandstand was abandoned, and the building was reinstated. A proper air-raid shelter was built at the bottom of the Recreation Field instead.

A large influx of London evacuees into Corsham at the time brought an increase in juvenile delinquent behaviour (to that already existing in the town!) Some damage to the bandstand and to the Band's instruments stored in the Methuen School (opposite the Alms Houses) was reported.

1942: The Royal Army Ordinance Corps gave a concert in the bandstand during the summer, as well as in the High Street on Christmas day.

1954: Some repairs were made, but the bandstand was now rarely used for its designated purpose.

1958: After many years of neglect, the bandstand was in a poor shape and little used, and was finally demolished. No sign of the bandstand remains today.

An interesting aerial photo of the bandstand's location can be found on the 'Britain from Above website here: *http://www.britainfromabove.org.uk/image/epw033512*

Chapter 3. Batters.

On the south side of Corsham, between the Pound Pill and the Ladbrook Lane bridges, lies approximately 1.5 hectares of narrow woodland called the *'Batters'*, which runs alongside the Great Western railway line. The Batters is owned by Corsham Town Council and has footpaths linking Prospect/Pound Pill with Brook Drive. Although there is no river in the town itself, the Ladbrook stream rises to the south and flows through modern housing eastwards through the Batters and out to the parish to Lacock where it flows into the River Avon. The Batters can be accessed from the west via the long footpath commencing at the end of the Pound Pill bridge, or via a shorter footpath at the east end alongside Brook Drive on the Prospect estate. A beautiful haven has been created here for wildlife, along with a tinkling stream which is always a joy to walk beside in any season.

This strip of 'hilly' overgrown wild piece of scrubland has had many uses since its creation as the result of; (a) the dumping ground for the thousands of tons of soil, excavated as part of the embankment leading into the building of Box Tunnel (between June 1838 and the last day of June 1841), and (b) later as a part of the development of the Broadmead/Brook Drive Prospect estate in the mid-1900s.

Previous to this, the only two things of note in this area of Corsham were;

(1) the old Corsham Tannery of the early 19th century originally set up by William and Uriah Goold (situated in the valley alongside the Ladbrook stream behind what are now the cluster of cottages on the Chippenham side of the Pound Pill Bridge; and (2) just beyond the cottages at the bottom of Pound Pill, an old stone quarry, now long hidden by trees.

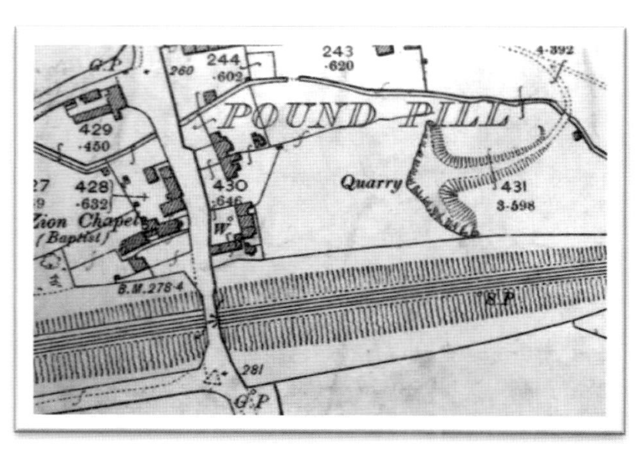

'The Ways of Corsham' book by John Poulsom, shows the word *Batters* = 'Railway Embankments'. This is in line with an obscure 1540/50s origin of the word *batter* = 'of the face of a wall or the upward slope on the face of a wall'. The noun = 'the slope of the face of a wall that recedes gradually backwards and upwards'; and the verb = (intransitive) 'to have such a slope'. Another first known use of the word *'batter'* (in 1743) = 'a receding upward slope of the outer face of a structure'.

Nearly eighty years after its construction, the 'Batters' was put to good use in 1915/1916 for trench building exercises by the Scots Guards before they went off to war on the Western Front. It was reported at the time that they had transformed the area into a miniature 'front', with trenches, dugouts, redoubts etc., after which they carried out many interesting night attacks.

Some of the trench building also took place just to the south of the Batters, in an open field where the Ludmead Road, Broadmead, Brook Drive and Woodborough Road houses stand today.

In February 1916 a Battalion Training Company was formed at Corsham and three detachments were sent here for periods of intensive training of about one month each. The Scots Guards were temporarily billeted in Corsham, in tents on the Corsham Court estate whilst they completed their training. Paul Sanford Methuen, 3rd Baron Methuen (1st September 1845 - 30th October 1932) the owner of Corsham Court was their Colonel in Chief. He was appointed colonel of the Scots Guards in 1904, then General, and in June was given the command of the IV Army Corps. He became instrumental in helping raise the standards of training of the British Expeditionary Force in 1914.

The trench digging activity gave greater credence to the area's name, as it fitted in nicely with '**Battery**' = a fortified emplacement for heavy guns: anti-aircraft missile batteries; a mobile battery of 105 mm guns. Put the two words 'BATTERS (embankment) and BATTERY (of guns)' together, and that is why this area of Corsham was called the *'Batters'*.

Officer's Dugout in the Corsham Batters.

In 1965 the Town Council tried to purchase this piece of land from British Rail, but were outbid by local Mr Frank Smith. In 1967 the land was generously gifted to the Council by Mrs F W Smith.

In 1968 a proper footpath was constructed and the woodland substantially tidied up, with the commencement of proper fencing being provided to stop children straying onto the railway line and squashing old pennies on the rail track.

The following year, the fencing company went into liquidation with the job only half done! Some of the new fencing was ripped out, presumably by those who wanted easy access to rabbits on the embankment to continue. The wire mesh safety panels were also removed from the bridge over the stream. These all had to be replaced.

In 1970 the neighbours were unhappy with the fencing at the bottom of their gardens, and with cyclists continuously passing by. Other neighbours deposited rubbish of all types onto the site, and whole sections of the railway fence were ripped out once again.

In 1975 several large trees had to be felled due to Dutch Elm disease - a few providing challenging bridges across the stream for the youngsters to balance across!

In 1977 the safety fence on the Batters Bridge was ripped to pieces and had to be replaced once again.

In 1979 the play equipment in the Batters had to be removed after constant vandalism.

In 1984 illegal horse riding on the footpath was stopped.

In 1988 there was an outcry when at times the Corsham sewage system was unable to cope with the town's demand - causing unpleasant consequences with the stream running through the Batters essentially becoming an open sewer!

In 1990 work commenced in the Batters, with undergrowth being cleared and footpaths repaired etc. This was aided by an anonymous donation of £500. Volunteers carried out scrub and vegetation clearance, replanted trees and re-laid paths. The Town Council continues this good work today.

In November 2016 the Batters (i.e. Corsham's Great War training site) was protected with the erection of a centenary plaque as part of a national initiative by Fields in Trust and the Royal British Legion to remember the lives of the Scots Battalions that trained there in preparation of the Western Front in the First World War.

These days, the Batters is regularly used as a 'shortcut' walkway between the residential area and town centre and is an important haven for local wildlife, with the lovely (now) clean flowing Ladbrook stream at its centre. The woodland area now consists mainly of Ash and Hawthorn, with Sycamore and Elm, in varying sizes and condition. Ground flora includes Ground Elder, Wild Garlic, Cow Parsley and Dogs Mercury.

Part of the footpath and brook – classified as a Main River by the Environment Agency in 2004 – crosses through the lower area of the woodland. There are several mature trees here, including significant Wych Elm, along with wildlife attracted by the stream, which has a range of ferns along its bank.

Thankfully the vandalism has all but disappeared, apart from the spray painting of the recently constructed railway bridge over the Ladbrook Road at the east end. It is hoped that the historical importance recently given to the site will deter future problems.

Chapter 4. Box Tunnel.

The building of Box Tunnel is recorded in many books. Hopefully, this version will give you a different perspective. *Photo shows the Corsham entrance with side tunnel to the underground station!*

This chapter is a testament to all the poor lost souls who perished in the building of Box Tunnel. The Newspaper reports of the time were unique in the way that they captured in so few words the horrors of the many who perished - with most of the verdicts being wrongly categorised as 'Accidental Death' at the inquests. A number of newspaper reports covering the deceased appear at the end of this chapter, ***but please BE WARNED, as some of the stories are not for the squeamish!*** These men must not be forgotten, as their sacrifice opened up a whole new world for many.

The following remark made by the Rev. J. East in the 1841 Thursday 29 April Bath Chronicle and Weekly Gazette just about says it all:

'The awful number of lives that had been lost between Bristol and the Box Tunnel since its projection - no fewer than 150! Through the recklessness and heedlessness of responsibility on the part of those who had the power in their hands.'

Had the Health and Safety Executive (HSE) organisation been around in the 1800s, most of the deaths would never have happened. The lack of protective clothing, safety barriers and proper working conditions were the main causes, with the majority of the deaths occurring in the huge deep multiple access Shafts of Box Tunnel.

This chapter is written in three parts:

PART 1. An Introduction.
PART 2. The writings of tunnel foreman Thomas Gale. A unique first-hand insight taken from the 1884 writings of tunnel foreman Thomas Gale, a native of Box, who later, finished his working career as an Office Porter at the G.W.R. Station in Bath because of injury and ill health.
PART 3. Newspaper reports. Numerous newspaper reports, including details of some of the men who perished in the building of the tunnel.

Corsham Revealed

PART 1. An introduction:

When the Great Western Company forwarded their Bill to the Committee of the House of Commons in early 1835 (i.e. the idea of digging a railway tunnel from Corsham to Box), it was duly described as:

'The wildest scheme that was ever brought before Parliament'.

Initially, when it was thought that the smoke from the steam trains travelling through the long tunnel would kill the passengers by the time they reached the other end, it was proposed that the passengers were to be *'dragged up and lowered down the Box tunnel and plane by a rope five miles in length, which must be productive of a dreadful and perpetually recurring sacrifice of human life'.* An attempt to stop Sunday use was defeated.

Opponents to the Box Tunnel project were worried about loss of life or noise when two trains passed. *'No-one,'* it was said, *'would ever go through twice'.* There was a fear that if the brakes failed, the steep slope down into Box village would accelerate the trains in the tunnel and make them reach a speed of 120 mph. Brunel calculated that friction and air resistance would reduce this to 56 mph!

The Bristol to London railway line would commence at, or near a certain field called Temple Mead within the parish of Temple, otherwise Holy Cross in the City of Bristol, to a certain field between Paddington Canal and Turnpike Road in London. A branch line would be included from near Thingley farm in the parish of Corsham to a field near the gas works at Trowbridge (in area known as Islington), from there another branch line would go to the farmyard of Kingston Farm adjoining Bradford-on-Avon.

Before the Box Tunnel route was agreed, the original course was planned to go overland from Chippenham via Pickwick to Box. The entire track would have been above ground. This scheme was not adopted due to the great difficulties envisaged in the disruption of many farms. The tunnel project was substituted and this, in turn, led to the finding of the great oolitic limestone beds of stone. This proved to be a great boon to Corsham as a huge stone trade was developed. An added bonus was that the stone could travel down a natural gradient to the railway sidings at Box and Corsham.

In August of 1836 a contract tender was put out to sink six permanent and two temporary Shafts for the proposed tunnel at Box, near Bath. The Shafts would be 28ft in diameter and sunk principally through stone oolite.

In February 1837 a tender was advertised consisting principally of *Cutting* and *Embankment* earthworks, construction of all bridges and culverts and other masonry requirements and laying the permanent rails of that portion of the railway extending from the east of Box Tunnel (i.e. the Corsham end) to the boundary of the fields No's 18 and 19 near Chippenham - a distance of about four miles and fifty chains. This was a major task as there were many hills to dig through!

On the commencement of the build, not all was running smoothly - for in 1837, several of the contractors were defaulting on their commitments, leaving the poor workmen (many of them strangers to Wiltshire) in a state of destitution due to a large amount of wages being unpaid. These poor men and their families depended from week to week on due payment of regular money. At first, the men resorted to begging in small gangs at the houses in Corsham and Box for food. As a form of protest, the labourers removed carts, wheelbarrows, planks and various tools from the tunnel site and deposited them in the Corsham Market House (now the Town Hall). Thankfully, the poor fellows were helped by the generosity of the people of Corsham and its neighbourhood with the provision of food and money. Many of the men's families depended solely on a large portion of the wages being sent home for their wives and children to survive; some families were now reduced to a state of starvation. One desperate and pregnant wife from Wales came all the way to Corsham with one of her children and was broken-hearted to find her poor husband famishing! The *Company* promised to look into matters without delay.

In January of 1838 contract tenders were released for excavation and completion of lengths of Box Tunnel to be excavated east and west; below are some examples:

- Contract No. 4: Both lengths to be worked east and west from the bottom of the Shaft No. 6 forming a total length of 1375 feet.
- Contract No. 5. Four lengths to be worked east and west from Shafts Nos. 4 and 5 forming a total length of 2400 feet.
- Contract No. 6. Four lengths to be worked east and west from Shafts Nos. 2 and 3 forming a total length of 2400 feet.

The excavation of each section of the tunnel was commenced at the bottom of each Shaft, by digging east and west to meet up with the nearest Shafts. Contracts were let for each section. By February 1838 all the permanent and temporary Shafts had been completed.

The ingress of water was a major problem, particularly in the winter months. Shaft No. 7 was a particular problem, with immense volumes of water seeping in from the surrounding springs. Large steam engine pumps had to be installed to drain out the water, working both day and night.

On the 19th October 1839 a small portion of the tunnel collapsed at an estimated cost to the contractor of £800 (£6,000 in today's money).

At the beginning of 1840 much water was still impeding the progress of the work. Three additional Shafts were sunk to enable the tunnel's progress to be much accelerated.

At the Worcester Natural History Society in June of 1841, it was explained how the final alignment of Box Tunnel was accurate to within an inch. Mr. R. Varden Esq., a Worcestershire Architect and Civil Engineer, reading from the scientific paper entitled. *'The Geological Character of some of the cuttings of the Great Western Railway'*, explained how it was done.

Shafts were sunk as usual and on the brink of each, exactly over the intended tunnel route was placed a telescope which could point upwards or downwards, but once fixed in place would not move in the slightest degree either to the left or right. The tube of the telescope contained two cross-hairs to enable the engineer to fix his eye exactly on the object he is viewing. The telescope was fixed in a position so that it could see a pole fixed at the western end of the tunnel and a pole fixed at the eastern end, consequently every object between the two poles to which the telescope could be pointed to was *exactly* over the top of the trajectory of the tunnel. Once this was set up on the surface, a thin straight stretch of wire was placed at the bottom of the Shaft and stretched horizontally so that it could be seen from end to end through the telescope.

The position of the straight wire was then readjusted to line up exactly with the cross-hairs of the telescope which was now pointing downwards. This produced the exact course to follow and was so precise, that when the *tunnellers* from both the Box side and the Corsham side eventually *broke through*, there was only a deviation of one and a quarter inches from a straight line.

PART 2. The writings of tunnel foreman Thomas Gale: (Photo shows Brunel).

'A Brief Account of the Making and the Working of the Great Box Tunnel' by Tunnel Foreman Thomas Gale 1844'.

In 1880 after spending many years employed in the construction of Box Tunnel, ex-tunnel foreman Thomas Gale relied on a meagre 10s per week sick fund to keep him alive, owing to failing health including grievous asthma. Thomas was persuaded to write out some notes of his experience and this was transposed by R.E. Peach, into a small book, i.e. a pamphlet which was sold at sixpence a copy to financially help Thomas. The book written in 1844 was called, *'A Brief Account of the Making and the Working of the Great Box Tunnel' by Thomas Gale'.*

Below, are some extracts on what it was like working inside the tunnel below Box woods.

Sinking the first *'ventilation and light'* trial Shaft took nearly a year. It took another two years to finish all of the Shafts before work on the actual tunnel could begin. Tunnelling commenced in June 1838 and was finished on time, three years later on the last day of June 1841; celebrated by a day's rejoicing in Box village. It had taken six years in total to complete Box Tunnel.

Thousands of people came from all parts to enjoy the free beer, music and hogsheads given away by the tunnel Contractors on the opening day. In the evening, the principle men of the tunnel were entertained in the Queen's Head. Rail travellers were now able to journey from London to Bristol in about four hours! This heralded the end of the daily horse-drawn mail and passenger coaches travelling along the London to Bristol turnpike road.

In the last six months of the build, to get the tunnel finished by the *planned* completion day, there were about 4,000 men working on it. Work went on apace via two shifts. In the neighbouring villages of Box and Corsham, the workers beds were never cold and empty; for as soon as the dayshift finished, the beds were taken over by the nightshift workers!

The original contractor was Horton, but he failed before the Shafts were finished, and the work was completed by the *Company*, the chief being Mr. George Burge of Herne Bay; Thomas Gale was his Forman. Burge was responsible for the three parts of the tunnel that had to be completely bricked up. The tunnel was all constructed by manual labour along with up to three-hundred or so horses. As many as forty boys were employed to drive the horses. On average, there were as many as eleven or twelve hundred men working day and night to draw up the earth and stone from out of the tunnel up to the surface or otherwise engaged at different works in the tunnel. The machinery for lifting the soil was worked by horse power as the use of steam was impracticable due to the lack of water at the summit of the hill. The daily wages for Burge's workers were: Bricklayers 6s 0d, Miners 5s 6p, and Labourers 3s 6p. The contractors for the Corsham end were Mr. Stothert and Mr. Lewis, but they later gave up after being continuously *drowned out* by water! A sixty-horse powered steam engine was brought in to pump out the water. Brunel's personal assistant, William Glennie, was in overall charge of the whole workings. The bricks were made by Mr. Hunt, on the Chippenham side in the nearby meadows, using a hundred horses and carts to transport the bricks to the tunnel.

Box tunnel is 9,680 feet long. Of the twelve or thirteen ventilation and light Shaft holes, only five remain; the others being arched over and filled up on completion of the tunnel. The depth of the deepest Shaft is about 306 feet, the smallest 70 feet. Thirty million bricks were used, and 414,000 cubic yards of earth and rocks were extracted. Over one hundred men were killed in different parts of the works and in different ways - and many more were injured, some for life.

Note: It is said that Thomas Gale overestimated the number who died. GWR only reported 10 deaths and the local papers only a handful. Others such as David Brookes, in his book 'Journey of the Railway and Canal Historical Society No.142 July 1989' states that there were only 19 fatalities.

If you look at the *genuine* national and local newspaper reports at the end of this chapter - you can make up your own mind up as to who was correct! [Ed]:

Every week, one ton of gunpowder was used and one ton of candles (made in Box) consumed during the time the tunnel was built. On the 23rd January 1849 gunpowder stored in Spackman's shop in the High Street (where Ultra Warm is now), led to the death of owner Mr Henry Spackman when his grocery and drapery shop burn down. Loud explosions due to the gunpowder stored in the attic for use in the construction of Box Tunnel, caused several huge explosions, some being heard eight miles away in Bromham. Henry lost his life after re-entering the building with his nephew, to try and retrieve *'a little of their wearing apparel'*. As the fire reached the stairs behind them, the nephew escaped from an upstairs window but was unable to reach his uncle who was found later with scarcely a feature left on him *(see Chapter 13 for more on this). Photo shows rear of the shop.*

On one occasion, Brunel refused to accompany a contingent of visiting GWR directors as they descended down one of the Shafts, in what can best be described as a wooden tub lowered by rope. Brunel stated that his wife had prohibited him from being lowered down in such a contraption. Halfway down, the *pilgrims* found themselves slipping about in the muddy greasy tub, suspended one-hundred and fifty feet from the dark bottom until the *'blastings'* that had been prepared, roared and reverberated around the long drawn caverns and up through the Shaft where they were temporarily suspended. On their eventual return to the top, more than one of the Directors (who had originally laughed at Brunel's concerns) later received a similar prohibition from their own wives, after describing the experience!

On another occasion, when Brunel was travelling on a shaggy pony at a rapid pace on his way to inspect the shafts, the animal stumbled and pitched the engineer onto his head with great violence. Brunel was taken for dead, but eventually recovered!

For two days each year, the sun can be seen shining through Box Tunnel, providing it was clear of smoke! As railways were little known in those days, the building of the 'Great Box Tunnel' was considered a wonderful undertaking.

These days, it's even more wonderful to contemplate how they ever managed to build it without any mechanical means. The opinion was widely held at the time (even by some doctors) that no passenger could possibly survive two journeys through Box Tunnel. The following public notice soon appeared, regarding the 'Star' coach:

'Persons fearful of Box Tunnel, may go overland by this coach, and then rejoin the train at Chippenham'.

The Railway Hotel at Corsham was also available for the benefit of those who wished to avoid the journey through the new tunnel. As it turned out, the only danger was by the passengers themselves, who lit up foul smelling brimstone matches, which suffocated the passengers inside the coaches as they travelled through the dark tunnel! Thomas Gale continued working with the engineers at the tunnel until 1844. Then he joined the Company's service as a porter at Oxford. During a night shift in April 1852, Thomas had a severe accident, having three ribs fractured and otherwise seriously injured. He came back to Bath as a porter and remained there until 1880 when he was obliged to leave the Company's service owing to ill-health.

PART 3: Newspaper reports. WARNING: Some of these reports are <u>not for the squeamish</u>!

One of the first tunnel deaths reported, occurred in late 1837. Mason John Fowels aged 24 was working at the bottom of Shaft No. 3 at about 8 o'clock on a Friday with several others, when a *banksman [i.e. the person directing the operation of the rope crane]* lowered two stones weighing about three-quarters of a hundredweight, each suspended together on a rope sling. The standard orders were to let one stone down at a time.

About halfway down, they met the skip *[i.e. a cage or bucket in which men or materials are lowered and raised in mines and quarries]* on the opposite end of the rope and entangled themselves, resulting in both stones slipping out of their slings - one of them falling from a great height directly onto the head of the deceased and completely severing it from the body, leaving only the chin attached to the head. The remains of the head were collected the next morning. A brother of the deceased who was working in the same Shaft at the same time was also injured, but not seriously. The jury returned a verdict of 'Accidental Death' with severe censure upon the carelessness of the *banksman* who has received his discharge from the works.

It was a solitary life for the navvies outside of work. Norris, employed in making a cutting at Corsham, was found dead on 1 December 1838, in the hay loft of the Rail Road Inn (now the Great Western) at the bottom of Pound Pill. Chalked on an attic door in the Corsham Almshouse, is the inscription, *'J.C. A man killed on the railroad January 1837'*; the attic probably being used as a cheap dormitory for labourers working on the Box tunnel.

On 18 August 1839 John Howell, an 'aged' man, was crushed to death by an earth fall. Another man named William Vickers died at the Chequers Inn at the bottom of Chequers Hill near Corsham, following and evening drinking beer, and a considerable quantity of gin. Sailor Jack was blown 15 feet onto the air when preparing a shot for *'firing'*, and miraculously only suffered a broken ankle.

A young lad named William Olive slipped and the wagons passed over him slicing off both his legs killing him. John Simpson was burned to death after falling asleep next to a lime kiln. The bodies of the dead were held on the bar of the Tunnel Inn (which acted as a mortuary), now an ivy covered private home on the junction of White Ennox Lane and Boxfields Lane, near Rudloe.

In May of 1838 a man named Giles Long was killed when he fell down one of the tunnel Shafts.

On Friday 3rd August 1838 a serious accident happened to a 19 year-old bricklayer named Day in Shaft No. 3. He was working with two others on a stage suspended 50 feet up in the Shaft on ropes when he unthinkingly pulled a skip (basket) over-laden with bricks which was descending alongside. The construction, not designed for such a heavy burden, suddenly turned aside and precipitated the man to the bottom of the Shaft. A barrel containing cement, which was also on the stage, fell on top of him. He survived and lingered in dreadful agony until Saturday morning when he died. His companions had previously warned him of the danger. The two colleagues involved had a most narrow escape, and were only saved by their dexterity: One catching hold of the *stage* as he was falling and the other clinging round the neck of his colleague, both suspending themselves until the necessary assistance was rendered. An inquest was held at the Box Tunnel public house on the 6th August which concluded with a verdict of 'Accidental Death'.

On 21 August 1838 an inquest was held on the body of a man named Hall from the nearby village of Holt, a *banksman* at Shaft No.8. who came to his death on the night shift at 11 o'clock on Monday evening. He was engaged in lowering the empty wagons down the Shaft. Due to some aberration of his memory, caused partially by drink, he drew the wagon backwards into the Shaft and fell backwards pulling the wagon down the Shaft after him. His death was instantaneous - the distance was about 80 feet with the wagon falling on top of him crushing his legs and arms and the back part of his head to such an extent that his brain was protruding. Another workman at the bottom of the Shaft narrowly escaped death himself (the falling wagon missing him by about three feet), as he was at that moment engaged in preparing to start the ascending wagon. The verdict was once again 'Accidental Death'. The deceased left a wife and five children.

In September 1838 a young boy named Daniel Thomas from Wick Hill, near Bremhill, unfortunately fell into Shaft No. 6 and dropped a depth of about 200 feet. He had fallen into a considerable quantity of water which is thought to have saved him. But his injuries were so serious that he did not survive and he passed away on Sunday the next day. The following month in October, Mr. Hunt, the contractor for the brickwork in Box Tunnel had a narrow escape in Chippenham. He was getting into his carriage at the top of Rowden Hill when the horses took fright and galloped off at full speed through Chippenham. When he reached the Angel Hotel, the horses took a sharp turn and plunged into the canal along with the carriage and Mr. Hunt whose only injury was to his pride on receiving a thorough wetting! On 16 November a fatality occurred when one of the bricklayers employed at the top of Shaft No. 5 was walking near to the mouth of the Shaft on a dark night, when he unfortunately stepped into the pit and fell 290 feet to his death. His head was dashed to pieces by the fall and his bones broken in a most dreadful manner. His body was taken to the Tunnel Inn and presented a shocking appearance. The deceased had just come up to the top of the Shaft to receive some refreshment when the accident happened which precipitated him straight back to the bottom!

Another fatal accident occurred on Tuesday 23 April 1839 to a young man named William Wait aged 18, a native of Biddestone. He had been employed on the *works* for only a few days. When he was working at the bottom of Shaft No, 7, a stone about 45 lbs in weight fell from a loaded wagon as it reached the top of the Shaft. The stone fell onto William's head by which part his brains were beaten out! He died within two hours after the accident. Ten months later in February 1840, William's father Daniel Wait (in the service of Mr. Thomas Little of Biddestone) was employed in pecking the roots of a large tree which had blown down. When Daniel chopped away at the root which was still in the ground, the tree rolled over on top of him and killed him instantly. It required the strength of five horses to remove the tree before the body could be extricated. His daughter was burnt to death a few years since. He left three young children to lament his untimely end.

Verdict - 'Accidental Death'.

On Thursday 23 May 1839 a labourer named J. Sargent was engaged in No. 3. Shaft when a stone of great weight fell from the skiff whilst ascending and struck the poor fellow on the head, killing him instantly.

On Saturday 6 July 1839 a shocking accident occurred at Shaft No. 4. to a man named Falkin who was blasting rocks. Not being aware that the match was lighted he advanced too near when suddenly the mine exploded and the stones cut his head dreadfully. He is now lying in a shocking state and little or no hope is entertained of him.

In October 1839, Joseph Daniels aged 22, a native of Cornwall was blown into the No.4 Shaft in consequence of a trail of gunpowder having ignited accidentally. The Shaft in question is of a great depth and the body on being taken up presented a melancholy spectacle. The symptoms of life were just about perceptible but the vital spark quickly became extinct. The jury at the inquest held at Box before J. Ady Esq., the coroner, recorded a verdict of 'Accidental Death'.

On 15 November 1839 John Walker a native of Bristol, employed at the Box Tunnel was wheeling a barrow over a plank laid across on of the Shafts. He missed his footing and was precipitated to the bottom and killed. A week later on Friday 22 November, Mr. David Lee the sub-contractor of the No. 2 Shaft had just returned from a journey and had descended into the pit to inspect the proceedings of his workmen, when suddenly a piece of timber gave way and fell on his head crushing it to pieces causing instant death. He left a wife and a small family.

On Friday 29 November 1839 Thomas Walker from Bristol was waiting to descend Shaft No. 3 when he asked one of the workmen if he could wheel a barrow of mortar to the skiff, as he was cold. Just as he accomplished it, the wheel of the barrow broke asunder and the poor fellow fell 302 feet along with the wheelbarrow. The back part of his head was smashed to pieces and there was scarcely a whole bone left in his body. He has left a widow to lament his untimely end.

On the 14 February 1840 another fatal accident occurred at Shaft No. 4. Whilst working above ground, Robert Price (a native of Bradford-on-Avon) unfortunately advanced too near the mouth of the pit and fell 296 feet and was literally smashed to pieces. Ten days later on Tuesday 24th, a fatal accident took place at No. 3 Shaft. As the workmen were lowering the skiff filled with bricks, the rope broke and the skiff fell 200 feet upon two men working at the bottom killing a man named Bailey on the spot and very much injuring the other. On Wednesday 25 February another accident took place at No. 5 Shaft. As a man named Osborne was coming up in a skiff, a stone fell from the top which knocked him out of the skiff to the bottom, breaking his leg and arm in two places and very much injuring his head. He was taken to the Bath Hospital, where his arm was amputated. But we hear that there is not the slightest hope of his recovery.

On Tuesday 3 March 1840 another accident occurred at the No. 3 Shaft, which proved fatal for a young man aged 21, George Bailey. Whilst working, some of the tunnel's brickwork gave way and the poor fellow was crushed to death. Shortly after, at the same Shaft, a man named Richard Orborne was descending from the heading to the bottom of the tunnel when his foot slipped and he fell a depth of 20 feet on some rough stones which so mangled him, that on being removed to Bath Hospital, it was deemed necessary by the surgeons to immediately amputate one of his arms at the shoulder. He is now lying in the hospital in a hopeless state.

On 19 March 1840 a fatal accident occurred near the Chequers Inn on the Chippenham road to a young man named James Martin from Corsham. The deceased was a carter for Mr. John May of the Hare and Hounds Inn, Pickwick and was employed in conveying bricks from Mr. Hunt's brick-kilns in Chippenham, to one of the Shafts of the Box Tunnel. Being anxious to arrive at the brickyard early, in order to obtain his load first, he drove rather furiously and being seated on the shaft of the wagon which passed over a heap of stones on the roadside he fell off and both wheels passed over his body, so injuring him that he only survived about three hours. Verdict 'Accidental Death'.

On Tuesday 24 March a man fell down No. 1A Shaft and was killed. He was buried at Box the following Saturday. Another man was much hurt by a stone falling on him at the No.2 Shaft.

On Saturday 21 April 1840 a melancholy accident occurred at No. 6 Shaft to David Neate, a person engaged as a centre-setter. One of the centrons unexpectedly gave way, one of the ribs of which fell across the neck of the unfortunate man, occasioning the blood to flow profusely from his mouth and ears and depriving him of his reasoning faculties. Twenty minutes elapsed ere he could be extricated from his perilous situation. He has remained senseless since the occurrence of the catastrophe, and the injuries are of a kind to preclude any hope of his recovery.

On 4 July 1840 an inquest was held at Box on the body of a man named Picket, whose death was caused by the collapse of one of the supports of the Box Tunnel. The jury returned a verdict accordingly? A fatal accident took place on the morning of Wednesday 15 July 1840 at No. 5 Shaft as seven men were at work sinking the Shaft. The sides of the pit fell in, killing one man on the spot, another died in the course of the day, two more are not expected to recover and another three are much injured.

On the evening of 3 July 1840 a dreadful accident took place at the engine house of the No.7 Shaft to a young man named Sheppard from Atworth. The deceased (who it is feared was in a state of intoxication) had gone into the engine house to lie down. There he fell asleep and during his slumbers he rolled himself under the sway-beam (i.e. a pivoted overhead beam used to apply the force from a vertical piston to a vertical connecting rod) which in its action came down violently on his head and crushed it to pieces.......ouch!

In the middle of December 1840 a fatal accident occurred at the No. 6 Shaft. It was occasioned by the negligence of one of the workman who used a lit flame where some gunpowder was stored. The consequence was an explosion by which the man was killed on the spot! On the evening of 10 April 1841 a fatal accident occurred on the open cutting near Shaft No. 8 to a poor man named Stafford, of steady and industrious habits. It appears the deceased was following his work at a short distance from the place where others were blasting the rock, when a large stone fell on the head of the poor fellow, which so injured him that he survived only a few hours.

On Sunday 23rd May 1841 two boys named Rawling and Aust, residing at Corsham, prompted with a curiosity and daring beyond their years, proceeded to the entrance of that huge bowel of the earth (the Box Tunnel), with the intention of prying into its most secret recesses; but here they were a little opposed by an Inspector, stationed for the purpose of preventing their passing at the Corsham tunnel entrance. Disappointed, yet nothing daunted, they immediately visited the different Shafts, hoping to find some means of entrance.

At an air hole near the No. 5 Shaft they discovered a rope hanging down, and supposing it reached the bottom, (a distance of nearly 280 feet from the surface) commenced to descent, sailor-like, hand under hand, having nothing to trust to but the rope for support.

They managed very well for 100 feet when the rope was found to be so wet and slippery that they could hold on no longer, so down they went at railroad pace about 30 feet, where alas the rope ended! and fell the remaining distance. Happily, Mother Earth, as in expectation of such visitors, had a soft bed prepared of soft blue marl (watery clay and limestone) 5 feet in depth, (formerly used as a well) into which they soused head over and ears; the uppermost boy falling upon the one first down who scrambled out and succeeded in pulling out his fellow traveller. Neither was seriously hurt, considering what a fall was theirs; so changed indeed were they in form and colour that they hardly knew each other. On making their way back to exit by the tunnel entrance, the Inspector on seeing such questionable ghostly shapes approaching, did not wait to demand their business, but started up the rough rock work of the open cutting and fled across the quarries, alarming and astounding the peaceable inhabitants of Corsham with his fears of what he had just seen in the tunnel.

"I heard a sound as of many echoes", and this is a full history of its cause. *Your faithful correspondent, A DISTURBED FOSSIL.*

In the last week of October 1890, three more men have lost their lives at some of the Shafts of the Box Tunnel, by material falling upon them and two others have sustained dreadfully mangled limbs.

In September 1893 the Wigmore Castle *up train* express came off the rails in the centre of Box Tunnel. The driver managed to bring the train to a halt, but unfortunately another passenger train came into the tunnel and smashed into the disabled engine. A dozen passengers in the *up train* were trapped in the wreckage and seriously injured, including two from Corsham, Emily Fisher aged 25 who suffered a contused leg (a bruising/haematoma of the lower leg), and Anne Porter of with a critical fracture of ribs that gave the doctors some concern.

The trapped passengers were fearful of a fire starting. When the engine of the up train was eventually brought out at the Corsham end, its frame was shrivelled like matchwood. It was a miracle how the driver and stoker managed to escape from being killed.

In 1897 a 22 year old man named William Beard, a labourer aged 21 from Biddestone, met his death while working 150 yards inside Box Tunnel. He was working with his colleagues J. Hemmens and W. Hayes relining the roof, when the 6:40 ex-Corsham goods train came along the track.

They stepped away from the rails to let the train pass but when it was only five or six yards away, Beard pressed his hand on the breast of Hemmens and suddenly sprang over the line, evidently trying to drag down a dangling rope which they had been using for hoisting up the mortar bucket. He apparently fancied that it would somehow interfere with the train. One of the train's buffers stuck Beard's head. Even though the train had only been travelling about 7 miles an hour he was dragged underneath. Beard's corpse lay on the line about seventeen yards away, with his head across the metals. His neck was broken, a leg fractured and he was cut about the shoulders. He lost his life from an excess of duty, fearing that an accident would happen to the train if the rope remained hanging down. What makes this accident sadder is that Beard was the mainstay at his home where he resided with his widowed mother, grandfather and grandmother.

Chapter 5. Brewers Yard Quarry

In the *Rudloe Firs* wood at the very top of Box Hill, there was once a huge water tower *(much higher than the replacement tower standing there today).* Several huge metal water tanks were suspended high up in the air on long legs of criss-crossed iron. In the same wood, is a very steep, slippery and narrow rubble-strewn inclined shaft that leads into the small underground quarry called *Brewer's Yard.* Mr Brewer had worked on the Box Tunnel excavations some forty years earlier. The entrance is fenced off these days, as the incline is too dangerous to descend without proper equipment. The underground workings are on two different levels, with a shaft passing through to both levels. The bottom level is accessed by a flight of stairs cut into the rock. The roof of the quarry has collapsed in several places!

[Ed] In the 1960s as a teenager, Mick Walsh *(from Rudloe)* and I used to regularly explore this underground quarry; but prior to descending the incline shaft, we would climb up the long ladder to the very top of the water towers. Once up, we would *dare each other* to jump between the separate tanks (a leap of about two metres) with a drop of about 60 odd feet if you failed to make it! The leap was made the more dangerous, by the fact that the tops of the metal tanks were completely rusted through in many places! Thankfully, the tanks have long since been replaced with access denied to its top.

The climb down the long narrow Brewer's Yard quarry entrance shaft was always made in trepidation in the summer, as we knew that once halfway down, the *Bats* would hear us, and would come streaming out in their hundreds. On several occasions, we had to lie on the ground in the narrow shaft for at least five minutes and cover our heads as they flew over us. It was not an experience for the faint-hearted! We never knew who were the most frightened, the *Bats* or us!

You also had to be careful not to dislodge too many stones on the way down the incline shaft, in case they blocked off the small exit passage into the quarry at the very bottom of the slope. Near the bottom of the slope shaft, is the opening to a round vertical shaft *(see photo Courtesy of Steve Higgins www.higgypop.com)* that opened out onto the blue skies above; this has long since been capped off in the woods above. The shaft would originally have been used to remove stone from both levels up to the surface.

Corsham Revealed

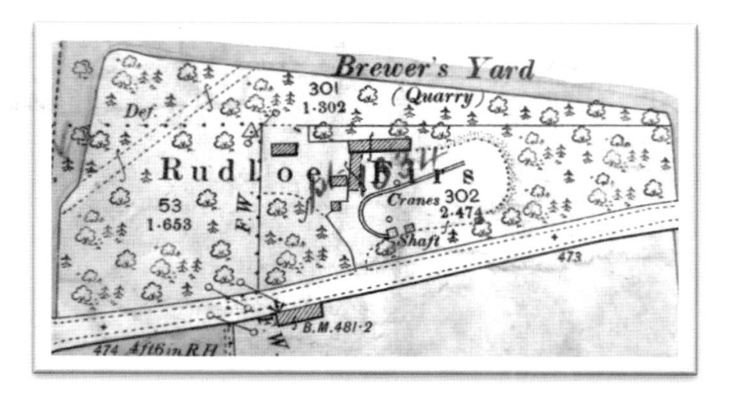

At the bottom of the shaft, were the contents of the Rudloe Council Estate rubbish of many years, e.g. old beds, mattresses, fridges and prams etc. some of the rusted frames are still there now! Once, somebody set fire to a double bed mattress which lay on the top, and it took many weeks for the smoke to stop funnelling out of the shaft!

The unique Brewer's Yard quarry was worked around 1880 and has two distinct levels. From the bottom of the sloping entrance shaft which leads to level one, access to the second level is via the narrow flight of stairs, but there was a lot of rubble and infilling to contend with.

On our first visit, when we explored the higher level, we turned a dark corner and almost fell down into the vertical interconnecting shaft *(which we were unaware of!)*. Our means of illumination, were long thin pieces of white Perspex, purloined from the waste heap of a local factory *(we could not afford torches or batteries in those days)*. The burning Perspex smelled awful and the light was minimal to say the least! [Ed] The memory of this shaft and the thought of nearly falling down it has remained like a *deep saw blade gouged into the quarry walls of my memory.* In the gloom across the other side of the shaft, you could see other tunnels, leading into the black darkness beyond, *like the entrance to Hades*.

In the lower level of the quarry, many sawn blocks of Bath stone are stacked up but were never removed; this was possibly due to a partial collapse at the smaller shaft in the centre of the mine which prevented the safe removal of the stone blocks.

When I recently discovered the photo of the shaft (*courtesy* of *Derek Hawkins'* book, *'Subterranean Britain, Bath Stone Quarries)* it brought back all my nightmares, especially seeing dear old Mick Walsh's initials **(MW)** which can clearly be seen on the left brim of the drop! ***R.I.P. Mick.***

Chapter 6. Castle - Tumulus/Mound Hartham.

(Motte castle 150m south of Jubilee Wood in Hartham Park, Corsham.)

Hartham *(mentioned in the Doomsday book)* was previously the site of a medieval manor house *(Hartham Manor)* probably being where the current Hartham Park house now stands.

The only current sign of anything remaining from that era is the Hartham Castle Mound.

Mounds *(known also as 'tumulus')* were once thought to be the defence posts of pre-Conquest occupying invaders, i.e. medieval fortifications introduced into Britain by the Normans.

Such a mound can be found a quarter of a mile to the north of the wooden Stické Court and the Tyning Wood at Hartham Park in Corsham.

The location is Latitude 50° 27' 1.26" N; Longitude 2° 12' 21.78"W

The grid reference is: ST 8948 7336 (map quarter sheet ST87SE) which is part of the Chippenham Without Civil Parish. The nearest postcode is SN13 0RN.

The mound, amidst much worked oolite stone could probably have been a mediaeval timber-castle mound, but there are no signs of a bailey or moat *(Lindley).* It has been described as a Rejected Timber Castle *(Motte)* as there are some earthwork remains. It could also have been a barrow, a windmill mound, a medieval mill mound, or even the base for a gazebo.

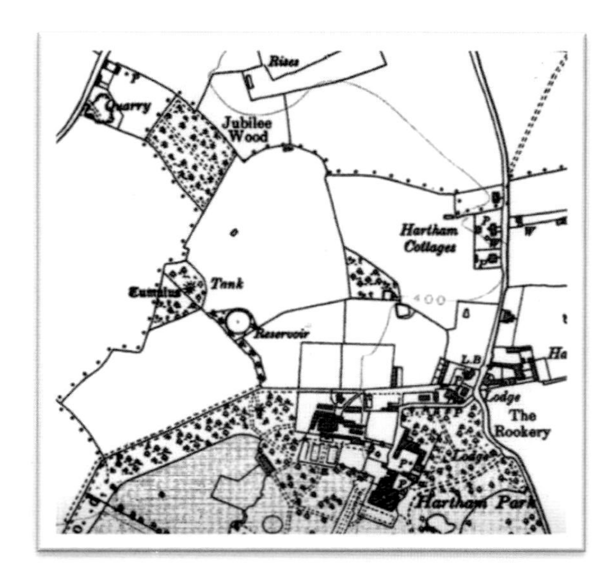

The mound, is described as a 'Tumulus' in the 1828 *(1st edition Ordinance Survey Map)* and in the 1837 *(Tithe map)* as being unenclosed and part of the Great Rookery field.

1923 map shows *Tumulus, Tank* and the *Reservoir.*

The mound composed of earth and oolite rubble, is 25.0m in diameter at the base, 9.0m across the flat top and 3.4m high, *(i.e. 30 paces in diameter and about 10 ft high)* of conical appearance with a small flat top and is situated inside a small copse of undergrowth and Beech trees 150m south of Jubilee Wood, Hartham Park. A large Beech tree now stands guard on the very top! Locations of motes being built near settlements meant that many were often modified continuously after their military functions had expired. This is a distinct possibility for the Hartham tumulus.

The area is overgrown, and there are also signs of pipe trenching of years gone past. The hidden stone and earth ramp running up the Southern side, gave access to a massive late 19th or early 20th century water tank and pumping equipment which were set upon cast iron pillars *(or a timber tower),* marked by a rectangular depression at the top in the centre with three square concrete plinths over bore holes drilled down through the mound.

There is a brief mention of the mound in the Wiltshire Archaeological and Natural History magazine Vol. 93 p. 115 which exemplifies the problem of distinguishing genuine motes from post-medieval garden features. Although the mound may seem questionable as a motte *(i.e. a mound forming the site of a castle or camp),* it has been classed as a monument *(List entry Number: 1011307),* scheduled under the Ancient Monuments and Archaeological Areas Act 1979 and therefore protected in Law, as it appears to the Secretary of State to be of national importance.

In Hartham House's heyday in the late 19th/early 20th century, water was pumped up from a hydrant in the large Stew Pond (*medieval name for a pond used to store live fish*) at the bottom of the valley in Collett's Bottom Woods near Weavern Farm. The water was pumped up the hill and into a huge water tank placed on top of the Hartham Castle mound. The water then fed a large concrete reservoir some 50 meters south-east alongside the mound.

The reservoir would have been used to nurture the Manor house's plants and vegetables in the huge red-bricked walled vegetable garden *(now just a grassy field)* at the rear of Home Farm.

The left wall of the red-bricked walled garden was built in a strange wavy line design that can best be seen from above on Google Maps. The reservoir is now completely overgrown with trees and shrubs, but there are still clear signs of cast-iron pipe-work and huge chunks of the old concrete perimeter peeping through the undergrowth *here and there.* It's another hidden gem of Corsham.

The Legacy Scheduled Monument Number for the mound is 19044. Historic England (Pastscape) DEFRA or monument number is 208396. Please note that the mound is on private land not open to the public. Permission to visit a site must always be sought from the landowner or tenant *(The Hartham Estate, and Church Farm and Home Farm).* Many thanks to Eileen Cook who *unearthed* this long lost gem and to Kate Jones of the Church Farm Bed & Breakfast for access.

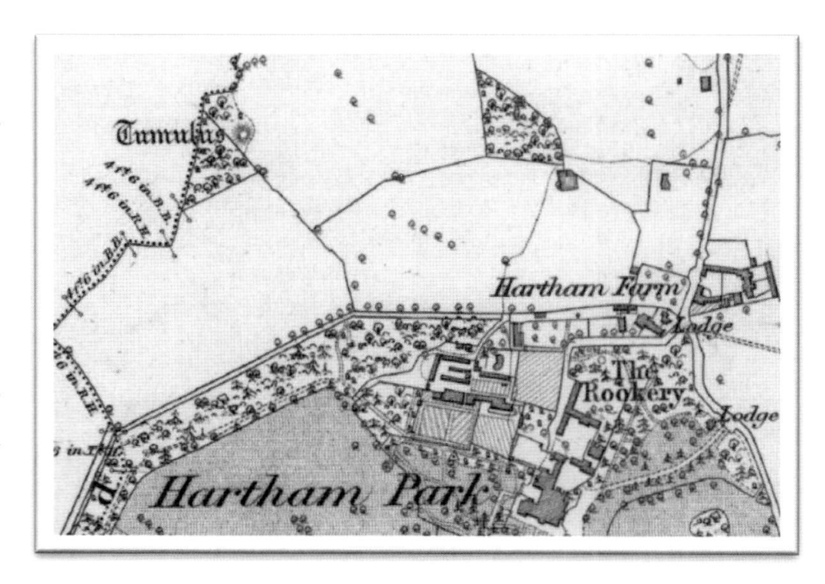

Chapter 7. Cathedral - Corsham.

Getting lost in the 'Cathedral' [Ed]:

'Warning do not enter the Box Caves unless under supervision of experienced guides.'

At the top of Box Hill in Hazelbury Quarry underneath Box Fields, is the *Cathedral* quarry worked by John Pictor between 1829 and 1850. This was created by quarry workers using the old digging method prior to the saw. This involved a 'jadding iron', a bar of iron about seven feet long and seven-eighths of an inch diameter, with a chisel end. Using this, the quarrymen were able to do amazing neat work with just a primitive tool!

In normal quarrying, a vertical shaft would be dug out to reach the best quality stone bed, after which quarrying would continue along tunnels fanning out horizontally; but here, all of the stone beds were excavated as the quarrymen moved downwards. Over the years, this resulted in a vast chamber being created underground, known appropriately as the *Cathedral.* Once the quarrymen had reached the bottom of the bed rock, they continued tunnelling horizontally creating a maze of tunnels, some joining up with other nearby quarries under Box Hill. These stone beds are remarkable in the fact that they exist 70ft-100ft below the surface. The 190 foot long, 100 foot high, thirty feet wide *Cathedral* cavern was a *'must see'* for the local youths of Corsham in the 1950s/1960s.

The *Cathedral* was first started from above ground, by excavating a vertical shaft down from the surface to where the *bed stone* lay. Starting at the surface, the quarrymen would chisel out the first 2 to 3 inches of stone off the roof, using a *picking jad* or long bar together with hammers and wedges. The shaft was then worked downwards and galleries driven off at three levels narrowing into a passage at each end. Stone was pulled out through the roof by chain and jinny-ring (a wooden wheel made of rope and spindle that was pulled round by a horse) that raised or lowered loads up and down the shaft. On the roof of the tunnel entrance at the very bottom of the *Cathedral*, you can see the deep grooves worn into the tunnel roof, made by the ropes used to pull along the heavy blocks of stone and then winching them up the shaft. The *Cathedral* is a supreme example of vertical shaft entry, essentially a shaft which has been widened into a huge bell shaped cavity. Ten feet away from the main shaft opening is a small round opening in the ceiling that was originally an old well, the bottom of which you can see when you are inside the Cathedral. The easiest entrance into the *Cathedral* is via the *'Backdoor'* entrance at the front of a large cliff face which was roughly rectangular before the entrance was blocked off. Now, the entrance is gated off and access inside is via a very restricted crawl through large stone blocks. The entrance leads to the *Cathedral* by a passage called the *'O'* route, and is 200 yards to the North East of Eastgate.

[Ed] On one occasion in the late 1960s, a friend and I accompanied by two girls, decided to visit the *Cathedral* on the premise of what my boastful friend said, *"That he knew the way!"*. We did find the *Cathedral*, but then ended up getting completely lost. Our light source (thin strips of burning noxious 'Moon Aircraft' Perspex from their waste pile at the rear of the factory in Beech Road) was beginning to run out. Unbeknown to us, a group of our friends had decided to wait for our return by the quarry entrance. For some unknown reason, they decided to light a wood fire by the entrance, and the smoke billowed into the tunnels where we were. We were lost for the best part of an afternoon and beginning to panic, as the density of the smoke was hindering our feeble and diminishing light. In the end, I decided to head in the direction where the smoke was coming from, in the hope that my *'Tonto'* instinct would eventually lead us to the exit. At one stage, we had to squeeze through a very narrow tunnel, but eventually we did surface coughing and with blackened faces from the smoke.

[Ed] I leave you to imagine the words exchanged with our friends for their stupidity, and I hope that my God forgives me for a temporary lapse in my faith.

I revisited the *Cathedral* on a guided tour a couple of years ago. It's almost 50 years since I was last there! And it's just as scary! But when the sun shines down the shaft and lights up the chamber, it still looks magical.

The above, is just a very small taste of what we (the local Corsham youths) used to get up to, in the vast Corsham underground in the 60s and 70s.

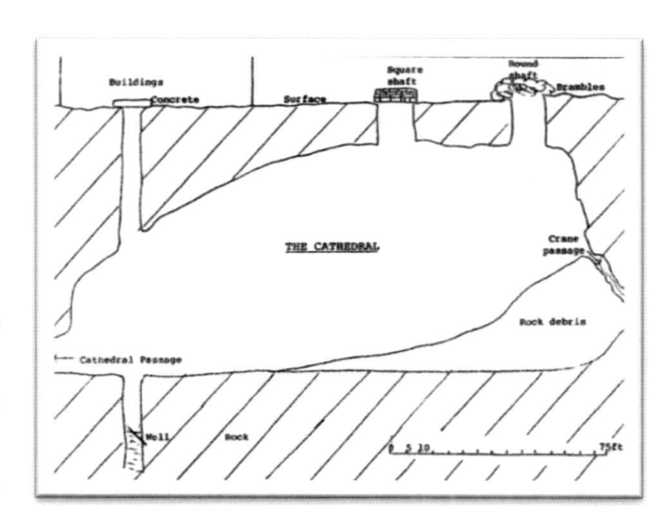

In the Box Woods at the top of Quarry Hill, there were many deep open pits and several underground cave entrances. Most of these have now been filled in, but there are still one or two open entrances there. In the sunshine, this wood is a beautiful place to walk, as the light streams in through the leafy canopy. But deep below, there are miles and miles of maze-like tunnels under the floor of the wood. It's now a very dangerous place where roof collapses are becoming more prevalent. It's not a place that I would want my grandchildren to explore on their own!

'Warning do not enter the Box Caves unless under supervision of experienced guides.'

Chapter 8. Charabanc Trips.

Here is a lovely *postcard* photograph taken at the corner of the High Street where it meets Pickwick Road - of twenty or so Corsham people on 16 June 1913, getting ready on the local charabanc *(often pronounced "sharra-bang" in colloquial British English)*, for a daytrip to Wells, Cheddar, and Burnham-on-Sea. In the photo are Herbert Head, Harry Wait and Mr. Spackman standing centre.

Charabanc outings were popular at the time, and were the result of commercial use of First World War surplus lorry chassis being fitted with charabanc bodies. The body was built separately to the motor chassis, thereby allowing a second *goods body* to be fitted in its place during winter, thus keeping the vehicle commercially occupied. This was a big business in the post war years. Charabancs were hired from Crook's of Melksham and also from Brownings the haulage firm at Box, *(whose charabanc served as a coal lorry on other days.)* Charabancs were usually open-topped, with hard wooden *'benched'* seats arranged in rows, looking forward - with each row having its own door on the near side of the vehicle. They were especially popular for sight-seeing or 'works outings' to the country or to the seaside, organised by businesses once a year. The name derives from the French *char à bancs* ("carriage with wooden benches").

If you were prone to being nauseous, charabancs were not the transport for you, as they were noisy, uncomfortable, smelly and often poorly upholstered with low-backed seats! After a long trip, one can only imagine the state of the traveller's bottoms after a day spent traversing the bumpy roads of the early 1900s! They sometimes had a large canvas folding hood stowed at the rear in case of rain, which offered little or no protection to the passengers in the event of the vehicle overturning, particularly if overloaded and traversing down the steep and winding roads leading to the coastal villages popular with tourists. The vehicle had to stop for the hood to be raised, with each row of passengers helping to manoeuvre it forward as it reached them, before it could be fixed onto the front windscreen. The back seat was the most sought after, as it offered some protection from the rain. Those seated on the front seat alongside the driver - took the full force of any bad weather!

If you were lucky to have any side windows, they were made of thin mica which was a contributory factor in fatal accidents - *which in turn, contributed to the early demise of charabancs.*

The following is a typical description of one of the Corsham trips: **Choir Outing 16th June 1913.** On Monday, favoured by beautiful weather the whole day, one of the most popular *(for many years)* of these annual outings took place. So popular was it that upwards of 80 participated, nearly double the usual number. In previous years, only a few members of the choir, Sunday School teachers or bell-ringers had been unable to attend, but this year almost all of them rolled up, and many outsiders joined, making in all sufficient to fill three motor char-a-bancs. The party included the Parish Church and Gastard Church choirs, Sunday School teachers and the Corsham bell-ringers, accompanied by the Revs. H. B. Ellison (vicar), A. J. Winnington-Ingram (curate), and Mr. Lewin Spackman, organist and organiser.

A start was made at the Methuen Arms shortly after six o'clock and Wells was reached at 8 o'clock, where, after a delightful promenade through the Palace gardens, an excellent breakfast was provided for the company at Wickenden's. At 10 o'clock, the choirs attended matins at the Cathedral. This beautiful, dignified and restful service, with the perfect singing of the choir, will long be remembered. Dr. Davies the organist, expected the company and kindly invited Mr. Spackman to his loft during the service. The anthem on this occasion was by Attwood *'Turn Thee again, O Lord, at the last and be gracious unto Thy servants'* and nothing could exceed the perfectly devotional rendering of this composition. Through the kind thought of the Rev. A. J. Winnington Ingram (at one time a student there) some of the party were enabled to visit the library of the Theological College and the Bell-Pulling swans on the moat and the wonderful mechanical clock were observed with interest. About 11 o'clock the journey was resumed and Cheddar was next attacked, the majority visiting Gough's wonderful caves and the cliffs clambered over, and strawberries now in full season, consumed. Here the first check to the programme occurred, one of the motor-char-a-bancs, having had enough of the dusty roads, refusing to continue its journey to Burnham. Strenuous effort on the part of the chauffeur was unavailing and telephone messages were despatched to Bath and Burnham for aid. Car No.1 came back from Burnham and fetched the stranded ones, while a fresh car arrived later in the evening at Burnham and conveyed the party home.

At Burnham the party were regaled with a cream tea at the *'Clarence'* and the usual seaside amusements enjoyed. Owing to the delay with the cars the intended visit to the Clare street (Bristol) Picture Palace was abandoned and the first car left for Corsham at 7.30, arriving home after a lovely drive, about 11 o'clock. Those who prolonged their festivities till a later hour, were not so fortunate, the second and third cars varying the events of the day, one by careering about Somerset, in various directions, giving Weston a call and the other being held up on the road for repairs, so that Corsham was not reached until 2.30. In spite of this, the trip was voted by one and all as most enjoyable, and no little thanks is due to Mr. Spackman for making the necessary arrangements.

Photo shows the Choir outing, on 22 June 1914.

Chapter 9. Cinemas - in Corsham.

Introduction: In its day between 1930-1976, the Regal cinema on Pickwick Road was very popular in Corsham, particularly the Saturday matinee in the 60/70s, where a *supporting* film would be shown first, then an interval where a nice young lady *(Pat Osborne)* would gradually appear out of the gloom at the front with her tray hanging down from her neck, containing sweets (e.g. boxes of scrumptious Toffee Poppets and proper sized Wagon Wheels!), cigarettes and ice cream tubs, all counter-balanced precariously with great skill perched on her hips! The cinema's seats were *'nothing'* compared to the modern cinema seats these days and were guaranteed to give you back ache for the next few days. Canoodling couples used to clamber for the double seats lined along the periphery and the darkest recesses of the back rows were responsible for many local romances in its time, and a lot more besides! The main movie came at the end of the sitting, usually viewed through a cloud of smog from the numerous cigarette smokers.

Canoodling couples used to clamber for the double seats.

For Corsham children on Saturday mornings, 'Zorro', 'The Lone Ranger', 'Flash Gordon' and a variety of cartoon films such as 'Popeye the Sailor Man' with his lover 'Olive' and arch-enemy 'Pluto', were very much appreciated. And if you were lucky, you were allowed to sit upstairs in the tiny balcony to watch the films and secretly drop chewing gum down onto the unsuspecting trendy bee-hive hair dos below! Another popular 'dare' for the young local scallywags at the time, was to crawl all the way from the back to the front, under the seats when the film was showing, with the reward of being covered in goodness knows what! Boys will be boys!

The film industry was vibrant in those days, with fond memories of watching epics such as *'Ben Hur'* in 1959 and the 1964 Beatles *'Hard Day's Night'*, *'Help'* in 1965 and their animated film *'Yellow Submarine'* (1968) still etched into the *'Yesterday'* memories of those of us who where there.

Below is a brief history of the cinema in Corsham.

In the 1920-1930s the Town Hall was often used both as an entertainment venue and as a cinema.

1926: Entertainments in the Town Hall included a concert by the Scots Guards String Band with soloist Mrs. Kelly, entertainment by the Bath Operatic Society, music by F.H. Bowden and the showing of the celebrated recently released film *'Don Q Son of Zorrow'* (the 1925 sequel to the 1920 silent film *The Mark of Zorro*).

1929: On 25 November a film was shown in the Town Hall illustrating a complete day's work in the Bath and Somerset and Wilts Central Children's Orthopaedic Hospital, with the little patients appearing for the first time as film stars, thus providing a lighter side to entertainments. In 1929, Mr. H. Andrews a fairground operator submited plans to build a cinema in Pickwick Road, at the roundabout junction of what is now Newlands Road/Pickwick Road. Mr. Andrews was *'stone deaf'* but coped well with the introduction of *'talkies'* helped by his sons.

1930: The new 350 seater £1,500 Corsham *'Picture House'* on Pickwick Road opens on Monday 13th October, built out of Bath stone and brick by the local builders Osborne and Sons. The Gents toilet was outside, behind the right hand side of the building, next to a small boiler house. On the right of the foyer were the Ladies toilet and a tiny pay box and to the left a staircase that led up to a shallow balcony, with room for two or three rows of seats.

Access to the projection room was up a further four stairs. The cinema was later lovingly nicknamed by the locals as, *'The Flea Pit' or 'Bug Hut'*. The tiny pay box (where you would be encouraged to buy chocolates and sweets), was immediately to the right of the entrance. An iron ladder (under the top right window on the outside of the building), was the fire escape to the outside from the projection room.

'You would be encouraged to buy chocolates and sweets.'

Mr Andrews' sons helped with the day-to- day running of the cinema. Prior to the commencement of the film, the dark interior would gradually glow with an eerie blue/green colour when an electrical charge was introduced into the projector's rectifier, consisting of a large glass bulb with tubes (nicknamed 'the octopus'), which gradually glowed mysteriously and filled with mercury. On the opening night there was a full house, with many others being turned away. The films on show were, *'King Of Jazz'*, a 1930 musical review staring, among others, Bebe Daniels and Bing Crosby.

1934: The cinema was also occasionally used for religious gatherings; such as the *'Peace Ballot'* held there in November and presided over by the Rev. G.W. Hodgson. The audience which included Lord and Lady Methuen were also entertained by Mr. A.C. Osborne's orchestra. Mr. Statford the owner at the time, also laid on matinees for the 'old folk' of Corsham such as the Saturday afternoon showing of 'Love, Life and Laughter' staring Gracie Fields which was attended in November of 1934 by up to eighty senior Corsham residents (conveyed to and fro to the cinema by Mr. J.T. Barley), many never ever having seen or heard a *'talkie'* movie before and thoroughly enjoyed themselves.

In July, Messrs. Andrews and Sons (the owners) sold the Corsham cinema to raise funds for a new cinema to be built by them in Bythesea Road, Trowbridge.

1935: Mr A. J. Stratford purchased the Corsham *'Picture House'* cinema in Pickwick Road and changed the name to *'Regal'*. The Kinematograph Year book of 1947 shows the Corsham *Regal* cinema having a capacity of 320 seats. The population of Corsham at that time was 3,941.

1941: During 'War Weapons Week' 24-31 May in 1941 special services were held in the County, attended by Civil Defence and other services in each town. The objective of the Chippenham District was to generate events that would raise £150,000 in support of the troops and provide equipment. Proprietors were asked to decorate their shop fronts with any money made from events to be sent to the *Air Raid Relief Distress Funds.* The Regal cinema played its part by showing the official *'War Weapons Week'* trailer film prior to performances throughout the week.

1942: Mr. Stratford had plans drawn up for a grand 588 seater Art Deco cinema to be built at the end of the *Tynings* opposite the Regal site but planning permission was not forthcoming due to lack of proper access. The Buildings Committee reported that the site had already been zoned as a residential area of eight houses to the acre, and that the front elevation of the proposed cinema, is unsuitable as the roof would form a very prominent objection and be detrimental to the amenities.

The intruder helped himself by scooping out some ice-cream in the café with his fingers!

Yet just a few years later, this location (at the end of the Tynings) became the entrance to the Corsham School, a much, much larger building than the cinema could ever have been!

1943: Mr. A.J. Stratford the proprietor of the Corsham cinema passes away in November. He had not enjoyed good health for some time. During the early stages of WWII, a building in the rear of Cheviot House was used as a cinema. The proprietor was Mr. Chipperfield of circus fame. The building later became the Corsham Laundry and was sold in September 1941.

Between the years **1946 and 1960**, the Regal had a rival; there was another popular cinema in Corsham, the Hawthorn Cinema situated at the bottom of Westwells Road, opposite to the Basil Hill Army Camp. The Kinematograph Year book of 1947 shows the larger Hartham cinema having 525 seats. Shows were once nightly and changed weekly. The owner was Councillor Mr. J.W. Andrews of Bath.

1948: During October, an intruder broke into the Hawthorn cinema. The cash box had been opened but fortunately only a small amount of money had been left in it. Business records were scattered over the floor and the intruder helped himself by scooping out some ice-cream in the café with his fingers!

1951: Further plans for a replacement cinema were put forward on a site at the end of the Golden Path, behind the houses at the southern end of the recreation field (roughly where the current Royal British Legion Club is today in Newlands Road). Again, this was turned down.

1953: In July, *'The Public Health Committee'* reported to the meeting of *'Calne and Chippenham Rural Distinct Council'* that Mrs. A.I. Williams had called their attention to the nuisance created by litter left on Saturday film nights in Pickwick Road, which caused particular nuisance to the residents on Sundays. The Senior Sanitary Inspector had made inquiries with the County Surveyor with a view to road sweepers undertaking additional work to remedy the nuisance, but the County Surveyor had not been able to co-operate in this matter. The Senior Sanitary Inspector was asked to interview the

Manager of the Corsham Cinema, to try and arrange publicly by a screen notice asking for the co-operation of the public.

1956: Mrs D. E. Tilley, Director and daughter of Mr Stratford, took over the day-to-day running of the town's *Regal* cinema in Pickwick Road. The building was beginning to *look its age* and some upgrades were made to bring it up to the current regulations. A telephone line was fitted. Previously in an emergency, the cinema had to use Mrs Tilley's home phone line, which was in her *Tynings* house opposite the cinema.

1958: On the 3rd August the cinema's projectionist Mr Norman Jefferies, took over the cinema's licence with his partner, June (they later married in Bristol on 13th February 1960). Norman also ran the local Regal Electric Co. They made substantial improvements to the cinema in the early 60's, including modernising the toilets and installing a large CinemaScope screen. The wallpaper displayed a collage of film stars, such as Elvis, Steve McQueen and Humphrey Bogart. The billing was usually three films per week, Monday, Tuesday, Wednesday, then Thursday, Friday, Saturday, and a special film on Sunday. The costs were, 1s 6d in the front 1s 9d in the back where the double seats were, and 2s 6d (half a crown) for a seat upstairs in the tiny balcony.

1960: The stage was altered to accommodate a CinemaScope screen. Norman and June were married in Bristol on 13th February, and then rushed off after the service to open their cinema for the evening performance.

1962: A new false ceiling is installed in the *Regal* to retain heat in the auditorium.

1965: Proposals were submitted to build new modern toilets in the *Regal*, under the balcony in the rear stalls. A new heating system was fitted. The fire officer wrote to Mr Jefferies concerning the lights in the exit at the rear of the building, which had been found not working on several occasions

1966: The *Regal* cinema closes down, as it had become outdated and inadequate and was unable to compete with the much larger modern commercial cinemas in Chippenham and Bath. The closing films were "Von Ryan's Express", supported by "Days Of Thrills And Laughter" screened on Thursday, Friday and Saturday the 7th, 8th and 9th of April.

1969: Mr Jefferies sets about drawing up plans to convert the *Regal* into a twin cinema by building an extension for a second screen at the rear. Work was held up whilst terms were agreed for the purchase of some of the land to the right of the building by the local council for a new junction and road (Newlands Road). Norman and June did much of the building work themselves, with specialised jobs being contracted out to local firms. On 19th June, the cinema reopened under the new name of the *'Corsham Film Theatre'*, with the original *Regal* seats recovered and set out in glorious alternating rows of gold and red. A week of films was shown as a *fringe venue* of the Bath Festival!

1976: The *Corsham Film Theatre* eventually closed on Thursday 8th June 1976, showing *'Mr. Superinvisable'* supported by *'War Of The Planets'*. Norman Jefferies stated that the Corsham cinema was no longer viable and had little local support. When Norman and June closed the 'Corsham Film Theatre', they opened 'Robins Cinema' at St. John's Place Bath (near to the Theatre Royal). The Corsham cinema remained closed and never reopened. And is now sadly gone forever!

Chapter 10. Cricket Club.

THE 1ST XI., 1889.

L. Spackman C. J. Mayo A. C. Kinneir J. Smith W. G. Allard
H. E. Mayo H. Spackman W. Spackman W. H. Robinson
C. F. Spackman S. P. Kinneir

Corsham must have one of the prettiest cricket grounds, reputed to be the sixth oldest in the Country. The Club has always played on the same Station Road field which is owned by the Corsham Estate. The field (previously the Corsham Common) was the site of the ancient Fair which was granted by Royal Charter in 1285. Although cricket may have been played in Corsham for twenty or so years before, no organised Club appears to have been formed until 1848, when the Hon. Frederick Henry Paul Methuen, became its first President. A year later on the 11th September he became the second Baron Methuen following the death of his father.

One of the first press reports covering matches involving Corsham appeared in 1848. The *Devizes & Wiltshire Gazette of 13th July 1848* records a match played on 10th July between Greenpark (Bath) and Corsham, who scored 18 and 21. The Bath gentlemen won with ease, in one innings of 53 with 14 runs to spare.

In 1862 a grand cricket match was played in Corsham, between the 11 gentlemen players of the West of England team and 22 players selected from the Lacock and Corsham Cricket Clubs. After a well contested match played with great spirit, the West of England 11 were declared winners by 10 runs. The ground was in excellent order.

In 1866 a resolution was passed to fine *'any member heard swearing or using any profane language in the field'* the sum of 6d. In that same year, Corsham played against the local Marshfield Club, whose captain, the famous *W.G. Grace*, scored 48 not out of a total of 89.

1888: Mr. T.P. Stevens presided at a meeting, where consideration was given by the Cricket Club Committee on the application for the hire of a portion of the cricket field for use by the Corsham Tennis Club. It was decided to let part of the field for a tennis court, on the condition that it should be an open club and that tennis should not be played during a cricket match.

In 1893 W.G. Grace played on the Corsham ground.

In 1928 a fascinating booklet called *'Eighty Years of Cricket. A brief history of Corsham Sports Club 1848-1928,'* was written by H.S. Lakeman, and included many early facts and figures along with the club's history; such as, *'In 1864, J.H. having taken the ball from the cricket box without permission without leave, be fined 6d'.*

In the 'foreward' of the book, Fredrick Methuen's son Paul Sanford Methuen (*later to become Field Marshall Methuen*), who by now was the second President of the Club in 1864, wrote a humorous introduction including the following paragraph:

'I remember playing just before Lord Robert's manoeuvres, at Corsham, when again I was 'leg-before,' a corporal being umpire at the bowler's end. When he was asked why he did not give me 'out,' he said he did not as a corporal, like to give a general 'out '!"

Later, Field Marshall Lord Methuen arranged for improvement of the ground by cutting down some of the trees which threw their shadow across the pitch late in the afternoon.

He goes on to say, *"I had not the courage to ask the Honourable Cecil Parker to remove some trees on his side of the road, but I had a good friend in the gale of last year which removed them for me, and therefore makes the ground perfect."*

The extent of the club's inventory taken in 1866 shows how sparse the amount of equipment was compared to modern day requirements. It was a case of making do and swapping over the pads when it was your time at the crease!

2	Boxes.
1	Marking frame.
2	Pairs of pads, good condition.
1	Pair of wicket gloves, poor condition.
2	Pairs of batting gloves, poor condition.
1	Tape, good condition.
1	Match of stumps, good condition.
8	Odd stumps!
3	Newly spliced bats, good condition.
3	Bats of last season, fair condition.
2	Bails.
1	Lock and Key.
1	Scoring Book, used up!

In the early days the Club were unable to get onto the field until after *'haying time',* where preparing the field was a mammoth task early on match mornings. Nowadays, preparation for the coming season starts as early as March.

Match admission was, non-subscribers 3d. 1 shilling for pair-horses carriages and 6d for single-horse carriages and saddle horses.

The original pavilion was no more than a tent and was no longer considered befitting the dignity and ambitions of the club. A new wooden, thatched roof pavilion was built in 1878 using a £25 donation from Mr. Poynder.

The new pavilion lasted until 1908 when it was replaced by a corrugated iron construction with two dressing rooms, one containing the apparatus for the preparation of teas.

In the winter, the *corrugated* building was used for Social activities; such as Whist Drives and dances etc. The corrugated iron construction survived until the stone, single-story pavilion was erected in 1971. Following a significant contribution from The National Lottery, a second story was added, and the new two-story building was officially opened in 1999 by David Gower.

Lakeman's book goes on to say that. *'The British Olympic Association's definition of a sportsman in those early days was as follows; and I like to think that these (in the main) are still upheld in the modern game.'*

A SPORTSMAN.

1. Plays the game for the game's sake.
2. Plays for his side and not for himself.
3. Is a good winner and a good loser, is modest in victory and generous in defeat.
4. Accepts all decisions in a proper spirit.
5. Is chivalrous towards a defeated opponent.
6. Is unselfish and always ready to help others to become proficient.
7. As a spectator applauds good play on both sides.
8. Never interferes with referees or judges, no matter what the decision.

In the early 1900s a Corsham Sports Day featured on the annual calendar and by 1921 the *'Corsham Sports Club'* was established. The Sports Club amalgamate the interests of all the other sports that were now emerging in Corsham in the post-Victorian era, such as Bowls, Tennis, and Hockey.

The following paragraph from the *Wilts Gazette of July 1922* written under the heading *'Hedge-side Chance-Blades (gathered in Wiltshire)'* by M.K. Swayne Edwards, sums up the importance of cricket as part of Corsham's heritage.

In a delightful description of Corsham, the Church, and Park, Neston, the roadside, streams, etc., we find the following:

'In most places wayside football lasts through the summer. Not so at Corsham. In the evenings and on Saturdays, you can see little groups marching into the corners of the fields, and setting up little stumps solemnly proceed to play cricket. Cricket goes on in the roads and byways, with strange implements but a sporting spirit, and I have actually often been impeded by boys practicing catching and throwing!'

The article goes on to portray the importance of match days, *'The walls all around are lined with passers-by who do not pass, but stay; workmen run up for a minute to ask the score or see an over or two, and the crowd is quick to applaud - either side.'*

During the WWI years, matches were arranged for the wounded convalescent soldiers who were being treated in the Town Hall Hospital.

In 1954 The Rev. A. Glen Smith on behalf of the Corsham Baptist Church, strongly disapproved the Cricket Club's decision to allow the Corsham Sports Club to provide facilities for Sunday Sport in Corsham. 1955 saw the formation of what has become the nursery for a host of the Club's leading players. In 1957 a new scoreboard was installed. New sight-screens were installed during 1958.

The late 1960's saw a change in Club Cricket with the re-introduction of League Cricket into the County. Lack of foresight in the late 70's by the Committee of the time, failed to accept a place offered to become founder members of the newly formed Western League. This decision saw the standard of cricket at Corsham diminish in the late seventies and early eighties. A late invitation to join the 'Three Counties League' based largely in South East Wales, was accepted for the 1982 season. An invitation to join the newly formed County Alliance League for its second season (1986) was readily accepted. In 1996 Corsham finished at the foot of Division One and relegation to Division Two.

After sixteen seasons in the Premier Division of the West of England Premier League, Season 2017 resulted in Corsham's relegation to WEPL Premier 2 - Wiltshire / Gloucestershire Division .

Recently the club have fielded a number of former first class county players including Roger Sillence (Worcs and Glos), Wes Durston (Somerset/Derbyshire), Nick Harrison (Worcs) and Craig Miles (Glos), as well as one of its overseas players, Ranadeb Bose, who went on to tour with the successful Indian Touring party of 2007 to the UK.

The 'club's claim to fame' is that they produced two Test cricketers: firstly, Corsham born Septimus (Paul) Kinneir who went on to play for Warwickshire and later, Cedrick Ivan James Smith who played for Middlesex. The history of these two stalwarts is recorded in David Smith's September 2000 book, *'Corsham's Two Test Cricketers'*, some extracts of which are included in the narrative below.

SEPTIMUS (PAUL) KINNEIR:

Septimus, who liked to be known as Paul *(maybe to avoid the inevitable nickname of SKinneir)* was born next to the brewery in Pickwick on 13 May 1871. Sep never received any regular coaching yet he became one of Corsham's best ever cricketers. Sep went on to play for Wiltshire but not as a regular, presumably due to work commitments. His first match for Wiltshire at Lords was in 1890 and he last played for Corsham in 1896.

Sep was named one of Wisden's cricketers of the year in 1912. He also appears on an Imperial Tobacco card as one of Warwickshire's County Cricketers.

In 1896 Sep played for Warwickshire CCC. During a match against Gloucestershire in Cheltenham, Sep met a beautiful girl, after which he became seriously ill - but hopefully not as a result of meeting the girl! Warwickshire paid for Sep's treatment in Germany. Sep lost his hair and thereafter always wore some sort of head-gear. In 1911 he was part of Warwickshire's first Championship winning side when he scored 1,629 runs in 20 matches, including a career best 268 not out, at an average of 49.36. This performance led to him being chosen to play in his one and only Test match in 1911/1912 against Australia in Sydney, having turned forty.

The Albion Gold Flake Cigarette card No.5 in the 'Cricketers' series (see photo) shows Sep Kinneir wearing Warwickshire cap, full length, in batting pose, at the wicket. On the rear it describes Sep as, *'Particularly stylish with a left hand bat, and the scorer of 1,148 runs last summer for Warwick, including 268 not-out against Hants at Birmingham, and a double century a against Sussex at Chichester. Has 22 centuries to his credit in first-class cricket'.*

Sep passed away on 16 October 1928 when he was found draped over his motorcycle which he had carefully laid down on the verge, having suffered a stroke. The following portrayal of Seb, attributed by Warwickshire and England all-rounder Frank Rowbotham Foster, shows a great affection for a dear friend lost:

'This is what I admire about my old friend Sep Kinneir: He was let down by a woman, he was shunned by other people, he triumphed over other obstacles which very few men have had to face, he was loyal to Warwickshire C.C., he never allowed bitter thoughts to enter into his mind, he was a man who was gentle and kind to everyone, and above all, he never married. That is the end of that memory and one I shall cherish until my dying day'.

Jim Smith at the Scarborough Cricket Festival

CEDRICK IVAN JAMES SMITH: Born on 25 August 1906, Jim's family lived in Havelock Cottage at 72 Priory Street in Corsham for about 150 years until 1992. Whilst Jim's father Eli *(a skilled plasterer and stone roof tiler)* played cricket for Gastard, it was Jim's Uncle Jessie *(often mistaken for being Jim's father)* who played for Corsham. Jessie once took a hundred wickets for Corsham in a season. Jessie and Jim were both big hitters, bowled fast right-arm and had very fine physiques. Jim attended the County School (opened in 1895), the windows of which overlooked the Corsham ground. Jim began his career with Corsham in 1922 as a fifteen year-old, and became a first team regular during 1923 to 1925. Jim played his first match for Wiltshire against Kent 11 at Gravesend in 1926; his next appearance was some months later in August 1927 by taking 4 of Berkshire's wickets. Jim went on to become Wiltshire's most consistent bowler and wicket-taker. Jim was not a big hitter in those days, with his largest total of 82 in August 1933, coming against Dorset on the Bemerton ground near Salisbury after he took 5 wickets for 46.

An envious Yorkshire reporter of the times stated in his paper:

'The Smith a mighty man was he! This particular one is a Wiltshire Smith. But for a trifling qualification slip, he would now be a Middlesex Smith. He bowls fast, and bats in sixes. It is a pity he has been allowed to hide his light in minor counties' cricket so long. On Thursday he playfully hit Percy Fender over the tavern for six - a long carry.'

In 1929 Jim began to qualify for Middlesex, to enable him to be eligible for the 1932 season, but his oversight in advising Wiltshire CCC of his intentions, delayed his County Championship by a further two years, thereby missing out on playing against the Australians who were touring England in 1934. Jim, then twenty-eight, made an instant impact in County cricket. In four consecutive matches, three at Lords and one at Southampton, between 23 May and 8 June he took 39 wickets. No fast bowler before or since has, in his first full county season taken more wickets for his county (143) or a greater total in all cricket (172). To his astonishment he was quickly on his way to the West Indies under captain Bob Wyatt. He played in all four tests, making his debut in Barbados. The tour proceeded well but resulted in defeat in the Test series by two matches to one. It was West Indies' first series win against any opposition, largely brought about by superior fast bowling which proved too much on this occasion for England's senior batsmen. The team was reunited later to play a match in the Scarborough Festival in September 1935 (see photo on previous page).

Years later, Bob Wyatt wrote the following about Jim, to a cricket fan in the West Country:

'I remember in one match when he was batting, he connected and drove a skimmer into a tree outside the ground. There must have been fifty spectators up in the tree and they all came tumbling out when the branch broke....'

Jim's portrait as a young man. featured on the cigarette card - *'John Player - Cricketers 1938 - # 24 Jim Smith - Middlesex.'* The following summary of Jim's career is written on the back of the card: ***C. I. J. SMITH*** *(Middlesex and England).*

'Newly twenty-eight when first appearing for Middlesex, Jim Smith was ripe in experience both with Wiltshire, the county of his birth, and M.C.C.

Over six feet in height, he uses this advantage for fast, accurately-delivered, straight bowling. Naturally, with great power behind it, the ball is apt to rise if Smith finds a lively pitch. From a record of 172 wickets at 18-88 each in 1934.

Jim Smith declined somewhat in deadliness, but three years later, with 149 wickets for 17-47, he was our best fast bowler. His attempts at mighty driving seldom fail completely. Born August 25th, 1906.'

Jim, the largest player at that time in county cricket, was blessed with a large physique slightly over 6ft 4in tall, size 14 boots and rarely under 16 stones.

On 10 Nov 1994 Jim married Mary Vinnicombe (1909-1993) in Harlestone, north of Northampton, after which Jim sailed with the Middlesex County Cricket team to the West Indies for a fee of £200 *(about £400 in today's money),* where he opened the bowling in the first Test at Bridgetown. In the second Test at Port of Spain, Jim was cautioned for short-pitch bowling. It has been said that after 1934 Jim was never quite the same bowler again. His bowling became less varied and his occasional late in-swinger not quite so effective. But he was still selected to play in his first and only home Test against New Zealand at Old Trafford in 1937.

Jim's three-year contract with Middlesex CCC expired on 1 September 1939. At 39 years of age, Jim later turned down the offer to play for Middlesex again in 1946. World War II had deprived Jim of his main livelihood at an early age. During the war years at home in Harlestone, he used the building skills he had learnt from his father and tended a small-holding, along with a spell working in the ironstone pits.

There was never a more popular player over the period of 1934 to 1939. His deadpan expression, height and his large physique endeared him to all and made him a favourite of cartoonists and caricaturists, such as Harold Gittings, Mercer and Tipping.

Jim and his wife Mary went on to run the Millstone in Mellor, a local pub with farm buildings a few miles away from Blackburn. This big shambling man was sublimely happy whenever he went out to feed his animals. If he hadn't been a professional cricketer, he would probably have ended up as a farmer. Jim's weight had always been a matter for good-natured discussion. In his Middlesex days it was fourteen and a half stone going on sixteen. Now it was nineteen!

He later had several successful seasons playing league cricket for various teams. In 1950, Jim stumbled and fell down when he was coming up to bowl and broke his ankle.

'That's it then. Better stay home and polish the glasses on a Saturday afternoon,' he said.

It took four men to carry him off; the injury putting an end to his playing days.

In the mid 1950's Jim did some coaching at Stonyhurst College after his league career had ended. As his county service was too short for him to have been considered for a benefit, he was invited back to Lords in November 1953 to be handed a cheque for £1,250 *(about £35,000 in today's money)* in appreciation of his services.

Corsham remained much in Jim's affection and he returned whenever he could to visit his sisters in Prior Street. Jim and Mary later moved into a cottage a few hundred yards away from their pub near Blackburn, where he sadly passed away at 72 on the 8th February 1979.

In 1993 in David Foot's book *'Beyond Bat & Ball'*, David sums up Jim's character lovingly as:

'Indiscriminate hitting made him the greatest favourite of his day and a subject of fireside talk for the rest of the century.'

If you want to know more about the Corsham Cricket club's history, visit their website here:

http://www.corshamcc.co.uk/

Chapter 11. Dry Arch - Corsham Park.

When the Dry Arch was built c1803, the original London to Bath original turnpike coach road passed just outside, and alongside the north perimeter of Mynte Wood, just north of where the Dry Arch is situated. The new turnpike road was later repositioned *(along with a new dry stone wall)* a quarter of a mile to the north at Chequers Hill, where it is known today as the A4 route. Local legend has it, that the Dry Arch is where the highwayman Dick Turpin once held up the London to Bath mail coach! But the arch did not exist then.

Although Corsham did have a highwayman, his name was John Boulter who hid with his gang the other side of town in Chapel Plaister, and then robbed travellers as they went over Kingsdown. Boulter was caught and hanged on 25th, February 1755 *(see Chapter 18 for more detail).*

Lancelot Brown devised a panoramic walk to the north and east of Corsham Court called, 'The Great Walk' (now known as the 'North Walk). The private path runs north through the Court gardens, then meanders east through the planted 'Mynte' woodland, from the Corsham Court garden, up to the ornate entrance with its massive wooden gates on the wide *'Chequers Hill'* to *'Thingley Junction'* road. The gates have not been opened for many years and the path immediately behind, is completely overgrown. At the point inside Mynte Wood, where the private path was crossed by a public footpath, an ornamental arch (known as the Dry Arch) of 'petrified stone was built. The arch was constructed to allow the Corsham Court family and their guests to walk uninterrupted beneath the public right of way which passes over the top.

The public footpath still passes over the Dry Arch which is sometimes used as meeting place for the youths of Corsham, who always sadly manage to leave their littler behind to besmirch one Corsham's beauty spots! Newly carved names have also appeared recently in the stonework, but thankfully not obliterating the important ones of the past.

The Dry Arch is built of *'petrified'* stone gathered from a brook in nearby Ford. Petrified stone, is the result of a tree or tree-like plants having completely transitioned into stone by a process called permineralization.

The result of this is that arch looks as though it was built with the demon heads of a hundred *'petrified skulls'*!

The eyeless faces are not a sight to see when *'nights black agents do rouse'*!

It certainly is a very creepy place at night, but in the daylight, it is a lovely tranquil spot that has a certain magical ambience about it.

The Rev Colin Gordon-Farleigh sums this up very nicely below in his online blog:

'For Corsham children over the years, it has served as a fort, a jail-cell, a palace, or whatever childhood imaginations wanted it to be, and just like so much else in our childhood, it has a touch of magic about it'.

The arch bears the scars of several regiments, with the carved names and initials of many a WW1 and WW2 soldier still visible there. The most prominent inscription is dated 27th April 1917 and is attributed to ***Private W.L. of the 27th Battalion Canadians*** with the N's carved back to front.

You can get to the Dry Arch along the public footpaths. Start your walk from Corsham's Saint Bartholomew's Church at the end of Church Street (next to the entrance of Corsham Court), go into the park, bear left and then follow the sunken metal-railing fence right to its very end.

Follow the footpath signs into the wood to the right. Or you can park at the bottom of Chequers Hill (on the A4 between Corsham and Chippenham) and walk back up the footpath towards Corsham, and into the Mynte Woods to the Dry Arch. The Dry Arch is on a popular circular 90 to 120 minute walk that takes in St Bartholomew's Church the park with its lake, and the villages of Westrop and Easton; there is always something new to see on this walk each season.

PLEASE DO NOT STRAY FROM THE PUBLIC FOOTPATH AND DO NOT LEAVE ANY LITTER BEHIND.

Chapter 12. Farleigh Down Tunnel at Shockerwick Box.

Between 1881-1930 the hills north-west of Monkton Farleigh village were quarried for Bath stone, leaving 300 acres of tunnels. This secure space was put to good use, when due to the unrest in Europe in the 1930s there was a need to provide secure storage for munitions across the United Kingdom. The proposal was to create three Central Ammunition Depots (CAD) near Corsham; one of them being the huge underground Monkton Farleigh Depot where two and a half million square foot of space was eventually converted for storing up to 120,000 tons of ammunition. The other two CAD depots were the *Tunnel Quarry* in Hudswell, Corsham, and *Eastlays Ridge* at the top of Neston.

In November 1937 the Great Western Railway was contracted to build a 1,000 feet (300m) long raised (transit-shed) and a twin-loading platform at Farleigh Down Railway Sidings at Shockerwick (also known as *Ashley Wharf*). This would be used as a *railhead* for loading and unloading ammunition to and fro, firstly on an overhead aerial ropeway and later via a tunnel linked to the underground WWII Monkton Farleigh ammunition depot built high up on the hill; all done in preparation for possible hostilities to commence with Germany.

In modern times, most of the derelict remains of Farleigh Down Sidings were razed to the ground prior to a planned redevelopment which never happened. Very little of it now remains - but enough to recognise it in the old photos (particularly the rusty transit shed which leads to the underground tunnel) and enough to give the location a mysterious sense of importance; AND it was a very important place during WWII........for a large part of the D-Day ammunition would have come from here.

It is a great pity that the location was not preserved like many other WWII sites, as it is of significant historical value. In recent years, the northern end of the tunnel underneath the now dilapidated transit shed alongside the sidings has been secured many times, but more than often it remains open due to vandalism and over-inquisitive explorers. Even the massive blast-proofed welded doors just below the transit shed have been forced open several times allowing access to the tunnel. The security barrier that was built at the top end of the tunnel (sealed by a concrete and rubble installation) to prevent entry into the Monkton Farleigh underground depot, has also been vandalised by intruders trying to break through.

For a time, the sidings became overgrown and a travellers' camp became established on the site. In the early 1980s, thieves broke in and dug up the under-floor ducting and removed all of the copper power cables along the tunnel's one and a half mile length! In the more recent past, it has been used for raves, parties, filming of music videos and a gallery for the local graffiti artists who have covered the walls with (it must be said) some very stunning images! The floor is littered with empty beer cans, the odd discarded needle and hundreds (if not thousands) of small canisters, some laughing gas canisters and many discarded paint spray canisters.

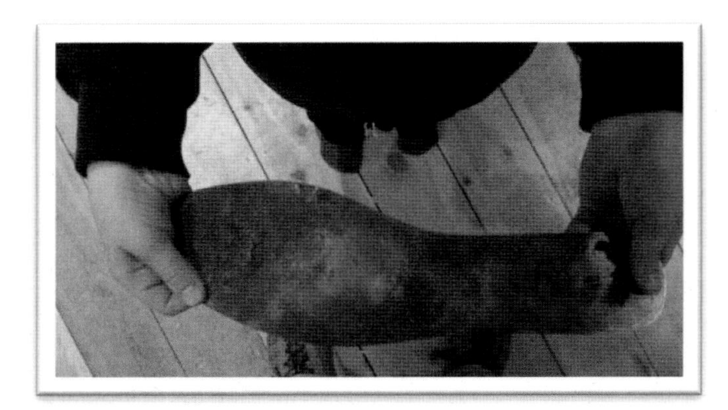

[Ed] If you look carefully, WWII mementos can still be found on site such as the soldier's metal boot insert, found by my grandson George during our visit there near the tunnel entrance in 2015. These were the type of protective inserts used in army boots more akin to jungle warfare, to stop the sharpened poison bamboo canes from penetrating through the bottom of the soldier's boots.

The Monkton Farleigh Depot some 450 feet above the valley floor, was built during WW2 and was decommissioned in 1965 and sold off in 1976. Originally, the ammunition made its way from the underground depot one and a quarter miles away (high up on the hill top), to the railway sidings (at the bottom of the valley) overland via an aerial cable ropeway. The ammunition was loaded into crates suspended from the aerial cable which was attached to short lattice pylons, much like the modern ski lifts of today. The 2000 yard mono-cable aerial ropeway stretched in a straight line from the sidings, up and over the brow of Farleigh Down to the depot. Later, the aerial ropeway was replaced due to its visibility and vulnerability to attack by enemy aircraft as the ammunition stored in the hilltop depot travelled above ground to-and-fro the railway sidings, making it more vulnerable to attack from the air.

To replace the temporary aerial cable ropeway, a spectacular 1:8 inclined underground tunnel was built to connect the depot with the sidings, thereby offering a secure route invisible to enemy aerial reconnaissance. The tunnel terminated at a loading platform below ground level and at a right angle to the main-line platform. The tunnel was scheduled for completion in 1941, and was designed to handle 1000 tons of ammunition daily.

Deep tunnelling was required for the top half of the tunnel; completed under contract by the Cementation Company. This upper half of the seven-foot-wide tunnel was constructed using a semi-circular brick-arched designed roof having maximum headroom of 69" and reaching a depth of 180 feet near the top edge of the Farleigh Down escarpment. The lower section of the tunnel was constructed using the much simpler *'cut and cover'* method, which hid an eight-foot-square reinforced concrete box-section. The concrete box sections were completely buried, but for much of its length, the tunnel here was hardly below ground at all and had to be disguised by forming a gently sloping earth bank over the top of it, and by building it in a trench of varying depth in order to maintain the specified gradient.

The lower end of the tunnel opens out into an underground marshalling yard with a large platform for loading and unloading the ammunition. During its construction, it was important to hide the excavated white stone waste from prying enemy eyes. Waste from the top shaft was carried by rail across the Monkton Farleigh village road and dumped in the old quarries. Waste from the air shaft in Ashley Woods was distributed among the trees where the dense overgrowth provided adequate camouflage from inquisitive enemy aircraft flying overhead.

Once the tunnel had been completed in 1942, aerial enemy reconnaissance flying overhead would see nothing but rolling countryside, with wooded hills, picturesque villages, and peaceful pastoral scenery. Many of the local inhabitants are unaware that deep under the earth, a wonderful feat of engineering had resulted in the creation of a vast bomb-proof store for munitions of war; those who knew, kept the secret inviolate.

To connect the end of the tunnel with the *sidings* transit shed, a slope shaft was sunk at the west end of the loading platform. This incorporated a narrow gauge railway which allowed rail trucks to be rolled down out of sight, along the thirty-foot deep slope and then sharply to the left into the underground ammunition sorting bay. In the photo, you can see the workers unloading 155mm propellant charges in the autumn of 1943.

Once the concrete lined tunnel had been completed in November 1941, engineers from Richard Sutcliffe Ltd started assembling the tunnel conveyors required to move the ammunition between the depot and the railway sidings. The task was completed by the following April.

Because of the long distance between the sidings and the depot and the heavy load carried against the gradient, it was necessary to use two separate conveyor belt units running in tandem and linked together by gravity rollers. Fixed rollers between the two conveyors fed ammunition from one belt to the other. The upper conveyor in the square half of the tunnel was 2,171 feet long and the lower one in the round tunnel 2,372 feet.

The belts were prone to jam from time to time. Whilst the conveyor belts were running, soldiers were stationed at intervals along the conveyor belt, charged with the unutterably boring and unenviable responsibility of keeping watch over the hundreds of ammunition boxes as they trundled past in the cold miserable gloom of the tunnel, checking that none slipped off or jammed. Emergency stop wires were attached to the side of the conveyor belts which would immediately stop both belts simultaneously from any point along the one and a quarter mile tunnel. Some sections of the two conveyors belt mechanisms are still in place but much of it has been stolen and sold for scrap. Ammunition was transported between the end of the conveyor and the main line loading platform above ground, via narrow gauge trucks.

Underneath the transit shed at the bottom of the 30ft slope shaft, the original heavy metal blast doors (much damaged and re-welded) lie askew giving access the large underground sorting yard. Alongside the yard, the adjacent offices, toilets, shower rooms, wash rooms and sub-station have all been completely stripped out and the walls are now covered in colourful graffiti. *Be aware that the large immersion heater in the washroom is lagged with dangerous white asbestos.* In the gloomy distance, you can see the square entrance to the bottom half of the tunnel. It's an eerie place to be these days, with the sound of the trains echoing around as they travel along the mainline above.

Even though the sorting yard is barely underground, its complete darkness, musty atmosphere and long history make it feel as though you are 100 feet down! To walk from the sorting yard to the tunnel's end (at the Depot entrance on the top of Farleigh Down escarpment) along the claustrophobic reinforced concrete tunnel and back again is a distance of two and a half miles. The tunnel is full of trip hazards and various graffiti images (some rude!) line the walls nearly all the way along. The halfway point is approximately where the concrete lined tunnel shape changes from round to square.

A number of other buildings still survive above ground within the railway sidings complex, including three pillboxes, three static water tanks and a surface air raid shelter.

The Monkton Farleigh ammunition depot closed at the end of WWII hostilities, but was kept in operational condition until the 1950s after the War Office decided that all ammunition movements should be carried out by road. The sidings were then cleared and not used again until 1984 when local Nick McCamley acquired the Depot and turned it into a successful museum until 1990 when the freehold was purchased by a Cambridge based company.

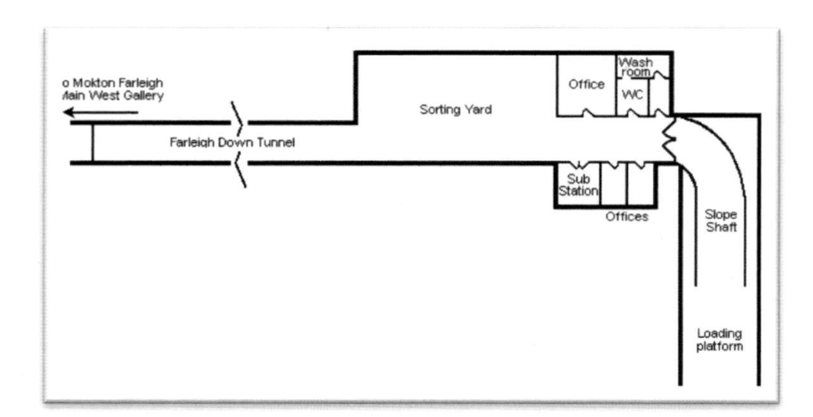

The mine fell into disuse once again and the vandals and thieves moved in to strip out anything of value. In 1996 the mine was acquired by Wansdyke Security, a secure warehouse business for secure storage of documentation .

The Farleigh Down Tunnel is not a place to visit if you suffer with claustrophobia or dislike rats.

Where is it? Turn left under the large railway bridge on the sharp bend on the A4 at Shockerwick just the other side of Box village. Three hundred yards up on the right, are three gates and several footpaths. Go back west towards Bath alongside the rail track footpath, and you can't miss it.

If you want to learn more about the Farleigh Down Sidings at Shockerwick; see Nick McCamley's wonderful book; 'Subterranean Britain. Second World War Secret Bunkers'. ISBN 9780992855420.

Chapter 13. Fire Brigade - a 200 year history.

The ***first*** Corsham Fire Station was for many years, thought to have been located at the end of Priory Street - but that was the ***second*** location!

THE FIRST FIRE STATION: An old Victorian postcard has revealed that the ***first*** location was just around the corner in the small Grade II listed Flemish Building at 94 High Street. The Corsham fire engine in those days consisted of a small horse drawn cart, with leather buckets and about 150 feet or so of leather hose. The men in the brigade would have been powerfully built and reliable. The building had an alarm bell on the roof and the name *'Fire Point Station'* can be seen emblazoned on the door in the old postcard. The alarm bell tower on this building is also evident in several other early Corsham postcard photographs. This building later became *A. Neate's 'Boot and Shoe Repairer's* shop. The building has had many other guises during its history, including offices and various shop outlets. Today in 2018, it functions as the Curtain Workshop. *www.jfgcurtainworkshop.co.uk/.* When this building was converted into an office some years ago, signs of the cobbled stable floor still existed, as did the crib loading traps in the ceiling. The joists of the upper floor were still covered up with old hay. This small building was originally the horse stable for the next door bakery cart, but doubled-up as storage for the original Corsham fire appliance, which would have been *drawn* by the baker's horse whenever the bell on the roof was sounded! If you go into the little Curtain Workshop building today, you can still see some of the original features.

1607: The following is a very early Corsham public order. *'It is ordered that no undertennante within ye town [of Corsham] shall at any time kepe or make two fiers in his or their houses whereby they may happen to endanger the towne with fier under penalty for each time 40/-.'*

The Corsham Fire Brigade has an intriguing history which is summarised in detail below:
1810: There has been a 'public fire engine' in Corsham since 1810. It was ordered that the fire engine should be taken out at least once in every three months.

1820: Firemen were alerted by the banging of a drum!

1849: Mr Henry Spackman's (grocery and drapery) shop in the High Street *(where Ultra-Warm now stands)* was completely destroyed after a fire started at two o'clock in the afternoon of Tuesday 23rd January. Henry lost his life after re-entering the building with his nephew, to try and retrieve 'a little of their wearing apparel'. As the fire reached the stairs behind them, the nephew escaped from an upstairs window but was unable to reach his uncle who was found later with scarcely a feature left on him.

The Corsham horse-drawn fire engine was at the scene in minutes, and battled in vain (along with the engine from Chippenham) to prevent the shop and the adjoining house occupied by Mrs J. Hulbert from being totally destroyed. Loud explosions due to the gunpowder stored in the attic for use in the construction of Box Tunnel, caused several huge explosions, some being heard 8 miles away in Bromham. *[Photo of Corsham Fire Brigade above is courtesy of John Cuthbertson]*

The Western Flying Post, Sherborne and Yeovil Mercury - 27 January 1849 - Corsham - Destructive Fire and Loss of Life (newspaper article)....................................

Between five and six o'clock on Wednesday morning, the house in occupation of Mr Spackman, grocer and draper, of Corsham, was discovered to be on fire, and within an hour or two the whole of the premises, together with the extensive stock in trade, account books, furniture &c was one heap of ruins, and Mr Spackman himself a corpse! so much of his body having been consumed by the fire that it was impossible to identify it! The accident, it is supposed, either originated in the back parlour, where there had been a fire on the previous evening, or in the stove leading from the shop into the chimney of the room. Mr Spackman's attention was first called to it by a suffocating smell; he immediately alarmed the family, who, with himself, effected their escape into the street, - the Misses Spackman, who slept at the back part of the house, getting through a trap-door into the adjoining premises. The drum (the usual means of calling the inhabitants together) quickly sounded the alarm, and assistance was soon procured. Within a few minutes the town engine was at work, and another engine was brought from Chippenham; every possible exertion, indeed, was used, but for a long time without effect. The flames spread to the adjoining house, occupied by Mrs T Hulbert, which was also destroyed, together with a large portion of Mrs Hulbert's furniture. Shortly after the engines began to play, there was a tremendous explosion from a quantity of gunpowder which was on the premises, but fortunately without injury to any one. From the combustible nature of the materials, the flames extended across the street and did damage to the windows of the premises occupied by Miss Fowler and Dr Dyke; and it was only by extraordinary exertion that these premises were saved from destruction, large flakes of fire flying to a considerable distance. Naturally anxious to save some portion of his property, Mr Spackman unfortunately re-entered the house, after the fire had obtained considerable ascendancy, and proceeded to his bedroom, where some valuable papers were kept; but the flames quickly burst forth from the back parlour door, at the foot of the staircase, and prevented his descent. His nephew, at the time, was in the back bedroom, and hearing him apparently gasping for breath, called upon him to follow him - the nephew at the moment leaping through the window into the garden below. It was to no purpose however. Mr S must have been instantly overpowered by suffocation and his body was afterwards found immediately under the spot where the floor gave way. His arms were on his chest; but his feet were completely burnt from his legs; and in this state his remains were taken to the Market House [now the Town Hall], where an Inquest will be held. Mr. Spackman was a widower, but has left a large family. His stock, which was valuable, was insured in the Sun Fire Office; but, nevertheless, the loss will be considerable. The deceased was a zealous member of the Baptist denomination, and has left a family of three children, and a large circle of friends, who deeply mourn his loss. This very shocking affair has cast a gloom over the whole neighbourhood, and will not be soon forgotten by those who witnessed the calamity.

Mr Spackman's pocket book, some valuable documents and a considerable sum of money were found unharmed amongst the ruins of the building. However, it appears that a number of records pertaining to local non-conformist Chapels, which were placed in the care of Mr Spackman were destroyed.

This was the first fire attended by the new Chippenham Fire Engine which was built according to specification. The Chippenham superintendent and a brigade of twelve powerful steady men *(all of them being good mechanics)* attended the fire. Their new engine was manufactured by Messers Mereweather at Long Acre, London, being complete in all its parts with four dozen leather buckets and about 170 feet of leather hose etc. It could start in 5 minutes notice by the attachment of four horses. Its services rendered on this occasion in Corsham was duly appreciated and gratefully acknowledged as, by its powerful application, a great amount of valuable property was saved.

1877: The first written record referring to the upkeep of a fire engine in Corsham, can be found in the Corsham Vestry Minutes dated 5 April 1877, which refers to a balance in hand of £18. 14s. 0d. (about £1,500 in today's money). This substantial amount of money was later handed over to the family of the recently deceased Mr Cole, for his years of service in maintaining the horse-drawn fire engine. This suggests that a fire engine had been available in Corsham during the years prior to 1877.

Note: A 'Vestry' was a form of Parish Council, before Parish Councils came into being; consisting usually, of a committee for secular and church government within a parish, which met in the vestry of the parish church. It was a fundamental unit of decision making within each parish, and acted as a miniature legislature for parochial government.

1880: Fires broke out in the premises of Mr. J.D. Horne, baker and confectioner, were attended to on two occasions by the brigade this year.

1884: The Vestry discussed a proposal to provide leather helmets for the Corsham Firemen.

1889: Corsham was connected to the mains water, supplied from the springs at Loxwell near the top of Naish Hill, Lacock.

During the formal opening ceremony, when Chairman of the Waterworks Company Mr. C. Mayo turned on the hydrant tap that was fixed to the Methuen Arms.......... *'the force of the water was such, that it was thrown over the top of the hotel*.' This would have caused some consternation to the new owner George Reeves, who had just completely refurbished the hotel!

1894: The newly formed Corsham Parish Council takes over the running of the fire engine.

1895: The care and management of the fire brigade was placed in the hands of the 'Lighting Committee'. Expenses were borne by the Parish Council. The fire brigade's Captain was paid an annual fee of £2.10s.0p, and the firemen, £1. A further £1.10s.0p was provided for the upkeep of the horse-drawn engine. The brigade now consisted of a Captain, Deputy-Captain and eleven firemen. The Corsham Blacksmith Mr. John Bull, described as a huge, larger than life figure of a man, became one of the new firemen, along with Alfred Butt, a tailor, and Arthur J. Hobbs, a saddler.

Rules and regulations were drawn up, which included a fine of two shillings for neglecting to attend a fire, and dismissal if the reasons were unsatisfactory. Use of bad language received a fine of sixpence. The stables containing up to forty horses at the Station Hotel caught fire, thankfully all were rescued.

Corsham Parish Council Fire Brigade.

RULES AND REGULATIONS.

1. This Brigade being formed under the authority of the Parish Council shall be subject to all regulations that have been or shall be made by them.

2. The Brigade shall consist of a Captain, Deputy-Captain, and Eleven firemen.

3. The Brigade shall meet in uniform for Drill and Testing the Engine not less than nine times a year, or oftener if required, and a record of attendance shall be kept by the Captain.

4. Any Member of the Brigade being absent from any fixed practice shall be fined Two Shillings; and any Member neglecting to attend a fire when called upon, without giving a satisfactory reason for his absence, shall, on the report of the Captain, render himself liable to dismissal by the Committee. Any Member using bad language shall be fined Sixpence, and the Captain shall have power to enforce strict silence during the practice.

5. All vacancies in the Brigade shall be filled up at a Special or ordinary Meeting of the Committee.

6. Each Member of the Brigade will be required to enter into an Agreement to keep his uniform in good condition, to use it only when on duty, and to deliver up the same when called upon.

7. Each Firemen shall be paid £1 per annum, and the appointment shall be subject to three month's notice. The Captain shall be engaged under special conditions as the Committee may from time to time determine.

8. The Captain or Officer in command shall have absolute control of the Brigade, with full power to suspend any Member guilty of any breach of discipline.

9. The Brigade and Engine shall attend all Fires in the Parish, and also in the adjoining Parishes, if the Captain shall consider it expedient—and, should the distance require it, the Captain shall have power to provide horses to convey the Engine to such fires.

10. No Member of the Brigade shall be allowed to leave a fire or place of Drill unless in case of injury, without permission of the Officer in charge.

11. At a fire the Officer in command shall when necessary, furnish his men with suitable refreshment—he shall also have power to engage extra assistance if required.

12. A List of the names of the Members of the Brigade together with a printed copy of the Rules shall be kept in the Engine House, at the Police Station, and at the Clerk's Office.

CORSHAM, JUNE 10TH, 1895.

1896: The £3 bill for dousing the Station Hotel fire in the previous year had still not been paid. The Parish Council accepted Lord Methuen's offer of £5 per annum for the use of a small building as a Fire Station at the end of Priory Lane (now Priory Street, and previously known as Stubbs Lane after a local clothier).

THE SECOND FIRE STATION:

1897: The Brigade eventually moves out of the Flemish Building at 94 High Street and into the small building at the very end of Priory Lane late in the year. The entrance was through high wooden gates onto the High Street at the very corner with Priory Lane (now Priory Street). A qualified *'fire-fighting'* instructor was paid £2.1s.0p to teach the new recruits. The installation of new one-and-a-half-inch water hydrants in the streets of Corsham, meant that the brigade now had to carry two hose sizes (one-and-a-half-inch and two-and-a-half-inch diameters). Fire hydrants were installed in the water mains under Hastings Road, Pickwick Road, Pickwick Street and Paul Street.

The launching of the fire engine in the second fire station must have been a complicated effort of cooperation. Once the alarm was given, nearby tradesmen would have assisted with the opening of the gates of the yard, then the doors of the station to drag the engine out on to the street. A fireman would then be dispatched to approach the local butcher, or baker or milkman for availability of his horse. The animal would be rounded up, brought to the station and harnessed to the engine. The addition of ladders, buckets hoses and other equipment checked and added by the firemen before all was ready. A wag once suggested at the time, that one of the firemen should be sent *hotfoot* to the scene of the fire to keep it going pending the arrival of the brigade, but this was a little unfair!

1898: The alarm bell on the roof of the Priory Lane premises was raised to increase its effectiveness. Following a fire at Corsham Court, Lord Methuen announced that he was to create a private Fire Brigade to look after his numerous Corsham properties. The old Corsham well in the Court's arboretum garden, converted into a *Conduit-House* (Grade II Building Listing NGR: ST8731370993), is a good reliable source of additional water that could be used to deal with any fires in Corsham Court.

1899: The new rates of pay for the firemen were 5s.0p for the first hour of a fire, after which the rate dropped to 1s.0p.

1900: The old horse-drawn engine was completely overhauled and repainted. Further hydrants were placed at the junction of Hastings Road with Station Road, opposite Mr James's cottages in Pickwick Road, at the top of Priory Lane, at Pickwick opposite Clay Lane, at the Cross Keys and at Pound Pill.

1901: The first case of arson associated with the Suffragette Movement occurred in Corsham. Corsham Hackney Business *Fly* Operator Mr Banks', alongside the Cricket field, was paid a tender of 10 shillings to provide horses for the fire engine at Corsham, Lacock or Biddestone. When Mr. Banks later retired from his horse driven carriage business with the advent of the motor engine, he became the manager of the Royal Wilts Pork Shop. Fire Chief Mr. Martin kept the horses in a nearby field behind Ivy House, and he was very often seen, frantically trying to gather the horses together whenever an alarm was sounded. On those occasions, when the firemen's horses could not be caught, other horses had to be unhitched from the baker or corn merchant's carts! New jackets were provided for the firemen this year.

1903: The poor state of the engine meant that it could no longer be used for practice. Mr Bolton's house (Pockeridge Lodge) caught fire, but by the time the fire engine reached the premises, the fire was out; Mr Bolton was still charged £1.

1904: The brigade is reorganised again, with the men having to reapply for their own jobs after receiving their notice. A Volunteer Fire Brigade (VFB) was formed with Captain A.W. Butt and Superintendent Ward leading the new team. Payment was made to members for loss of time when attending fires. The Captain and his twelve men received £45 for the purchase of new uniforms.

1905: Corsham Parish Council propose widening the bottom of Priory Lane to give better access to and fro onto the High Street. This would require demolishing some buildings including the Fire Station.

1906: The Chippenham Brigade gifted Corsham a fire escape *contraption*, but this was disposed later in the year after the Corsham Captain condemned it as useless! In December, the Parish Council approached Mr. J.D. Horne, of Swainswick, as to whether he would sell his cottage at the bottom of Prior Lane and if so, at what price, to allow them to widen the road there. Mr. Horne replied that he was not disposed to sell the property for less than £200 *(£17,000 in today's money).* The price was considered unreasonable by the Parish Council.

THE THIRD FIRE STATION:

1907: To widen the bottom of Priory Lane it would be necessary for the Parish Council to acquire, Mr. Horne's cottage, the old *malt house* opposite Ivy House and part of the buildings adjoining, plus 40 perches of land. The total cost would was estimated at £825 (£70,000 in today's money) £400 of which was the price of purchasing Lord Methuen's land. This estimated figure was reduced to £555 later in the year.

Lord Methuen donated some land and offered help to convert the larger building at the back of the Malthouse (directly opposite Ivy House in Priory Lane) into a fire station. This late 19th century *(incorporating C17 /and early C18)* Grade II Listed building now houses the Nursery at Heywood Preparatory School. The men were now covered by accident insurance when attending fires and new helmets were procured. The cost for the services of the brigade, hire of engine and horses to attend a fire at Biddestone was £6.16s.

1908: The brigade gets its own standpipe; previously, they were supplied by the Water Company.

In June, the estimate for widening the bottom of Priory Lane was now £794; of which £300 had been promised, leaving £494 to be provided. The actual cost of widening the road was only £120, the rest was required to purchase the cottages and land. In August, the Parish Council applied for a loan of £500 from the County Council to complete the road widening.

1909: The Fire Station building was valued at £120. The alarm bell on the roof was raised higher to try and increase its effectiveness. Work on widening the bottom of Priory Lane commences early in the year, after many years of discussion!

1911: Following discontent by the firemen, the rates of pay were increased to the maximum allowed under the rules of the National Fire Brigade Union.

1912: The following article appeared in the local press in June, *'There is a fire hydrant on the water main at Pickwick, Wiltshire, but it is of little value at present, as nobody knows where it is. .....We hope there will not be a fire before the oldest inhabitant has time to bring his faculties to bear on the subject'.*

1913: The ineffectiveness of the alarm bell on the station's rooftop is investigated once again.

1914: War breaks out and the membership of the brigade suffers, due to those being called up for active service. The Red Cross Hospital recently set up in the Corsham Town Hall requires a fire hydrant to be placed in front of the building, plus attendance of a fireman on duty at all times. The Parish Council pay Lord Methuen £5 gross annually (£400 in today's money) for use of the fire station building.

1917: The 40 year-old manual fire engine pump was modified and extensive repairs and modifications were made.

1921: Captain Butt resigns after 17 years of service. He is succeeded by Captain Reynolds at an annual salary of £3.30p. Captain Reynolds had previously been a Regimental Captain in the British Army.

1923: A fire at Boyd's farm took 36 hours to put out, and the disputed bill of £64 was reduced to £52 (just over £2,000 in today's money).

1924: It took two months for the manual pump to be converted to a petrol driven one. It was manufactured by Maundrells of Calne, at a cost of £195; during which period, cover for Corsham was provided by the Chippenham Brigade. The pump was now capable of producing a jet of water 80 feet high in 5 minutes. Because of the lack of available horses, arrangements were made with a local lorry driver to tow the engine to fires. The fee paid was 4s.0p per mile, but it very often happened that the lorry was also not available! On one occasion, the men had to man-handle the engine to the scene of a fire at Biddestone! On another occasion during the year, the weight of the alarm bell caused the brigade roof to crash through when it was being sounded. In future, the first fireman to arrive at the station had to call the other men!

1926: Captain Reynolds was replaced by Captain George Lodge, with the Second Officer being Arthur J. Hobbs who later went on to wear the silver helmet of Captain for 15 years (making a total of 36 years service). Arthur served in the Royal Field Artillery during the 1914 war and was an archdeacon of the Baptist Church in Priory Street; he was also a collector of local historical relics which included a set of Roman dice! Arthur also ran a cycle shop at 38 High Street (now a dental surgery) and spent a lot of time leaning on the door frame of his front door, watching the world go by. He was also the local correspondent for the *Wiltshire Times*. Electric lights were installed at the fire station. There were several fires to attend to this year; a fire in the workshop at the Lindleys near Gastard caused

£1,500 worth of damage. A fire occurred at Greenhill when Mr Hancock's lorry was not available to tow out the engine. A fire occurred at Pickwick and a bungalow at the Ridge was completely burnt down, plus there was a 24 hour blaze at Gastard Court farm.

1927: The first local joint fire exercise was organised at Corsham Court, with the local brigades from Corsham, Chippenham and Trowbridge, being joined by the private Corsham Court team. The Corsham pump was damaged during the exercise and had to be returned to Mr Maundrell in Calne for repair. A telephone was installed in the Clerk's office, where it would also be convenient for fire brigade matters.

1929: Six young men were enlisted as trainee firemen to fill future vacancies as they arose. Fireman J.J. Rossiter resigns after 20 years service and he was replaced by H.J. Rossiter.

1930: In November a long cherished hope was realised when Corsham received its own motor-drawn fire-fighting machine so that they would not be hampered as in past days. Those who had served for over 25 years said that it was very rare to get away without a *'wait'.* First it was for horses, and many a time they had to man-handle the engine to the fire. Then soon after the war, horses became scarce. Then the pump was converted to petrol-driven and the weary handling of the levers was gone for ever. Next it was made as a trailer to attach to a lorry. Then the same old trouble arose, but instead of waiting for the availability of a horse it was a lorry, and occasionally it was half an hour after the firemen were ready to get away before a lorry arrived to take them! At the last fire, the Brigade manually ran the engine a mile towards the fire before a lorry came.

It was then decided that something should be done and Messrs. Bately and Sperring (Pickwick Motors) found a Daimler chassis. Mr E.W Maundrell of Maundrell Foundries Ltd Calne were paid £50-£60 to make Corsham's first self-propelled fire engine! They took out the Lister engine and pumps and fixed them to the Daimler chassis. There was accommodation for all the men with a well for carrying the hose and the ladders being carried on top. At last, Corsham had its first self-propelled fire engine! The Firemen were delighted with their new engine and appreciated the efforts of the Parish Council and their Clerk (Mr. H.B. Coates) for all that they had done in bringing the fire-fighting appliances up to date. Maundrell Foundries also made pig-singeing apparatus for the huge C & T Harris pig factory in Calne.

Long Service Medals for 25 years were presented to Captain Lodge, Second Officer Hobbs, and Fireman W. Young. The fire station entrance had to be raised three feet to get the new engine inside. Lord Methuen offered the brigade the use of his fire escape ladder for practice drills.

1931: Chief Officer George Lodge tendered his resignation after 36 years of service. Although there was no shortage of volunteer firemen, only one of them could drive the appliance!

1932: For the first time, the locations of all of the water hydrants were noted on a six-inch Ordinance map, making finding the hydrants during a fire so much easier! The firemen's uniforms purchased nearly 30 years ago in 1904 were replaced at a cost of £32.10s, after the original ones were condemned; this improved morale. The Chippenham Co-operative Society supplied the boots at 28s per pair. Messrs. Spackman & Sons supplied the Chief Officer's and Second Officer's requirements for £9. 10s., and Messrs. Huggins & Sons from Bristol provided the firemen's tunics for a total of £15. 17. 6p. There were no new hats though, except for the Chief!

1933: After 36 years causing trouble, the high kerbstone in front of the fire station in Priory Street was lowered to facilitate easier passage of the fire engine in and out of the station! The station doors were painted with bright red vermilion paint, with *'Fire Station'* blazoned across in black lettering.

1935: The old troublesome alarm bell *(this can still be seen on the roof top of the Priory Street Heywood school building)* was replaced with an electric siren positioned on the roof of the Town Hall. The siren was sounded for the first time in November, by the Chairman of the Parish Council; but there were still areas in Corsham where the alarm could still not be heard. A fireman was asked to resign having been accused of stealing from a colleague. He refused and was discharged but did not return his uniform until legal action was threatened. Summer floods required the help of the brigade to pump out several High Street basements (see Chapter 14). The brigade helps out with the preparations in Corsham to mark the Silver Jubilee of King George V.

1936: The lack of heating in the station resulted in the water jacket of the jump engine bursting in January. A Minimax soda-acid extinguisher for use on 'chimney stack fires' was purchased for £4.12s.6p along with a foam extinguisher. A telephone extension was installed in the Chief Officer's house.

1936: The fire siren was sounded prior to a two minute silence in Corsham church, in remembrance of King George V who died on 20th January. There were no hydrants available in Gastard for a fire drill at the local school but a nearby pond provided an effective alternative!

1937: Air raid precautions were discussed, but there was no extra money to be had from the Rural Council for making any additional provisions. An appeal was launched for volunteers to assist the fire brigade in times of emergency. The brigade was thanked by the Corsham Council, for *the 'arduous work'* they did in preparation for the bonfire and firework display in Corsham Park, to celebrate the coronation of King George VI.

1938: The Parish Council asked the Town Crier to inform people that there would be testing in October of the fire siren on the top of the Town Hall, after it had been adapted to also give out a wailing sound to warn of air raids. Mr Dyke, the jeweller whose shop was opposite the Town Hall volunteered to sound the first test of the air raid siren which lasted 70 seconds.

The Corsham Brigade is now part of an Auxiliary Fire Brigade department that covers a wider area, formed as a back-up to assist others during the period of war. The Auxiliary Fire Service (AFS) was first formed in 1938 in Great Britain as part of the Civil Defence Service. Its role was to supplement the work of brigades at local level. In November, the Fire Brigades Act 1938 was the start of a take-over of responsibility for fire matters in Corsham, by the larger Calne & Chippenham Rural District Council; the Corsham brigade would now cover the additional larger area to the west of Chippenham to Malmesbury Road and out as far as Lacock.

1939: As from the 1st January there was no longer a Fire Brigade Committee in Corsham. The old horse-drawn fire engine known to have been in use prior 1877 *(which ran on sold tyres!)* was sold to an engineering firm in Bath for £35. The total sale of all the fire equipment came to £179. 13s 10p, far short of the original sum requested by the Corsham Parish of £248.3s3p.

The siren on the top of the Town Hall was rented back to the Calne & Chippenham Rural District Council for a rate of five shillings. The money from the sale was deposited in a Bank account by the Corsham Parish, in the hope that after the war, they would once again become the fire authority in Corsham. From 1st September four firemen were always on-duty but they had no steel helmets or protective clothing. Moral was low and they were stood down after a fortnight. No one had the authority to pay them for loss of earnings and they remained out of pocket.

THE FOURTH FIRE STATION:

1940: On the 29 January despite the failure of telephone calls getting through and the state of the local lanes, the Corsham men were promptly at their station to deal with a fire at the Neston Glove Factory. But not all was well, as the fire engine that had done them well over so many years, failed to start. To save time, Mr. Hobbs and some of the men went ahead with a hose pump and some fire extinguishers in the hope of mitigating the severity of the blaze pending the arrival of their Corsham fire engine and another one from Chippenham arriving. In the end, it was the prompt response by the Chippenham brigade that saved the factory. Since the Fire Brigade's Act of 1938, requests had been sent by the Parochial Committee to the Rural District Council, requesting that the Corsham brigade should be given the proper equipment needed to continue its good work. But red tape seems to have gotten in the way causing more discontent amongst the Corsham men.

After the factory fire, the Corsham Clerk wrote to the Parochial Committee, complaining that the Corsham Firemen who had attended the serious fire at the Glove Works in Neston were frozen stiff, due to their inadequate uniforms, compared to the fully equipped men from the Chippenham Brigade who also attended. It's no wonder that moral was low!

Having continued to answer calls up to March, the whole of the fire brigade resigned, as they had still not been paid for the on-duty work carried out on instruction from the Home Office the previous September. Their uniforms were handed in. The fire engine was sold privately, leaving the Rural

District Council to purchase the remaining fire equipment. Fire cover was provided by the Chippenham brigade whilst a new brigade was being raised and trained by Mr. A.V. Brown of Altus Engineering, with Mr. A.W. Cawte as Second Officer. New equipment and two fire tenders are purchased. The newly formed brigade resumes fire fighting responsibility in December, and they move into the Grade II outbuilding to the east at the rear of the Methuen Arms. This becomes the fourth Corsham Fire Station. The two storey building was originally a stable and a loft, and later used by Osbornes the local builders and stonemasons (see Chapter 30) who employed a huge team of men, working the stone. R. N. Gordon-Farleigh of The Wine Lodge, (now an Estate Agents), also rented this property for storage and bottling purposes in the late 1950's. It was built in the 18th century out of rubble stone with a half-hipped roof, slated to north, stone tiles to south. The west front has two blocks of five-tier dove openings on each side.

Meanwhile, war looms on with many London evacuees arriving in Corsham. In the summer, taps could not be used from 7pm to 9am because of a drought. Often, the drinking water was so polluted, that when it was available, it could not be used at all.

1941: Efforts to improve the water supply continued, but water pressure was a problem for the fire crew when early in the year, a *Lysander trainer* plane crashed into Mr. Moody's house at the top of 16 Station Road just up from the Gospel Chapel. For many years, you could see the black smoke stains on the masonry either side of the front door. The plane ended up stuck between the rafters on the roof for several weeks. The crash resulted in a letter being sent by the Corsham Council *(bypassing the Rural Council),* directly to Mr Herbert Morrison, the Minister for Home Security, complaining about the poor water supply which hampered the fire fighting operations on that day.

News was received that fire fighting was to be nationalised, with control passing to Company Officer A.V. Thomas at the main fire station at Chippenham.

1942: When the National Fire Service took over fire fighting responsibility in Corsham, the newly formed brigade's Chief Officer Mr. A.V. Brown resigned, after declining a *demotion* offer of reverting to the lower rank of Section Leader,

1943: Mr. Sheppard took over from Mr. Cawte as the brigade's Section Leader. The firemen eventually received their overdue Long Service Medals. The old fire station at the bottom of Priory Street (opposite Ivy House) continues to be used for parking the local ambulance and as a mortuary.

When Queen Mary visited Chippenham on 21 August she went to inspect a collection of *Fire Insurance Plaques* held by Joseph Buckle, a fishmonger in Chippenham. For most of the 18th century, before municipal fire services were formed, insurance companies maintained their own fire brigades which only extinguished fires in those buildings insured by the company.

To identify the buildings that were covered, a small plaque (the original ones were made of heavy lead) was attached to the front of the building at a height easily seen from the street but out of reach of thieves.

An original 'Sun Fire Office' *Fire Insurance Plaque (*a large sun with a face) from Corsham was previously given to Joseph Buckle by Field Marshal Lord Methuen who had it removed from one of his properties in Church Street. You can see a replica of this plaque on the front of the Old Post

Office (later the Halifax Building Society) building at 15 High Street. Each company had its own distinctive design which made identification of the property easier for their fire fighters.

1945: There was a public outcry in Corsham, when a press report in October covered a fire incident during the *'Victory over Japan'* night in Neston at 2230 hours, when a rick caught fire at Moor Barton Farm. The call bell system did not work, the siren was not sounded and the Police Station was not manned; the Chippenham and Military brigades could not find the farm at first (the engine from Chippenham eventually arrived 35 minutes later). When the local brigade finally got the message, it was only put on standby; nobody knew where the water hydrants were; the static water tank was under lock and key, but the key was not available! The hose was run out the wrong way and burst. And it was not until 0100 hours that a continuous supply of water was achieved. The Clerk of the Parish Council said that the Corsham fire bell had not been working for a month and the siren could not be used at night!

The Hon. Mrs Methuen said, *"If my house was on fire, I'd see the siren was sounded"*. She went on to say, *"Our old [Corsham Court] fire brigade was voluntary and cheap and whist things didn't always go right, we do expect these officers who have such great salaries to do better"*.

This was a stinging and forthright comment on the capabilities of the so-called professional fire services at that time, and it highlighted the confusion and lack of coordination between the different brigades in the area! Corsham Parish Council's hope that local control could be restored was in vain. This resulted in the resignation of Corsham's Section Leader Mr. Sheppard, in protest over the current system.

1948: The National Fire Service damaged the Town Hall roof during an inspection of the siren.

1949 - 16 April: Just before 2 p.m., Corsham's new Fire Tender driven by Fireman H. Bond, turned completely over on to its side as it was rounding the corner from the High Street into Priory Street when answering a call. Fireman H. Bond received bruises and abrasions, Fireman Ivor Leonard had a suspected fracture of the collar-bone and Fireman A. Hampton received slight injuries.

The fire was at the home of Miss Burchell, 118 Prior Street, her bed clothes had apparently become ignited. Her nephew got her safely downstairs and neighbour Mr. H. Batley, after trying to extinguish the flames, gave the alarm.

Two other neighbours Messrs. T. Rose and C. Collins crawled into the burning bedroom and threw most of the burning bedclothes out of the window and into the garden. By the time that the Chippenham Fire Brigade had arrived, the fire was almost under control!

On the 28th June the Chief Inspector viewed the following six sites in Corsham, with a view of providing a new location for the fire station in Corsham.

1. Corner of Grove Road and Station Road in a walled field of several acres.
2. Priory Street, High Street end in enclosed fields.
3. Near the Community Centre in open narrow space.
4. Pickwick Road near the Hare and Hounds.
5. Priory Street, Bath Road end in open space.
6. End of Grove Road in a walled field with a five barred gate, and occupied by a timber built garage.

A further alternative site at the end of the Tynings had previously been considered unsuitable. Only four of these sites were deemed practical, as they were in central potions; but it transpired, that these four areas had already been earmarked by the Local Authority for new housing. Lord Methuen was also unable to agree to the use of any development at the Grove field.

26 July: News was received, that the Secretary of State was not prepared to exercise his emergency powers of requisitioning, in order to enable the County Council to retain possession of the premises occupied at the Methuen Arms Hotel. It now becomes all the more essential that alternative premises for the fire station should be found with the minimum of delay.

18 August: The County Architect, F.I Bowden, suggested that a portion of the land recently purchased by the Health Committee, west of the Health Centre Clinic (near where the Porch Doctor's Surgery now sits) would be suitable for the new Corsham fire station, if it could be released.

1950: The lease on the Methuen Arms Fire Station is soon to expire. This leads to the search for suitable land to build a new station in Corsham. Arthur J. Hobbs *(also known then as Mr. Corsham')* who gave 36 years of service to the Corsham fire brigade, passes away. On 25 January the Corsham Parish Council sent a strong letter of objection to the Wilts County Council against use of the land adjoining the Health Centre Clinic for a new fire station to be built, as for the last two years, this piece of land had been used as allotments, now in a good state of cultivation due to the arduous work by the plot holders! It was suggested that instead, the strip of land to the left side of the entrance to Beechfield Road *(i.e. opposite where the Porch Surgery is now)*, would be more suitable.

1952: In October a ***cat***astrophic incident occurred when a valuable Siamese kitten climbed a big Elm Tree at the back of houses in South Street. The inspector of the R.S.PC.A. was sent for but arrived with no equipment. He called for the Fire Brigade's help. Two ladders were lashed together and Sub. Officer C. Davies went up some 35 to 40 feet and brought down the kitten safely to the ground. The kitten's cries had been heard over a wide area!

THE FIFTH FIRE STATION:

1952: After several years of wrangling as to where the new fire station should be built, a letter dated 18th July from the Home Office, finally agreed in principle to the erection (alongside the Health Clinic), of the first phase of the proposed new fire station at Corsham during the current financial year. A letter dated 17th December from the Home Office gave the official go-ahead to proceed with the tender from T. Merrett & Sons of Box, to build the first phase for a sum of £5,002.19s.3p.

1954: In October a letter was sent by the *'burly'* Corsham firemen, to the County Architect at Trowbridge, complaining that the water heater in the men's ablution room was defective. It kept delivering sprays of water from the top whenever it was turned on!

One would think that it would be a good permanent training fixture to have left it as it was! It was also suggested, that the type of sponge rubber strip used by motor body builders could be used to stop a draft coming through the half inch gap under the new fire station doors!

Photo shoes volunteer Firemen Joseph Rossiter and Mr. Clitheroe.

1986: There were 20 men in Corsham Fire Service when it is fully manned. Depending on what rank they were, they were paid £700 - £900 a year retaining pay. For a turnout they got £7 if there were enough men to man the appliance and if they didn't get on, they got £3. For a practice or drill they got £5. The firemen were called out on average, four times a week.

Station Officer Maurice Hancock retires from the now part-time station after 26 years of service. Maurice was also the caretaker at Corsham School and was one of the instigators in setting up the Corsham's twinning link with the French town Jargaeu where he was made an Honorary Corporal. Note: In recent years, the Corsham crew were alerted to emergencies by the siren situated on the top of the tower at the fire station.

Then it went ' hi - tech'.......... a large bell connected to the phone line, was installed in each of the firemen's houses at the foot of the stairs. This system worked well, but if there happened to be an emergency during the night, the whole household knew about it. Also at 07.30 each morning, the bell was automatically tested with a short 'coded' ring. Thankfully, later with the arrival of mobile phone technology, the firemen were issued with personal pagers to alert them.

1991: Heywood School moves its nursery classes into the newly refurbished old [THIRD] fire station building opposite Ivy House at the bottom of Priory Street.

1995: After a number of years of being involved socially with the station, Corsham crew manager Keith Shackleford successfully applied to be a retained fire fighter in 1995, going on to the role of crew manager in July 2001.

2004: The old Methuen Arms [FOURTH] Fire Station site at the back of the Methuen Arms is restored following a large fire in the premises.

2010: A £200,000 refurbishment of the 1950s [FIFTH] fire station building in Beechfield Road Corsham, SN13 9DN is completed.

2013: Ex-fire fighter Martin O'Shea aged 49 passed away, only months after he was diagnosed with an aggressive form of motor neurone disease. Former colleagues from Corsham Fire Station accompanied Martin's coffin to St Bartholomew's Church. ***R.I.P Martin.***

Keith Shackleford who served with Martin, for ten years at Corsham Fire Station said at the time;

"I had the privilege to serve alongside Martin. He was a great friend of mine and a great fireman – just a great individual. And to face what he did with the attitude he did shows his strength of character. He was one of us, and always will be".

2018: The current Station Manager at Corsham is Ade Hurren. Corsham is now an on-call station, so its fire fighters have other jobs and obligations. They commit time to the Fire & Rescue Service throughout the week and respond to emergency calls when paged.

Keith Shackleford's words above are a fitting end to this detailed history of the brave Firemen that have kept the Corsham residents safe over the past 200 years.

Thank you all.

Corsham Firemen celebrating a wedding at the Baptist Church in Priory Street.

Chapter 14. Floods - The Great Railway Flood of 1935.

The photo shows a view west from Potley Bridge, towards the viaduct and Corsham Railway Station.

One of the largest recorded floods in Corsham occurred on Tuesday 25th June 1935 during a heavy thunderstorm which deposited three inches of rain within two-and-a-half hours. Charles Lanham may still have been the stationmaster there on that day, as he was certainly in the post in 1939.

The elevation *above mean sea level* of the old Corsham railway station is 276 feet, making it one of Corsham's lowest lying areas.

Nearly all the land surrounding the old railway station is much higher; e.g. the town centre is 308ft, Lacock Road 300ft, Hare and Hounds 376ft, top of Box Hill near Rudloe, 472ft, Rudloe Fiveways 479ft, Westwells 351ft, Neston Church 394ft, top of Rough Street 390ft, Leafield Trading Estate 335ft, upper Potley 318ft, and Prospect 299ft etc.

Only the land to the west of Corsham *(i.e. towards Chippenham and the Ladbrook Bridge)* is lower at 243ft. Therefore, the topography of Corsham is such that nearly all rainwater flows downhill towards the lowest part of Corsham to where the old railway station and its approaching cuttings lay in the Corsham hillsides.

On Tuesday 25th June 1935 the Yockney Brook which meanders along from the reservoir just west of the station at the end of Pockeridge Drive, burst its banks near the station, pouring water down the embankment and into the railway cutting alongside the station, completely covering the sidings and the main lines. The 3:15pm Chippenham to Bath train just about managed to get through, but by 3:33pm *[only minutes after the train had departed Corsham]* the track was completely flooded to a depth of 3 feet 6 inches. Within an hour, the level rose to 9 feet in the station, completely covering the platforms and the waiting room seats.

The signal box was completely isolated, leaving the signalman trapped for over two hours and all the electrical circuits were cut off. The track, nearly all the way to the Box Tunnel entrance was flooded, with the tunnel itself remaining dry due to the rising gradient on the track as it approaches Box tunnel at 328ft above sea level.

Passengers sitting in the 4.47 p.m., Bath-to-Chippenham train at Bath station were transferred by bus via Lansdown, Wick, Marshfield and Biddestone, arriving in Chippenham at 8:30pm, four hours later than they had originally planned! Would-be passengers travelling on the Great Western Railway between the hours of 5:30 and 8:30 were conveyed from Bath to Chippenham and vice-versa by a fleet of motor buses. The line was usable again by half-past eight.

The rail track at Corsham remains at risk, with floods *(albeit not as bad as in 1935)* occurring from time to time. The flooding risk was recognised in the Environment Agency's Bristol Avon *Catchment Flood Management Plan of 2012*, which stated:

'Undertake integrated urban drainage studies, in particular for main line rail flood risks, and implement any recommended improvements, discourage inappropriate development and reinforce contingency planning and self-help in Corsham.'

Wessex Water's Bristol Avon Catchment Plan for January 2016 also recognised the risk:

'Surface water drainage and sewer flooding, which has occurred in parts of Bristol, Bath, Midsomer Norton, Chipping Sodbury and Corsham. Several other towns have the potential to be at risk from surface water flooding.'

The drainage water these days is managed by the newly constructed aqueduct alongside 'Tramways' near Potley Bridge, where the rainwater is now funnelled down into the Ladbrook steam which meanders through the *'Batters'* on its way towards Lacock before discharging into the River Avon just the other side and north of Lacock Abbey.

The following depicts a dreadful accident which occurred at the Corsham aqueduct in 1881.

FATAL RAILWAY ACCIDENT AT CORSHAM. A STOKER KILLED. 20th October 1881.

A dreadful accident occurred on the Great Western Railway near the Corsham Station this morning. As the passenger train which leaves Bristol at eleven o'clock and is timed to arrive at Corsham at 11.55, drew near to the station the driver and fireman noticed the break rod to be out of order. The fireman, leaning far out and bending so as to look in under the engine to see what was wrong, did not notice that the train was approaching the aqueduct which crosses the railway about 200 yards from Corsham Station. In consequence his head came in contact with great force with the buttress of the aqueduct and he was thrown onto the line. The driver did not notice his absence until the train had nearly reached the station. Some packers who were at work close by, observed after the train had passed the aqueduct, a man on the line and upon going up to him found it was the fireman and quite dead; death being from the nature of the blow instantaneous. His name was, we believe, James Humphries, and he was an inhabitant of Bristol but a native of Saltford where his friends reside. He was a very steady young man, about 26, and was an experienced fireman.

Chapter 15. Football - Corsham Town Football Club.

Corsham Town football team. Chippenham & District league champions.
Season 1905 – 1906

There are two major influences in the history of Corsham Football Club: (1) the struggle (particularly in the early years) to generate enough revenue to keep the Club going, and: (2) the prolonged battle in the late 1940s to find an alternative venue after the Rural District Council drew up plans to build houses on the Club's first ground at Pickwick Road, which was in a field at the very top and above where the Recreation Ground is these days.

Apart from local newspaper articles, most of the Club's early history has been lost, nevertheless.......

1863: It's important to understand that the Laws of Football were only just beginning to form and that it was a different game to what we see today. The Laws of Association Football were first produced in 1863 and were partly based on Rugby rules. Although 'offside' was included in the 1863's original rules, it was vastly different to the Rules/Laws of Associated Football used today. Back then, any attacker ahead of the ball was effectively offside. This meant that the tactical arrangements of the time tended to feature up to eight forwards. It was in the late 1860s that *The Football Association* decided to adopt a three-player rule (later reduced to two), with the attacker called offside if positioned ahead of the third-last defender. This allowed the passing game to develop. At first, the referee stood on the touchline, tasked with keeping time and 'referred to' when the two umpires failed to reach a decision on their own. In 1891 a single person was introduced (The Referee!) with the authority to send players off and give penalties and free-kicks without listening to appeals. The two umpires then became linesmen, nowadays commonly called 'Assistant Referees.'

1884: Corsham Town Football Club was formed.

1887: The rival Chapel Knapp Football Club was formed in Gastard by the kind liberality of Mr. T. Fowler of Gastard House, who presented the club with the whole of the necessary paraphernalia and gave the team permission to practice in a field next to the park in Gastard. Mr. T. Fowler became the president, Mr. T. Merritt the captain and Mr. F. Aust the secretary.

1889: *A Summer newspaper report:* A match was played on the Corsham Cricket Ground between the Melksham and Corsham Clubs which resulted in a victory for the visiting team by 4 goals to 2. From the commencement of the game, the home team was closely pressed and Melksham quickly scored two goals. After a little *even play* Corsham obtained their first goal which was not long afterwards succeeded by another. A dispute arose as to the fairness of the last goal and the Referee from Chippenham being appealed to, promptly decided in the favour of Corsham. The Melksham Team declined to proceed further with the game unless the Corsham umpire was withdrawn and a fresh one appointed. The Corsham Captain consented and the game proceeded, terminating as previously stated!

1890: Another of Corsham Football Club's early newspaper reports featured a match played on Christmas day against Chapel Knapp. The match was played on the *away ground* and resulted in a win for Corsham by 5 goals to 3. The teams were as follows:

Corsham: Payne goalkeeper, Allard and Dew backs, H.E. Mayo, Little and Clark Half-backs, Smith, Hancock, E.G. Mayo, Elwin and H.C. Yockney forwards.
Chapel Knapp: E. Merritt goalkeeper, T. Merritt and T. Aust backs, A. Fox, William Shewring and Pearce half-backs; A. Aust, Lodge, T. Fowler, W. Fox and H. Fox forwards.

1893: Corsham Town Football Club become affiliated to the Football Association, i.e. they were now a proper registered football club under the new Football Association regulations. It is very likely that the Club used the cricket ground for their early matches before establishing themselves on the Pickwick Road ground circa 1900.

One of the Corsham's earliest Cup games on record was Corsham v Swindon Town Athletic played on 27 October 1893 in the initial round of the County Challenge Cup competition, with Swindon winning 2-6. The Referee was the Rev. W.N.C. Wheeler. In the return match at Corsham the following week on Saturday 4 November, the Corsham team (having advantage of their home ground) were expected to make the Swindon cup holders sit-up. The Quarrymen (a nickname then given to Corsham) made a good start, for almost as soon as the ball was in motion the Corsham forwards rushed through the Swindon backs and scored. Then the Athletes' turn came, and they went to work with a will. Strive as they would however, the Corsham backs and goalkeeper held them in check for a long time. Hayward, who was playing a clinking game with his partner, Bywater, on the left-wing, at last opened the Town's account scoring with a capital long shot. Bailey notched a second point and at half time the score was standing at two to one in favour of Swindon. Corsham anticipated that they would pull off the encounter with success when they restarted with the wind behind them, but matters went very much the other way and Swindon scored repeatedly.

Floyd, Bailey, Price and Hayward, notched a goal a piece for the Athletes, making the total up to a round half dozen. Shortly before the referee sounded the final whistle, the Corsham forwards broke through the Swindon defence and S. P. Kinneir (who later went on to play cricket for Warwickshire and was a Test cricketer - *see Chapter 10*) drove a splendid shot past Southall. Nothing beyond this was placed on the record and the game terminated to a second win for Swindon by 6 goals to 2. The Rev. Mr. W.N.C. Wheeler was once again the referee.

A few days later, the 25 November issue of the newspaper *Wilts and Gloucestershire Standard* reported the following concerning the Chapel Knapp captain:

'A shocking accident occurred at Messrs. Yockney and Co.'s stone quarries early on Saturday morning. While a man named William Shrewring was at work the ceiling gave way and about two tons of stone and debris fell upon him, literally crushing him to a pulp. A man named Tanner who was working near, at once went to his assistance, and with other help succeeded in extricating the poor fellow. A doctor was also sent for, but death must have been instantaneous. The deceased, who was married nearly two years ago, leaves a widow and one child, for whom great sorrow is felt. The deceased was well known in Corsham, and was captain of the [Chapel Knapp] Football Club for two seasons.'

1894: The first Wiltshire Football League was formed; three years after the Swindon & District League had been established and three years before the Trowbridge & District League came into being. Corsham became the first champions of the Wiltshire Football League by winning the league on goal average over Southbroom (Devizes), much helped by an emphatic 17-1 win over Calne in their final game!

1900: This would have roughly been about the time when Corsham Football Club established themselves on the Pickwick Road ground, which became their first proper venue in a field north of the present day Recreation Ground (where the top of the Arnolds Mead houses are today).

1906: Chippenham and District League Champions for season 1905-1906 (see first photo).

1907: Corsham Football Club started to hold annual sports days on their Pickwick Road ground in aid to boost funds.

1920: On 10 January, Corsham won a friendly match against Marshfield and later entertaining Sherston from the Chippenham League. The Corsham Town Prize Band promised to '*play selections*' in the Bandstand at the top of the Recreation ground alongside the football field.

1920s: William (Will) Smith born 29 September 1901, once an amateur footballer with Corsham Town in the Wiltshire League, *moved on* to join the Southern League team Bath City for a season and a half. Will later turned professional by signing for Notts County on the Trentside where he spent four years until his transfer to West Ham in 1927. He made his debut for the 'Hammers' in the 2-5 away defeat by Huddersfield Town on 7 January 1928. His only other appearance for West Ham was one year and twelve days later, again a 2-5 defeat against Aston Villa at Villa Park. In May of 1923, Smith returned home to Corsham for a short holiday before travelling to Denmark for a tour with the Notts County team, along with rivals Huddersfield.

1921: Corsham Club were suspended for 14 days for playing an unregistered player Mr.A. May in a match against Sherston. Corsham Club Secretary had told the FA Council that they had *'originally left*

May out of the team, but when they got to the ground, they realised that their team was one man short, so were bound to play him. I hope you find this satisfactory?'

The FA Council replied, *'That it was not only not satisfactory, but a serious breach of the rules'*! The player was suspended for 21 days.

1923: The Corsham Football Club's Six-a-Side tournament in June was not the success that the Club had hoped for, with the final resulting in Chippenham St. Paul's B Team beating Spencers (Melksham) by 9 - 2. At the annual general meeting held in the Town Hall, the Chairman Mr. F. Dyke received the treasurer's report showing that a deficit of nearly £16 (£700 in today's money) at the start of the year, had reduced to a balance in hand of £4. 1s 6p. It was decided to run two teams, the first in the Second Division of the Wilts League, with the reserves in First Division Chippenham and District league. Mr. E. Head was elected Captain of the first team with H. Boulter as vice-captain, with J. Andrews and Vere Gale taking up respective roles for the reserve side.

1928: At a special commission of the Wiltshire F.A held at the Corsham Town Hall, Corsham F.C. were ordered to post warning notices around their ground during the whole of next season. This was a result of happenings that occurred during a game against Trowbridge, where Corsham's centre-half Boulter struck Shepherd, a Frome Reserves player, both during the and after the match. Boulter was suspended until December 1st and Corsham were ordered to pay 10s towards Frome's expenses. In September, the Corsham Reserves played their first game of the season when they visited St Marks (Bath) and lost by four goals to three, after being three nil up!

1930: Corsham drew 2-2 against Chapel Knapp in the first round of the Chippenham Hospital Cup. A few weeks later, having been beaten by Chapel Knapp in the return leg, Corsham played them again for the third time in three weeks, and won by 8-4 in a Chippenham League game; with the scorers for Corsham being Swanborough 4, Baker 2, Hayes and Robinson with 1 each.

1935-1936 Final League Tables

WILTS TIMES LEAGUE: FINAL TABLES

DIVISION I.

	S.	W.	D.	L.	Agg.	P.
Salisbury	12	11	0	1	7.010	22
Swindon	12	9	1	2	7.060	19
Trowbridge	12	9	1	2	7.000	19
Marlborough	12	8	2	2	7.089	18
Corsham	12	8	1	3	7.026	17
Devizes	12	6	1	5	6.953	13
Wilton	12	6	0	6	6.963	12
Marl. Col. O.T.C.	12	4	1	7	6.924	9
R.E. Larkhill	12	3	1	8	6.913	7
Mere B.L.	12	3	1	8	6.907	7
Warminster	12	3	0	9	6.917	6
Pythouse	12	2	1	9	6.837	5
Westbury	12	1	0	11	6.872	2

DIVISION II.

	S.	W.	D.	L.	Agg.	P.
Swindon B	16	15	1	0	9.258	31
Marlborough B	16	14	1	1	9.274	29
Salisbury B	16	13	0	3	9.094	26
Trowbridge B	16	11	0	5	9.049	22
Corsham B	16	10	1	5	9.047	21
Warminster B	16	10	0	6	9.015	20
Westbury B	16	9	2	5	8.472	20
R.E. Larkhill B	16	9	0	7	9.013	18
Devizes B	16	9	0	7	9.001	18
Marl. Col. O.T.C. B.	16	7	0	7	9.025	14
Marlborough D	16	6	1	9	8.799	13
Marlborough C	16	5	0	11	8.919	10
Devizes C	16	5	0	11	8.552	10
Marl. Col. O.T.C. C	16	3	0	13	8.888	6
Westbury C	16	3	0	13	8.582	6
Mere B.L. B	16	2	0	14	8.725	4
Westbury D	16	2	0	14	8.675	4

1935: At the annual meeting held in August, it was reported to the President the Rev. G. Holborow that the Club's debt had been reduced by £7 (which was about £350 in those days).

1936: At the annual meeting held in June, it was reported to Mr. R.E. Fowles the Club president, that last season's deficit of £23 4s and 9 1/2p was reduced to £14 *(which is about £700 these days)!*

1937: At the annual meeting held in July it was reported to Captain Slater the Club president, that a deficit of £14 0s 6p had been reduced to £7 17s 9p by the end of last season *(about £350 today).*

In December, Mr Matthew John Tate, a member of Corsham Football Club, married Dorothy Maud Perry, daughter of the late Mr. W. Perry of South Wales, and Mrs. Perry of Pickwick Road. The bride was given away by her brother (Mr. C. N. Perry).

1939: At the annual meeting held in July it was reported that next season, the Club would share its ground on the Pickwick Road with the R.E.s (Royal Engineers) Corsham. Mr. G. Dyke the honorary secretary said that the R.E.s were putting up new dressing rooms with baths. Match fixtures had been arranged so that when one club was playing at home, the other team played away. The R.E.s were based in the Basil Hill Camp along Park Lane.

1946-1947: Wiltshire Junior Cup - Champions.

THE BATTLE FOR GROVE FIELD

1947-1948: Wiltshire League - Champions. In September 1947 Corsham Town Football Club sent a letter to the Council, inquiring whether they would be prepared to sell them a portion of Corsham's proposed central housing site, at present used as their football field. The Rural Council informed the Club, that it regretted that it was not able to sell this land which had specifically been acquired for housing purposes. During the year, the Council's house building program was cut back, allowing the football club to use their Pickwick Road ground for another year.

1948: Trouble looms for the Club, when they are told that the Rural District Council had decided to build houses on the Club's Pickwick Road ground and the Club were asked to find an alternative venue. Mr. W.G. Freegard, who presided at the Calne and Chippenham Rural District Council meeting, said that it must have been obvious after the war, that the Corsham Football Club would need a field to play on, yet the Rural District Council had decided to build houses on the Club's Pickwick Road ground, following 50 years of football being played there.

Lord Methuen had written to confirm that the Corsham Estate Company would be very pleased to *'Let'* the South Bank farm field along Lacock Road (currently occupied by Mr. Griffin) to the Corsham Football Club, on which a permanent pavilion could be built. But Mr. Griffin strongly objected to the proposal as he did not agree to the taking of further land from the farm. His objection was supported by Mr. C.W. Watson, County Land Agent who stated that the County Small Holdings Committee (who leased the land) had not been informed of the proposal.

Mr. A.W. Nicholson pointed out that providing services on the South Bank would be very expensive. He offered the use of land owned by him at Hartham for an experimental period of time but the Football Club turned this down as the land was quite unsuitable, having set their heart on obtaining the Grove Field (alongside the cricket field) which was not being used for agricultural purposes.

The Corsham Football Club wrote to the Finance Committee declining the South Bank ground because: it was not situated close enough to the residential areas of Corsham, it would need to be enclosed, and costly water, electric and sewerage facilities would need to be provided. The estimated cost of compulsory purchase of the Grove field (which was not serving any useful purpose to the community) would have been between £4,500-£7,000 (about £150,000-£180,000 in today's money). Apart from the allotments at the far end, the Grove field has remained empty to this day.

Mr Watkins said that he was officially informed that a loan of £10,000 could be raised over 60 years, at a cost of a half-penny rate over the whole Rural district, or 1 1/2p over Corsham alone. There was a genuine concern at the time that interest in a Club with an average following of 700 could *peter out* if a solution was not found soon.

The Council's concern was that if the Grove Field was purchased, the Council would land itself with a cost of £400-£500 per annum (now £10,000-£13,000), which would have to be funded by the ratepayers of the whole district and not just the Corsham residents.

Patience seemed to be running out at this time, with Mr. Freegard asking the question;

'Is there a town of its size in this country in such a position as Corsham, where we find ourselves with no football field, no houses, and practically <u>no-nothing</u>.' Mr. Hullyer, the Club Chairman, said, *'That the Rural Council had no right to take away Corsham's old football field for houses when there was other land zoned for building on.'*

A question was asked why the houses couldn't be built on the Lacock Road field instead.

Corsham F.C. initially turned down the offer from Lord Methuen for use of the South Bank farm field as a new venue in Lacock Road. Once again, the Club felt that it was too far away from the Town centre and that it was valuable farmland. At that time, the Club's preferred solution was to relocate to the Grove field which would have been ideal in terms of attracting a greater number of spectators and for its more suitable location alongside the Cricket Field in Station Road.

The Chippenham Rural Council applied for a Compulsory Order to be made in respect to purchasing Grove Field for the Football Club's use, but this proposal was rejected by their Finance Committee on the basis that it would result in high rental costs for use as a football ground.

Tempers were beginning to get frayed - at the Chippenham Rural Council meeting held on 9 August 1948 Mr. R. Watkins (one of the Corsham members) led a deputation from the Club and presented a petition signed by 1,200 townspeople in support of his case. Later, he left the meeting in protest against refusal to reconsider a decision regarding use of part of Grove field for Corsham Football Club. The Council stated once again, that it had refused to apply for an Order for compulsory purchase, because of the costs of purchasing the field.

Leaving all the battling politics of the new venue location behind, the team having won promotion to the Wiltshire League Division 1, Corsham Town embark on an ambitious programme in senior football. The F.A. Cup, Amateur Cup, and Wilts County Cup. At the end of the season in the last week of April, Corsham played four matches in seven days! Wanting two points to be sure of winning the Wilts League 2 championship, Corsham put out their best team on the Monday night and thrashed the visitors Atworth 7-1, making Corsham's position at the top of the league unassailable. The 100th goal this season was scored during this game from a penalty.

1949: The *'Grove Field'* battle continues. The Parliamentary Committee supports the objection to use South Bank, on the premise that it would interfere with agricultural requirements and that alternative sites had not yet been considered to the same degree.

1949: The battle for the Grove Field is lost, with preparations now well in hand to develop the South Bank field along Lacock Road. By August, the new South Bank field is ready and stages its first game, with the Reserves losing at home 4-1 to Malmesbury, whilst the first team win 8-3 away at Pewsey.

In early September, Corsham's first team begin their first season at home on their new South Bank ground in Lackock Road, by welcoming Pinehurst Y.C. During the interval, a £55 cheque was presented by Mr. W. Freegard to Mr. Ernie Horlock on behalf of the Supporters' Club. The attendance of 400 was quite good, but fell short of the committee's expectations. It was said that the ground was a little way from town, but it is hoped that a bus service could be run to and fro to the ground on match days! The match ended up a draw at 2-2, which is probably *much about the same* result as the battle for a new venue! A former Corsham footballer, Mr. A.J. Pearce of Priory Street, presented the Management Committee of the Chippenham and District League with a handsome silver cup which has since been allocated to that league's Youth Knock-out Cup competition.

1950: Now that the dust of politics had finally achieved a result in the quest for a new ground, Mr. L. Waterton stated at the annual general meeting that the club's assets were healthier than they had been for sometime and now stood at £238 (nearly £700 in today's money), with £60 owing on the dressing rooms. Gate receipts were £213 7s 5p, with subscriptions £50 and a profit of £112 for dances and competitions. By now, the money was being more wisely spent. Mr. A. Pinnel was re-appointed linesman, with thanks for past services. It was stated that some form of shelter would be available for spectators by the time the 1950-1951 season commenced. The Corsham Town Supporters' Club chaired by Mr. H. Curtis achieved the largest following that has ever gone away (so far) with the Town Club when 300 of their supporters watched the first team play Trowbridge Town. They made their presence felt in more ways than one! They all seemed to thoroughly enjoy the game and even though Corsham lost the game, the team were not disgraced. They appreciated the Trowbridge Town Supporters' Club who managed to send over two coaches for the Corsham supporters, when none locally could be secured.

Ron Lodge who was in the R.A.F., must be Corsham's keenest ever player. At the beginning of the season, Ron landed in Bristol at 1 a.m. in the early hours of the morning and had expected to get a lift to Corsham in time to play his match. The lift never turned up, so Ron walked all the way to Corsham on foot and then played at outside left in the game against Odd Down!

Trouble looms once again - when the South Bank field (previously rated as being agricultural) is reclassified by the County Hall Trowbridge, resulting in a higher rateable value being placed on the four acre site of £16 per year, net £14 (about £350 today). An appeal on the Club's behalf was made for a reduction, pointing out that they were amateurs and had fallen on hard times, having lost £75 in this season alone. They finished last season with certain assets, namely a hut to which they had added a 30ft loft extension and upon which they owed £60? Their funds were practically nil *[this is not quite the same picture painted at the last general meeting!]*. The committee was working every night to get the ground in a good condition for the ensuing season. The Council were asked to pay 50% of the suggested rate but the Club were told that the rate charged must not have regard to the means of the occupiers (otherwise everybody would ask for a rebate)!

1953: The death took place in October of Mr. H Hullyer aged 62, who was for some time the Chairman of Corsham Football Club. He had served 21 years in the Royal Northumberland Fusiliers, finishing as Sgt. Major. He was gassed in the First World War and came to Corsham for treatment in the Town Hall Hospital. Whilst there, he met his wife and settled in Corsham over 30 years ago. He also served locally in the Admiralty Police at Copenacre for 14 years. The funeral was held in the Baptist Church. R.I.P.

1954: Bob Westwood, a Corsham Town Footballer had a narrow escape when met with a nasty accident on 13 September Monday morning. He was on the staff at a bank in Corsham and lived in Swindon and was on his way to Corsham when the accident occurred. His motorcycle was very badly damaged. He had no bones broken, but there were severe abrasions and bruising of the left leg.

1955: At the end of the 1954-1955 season the Club find themselves once again in financial difficulties, which necessitated finding new sources of income if the Club was to survive. The balance at the bank amounted to only £22.15s 11p (just over £400 in today's money), but outstanding accounts were £136 (£2,500). The Club's assets were valued at £273 3s 2p (£5,000). It was agreed that players would now pay 1s per match and Committee members and adult supporters travelling with the team should pay 1s and 2s respectively. It was said that the Club could not have carried on in the past without the help of the Supporters' Club.

Christopher Dyke, the 17 year-old youngest son of Corsham Town's secretary (and former Corsham goalkeeper) Mr. G.F. Dyke signed amateur forms for Bristol City. Standing 6ft in height, Christopher was an inside left forward and had appeared for Corsham Town in season 55/56. Christopher joined Corsham Town's reserves team on leaving Corsham Council School. Christopher's talent was spotted at the Wiltshire County Youth trials at Devizes in early September and he was invited to have trials (accompanied with his father) at Charlton Athletic as well as being chosen to play for the Wiltshire County Eleven team.

1960-1961: Wiltshire County League Division 2 - Champions.

1973: Corsham Football Club loses its HQ and gear in a fire during its 80th season. The recently renovated and re-equipped building at Corsham's ground is completely destroyed by fire at a considerable cost to the Club. By the time that the Fire Brigade had arrived, it was too late to save the pavilion which was ablaze from end to end. The two dressing rooms were also destroyed including new baths and the new gas fired heating system. Temporary changing rooms were quickly provided to enable the Club to honour its fixtures. It was estimated that £2,000 (nearly £20,000 in today's money) would be needed to rebuild. Due to the terms of the lease and repeated vandalism, there was no insurance policy covering the old premises. Corsham Fire Brigade believed the fire was started by a tramp that had lit a fire outside. A replacement building was erected soon after.

1976: The first known major honour was achieved by winning the Wiltshire Senior Cup, the same year promotion was achieved to the Wiltshire County League Division One. Incidentally, the team contained a certain Colin 'Nobby' Bush, who would go on to manage the team to their first Western League title some 30 years later in 2006/2007. Over the next 20 years the club produced some fine players but was never able to retain them for long with local Western League clubs snapping up the best talent Corsham had to offer.

1976-1977: Wiltshire County League Division 2 - Runners Up. Wiltshire Senior Cup - Champions.

1976-1978: Dave Pearce was the first team manager.

1984-1985: Andy Short was the first team manager.

1989-1990: Wiltshire County League Division 2 - Runners Up. Chris Ashe was the first team manager. It can be assumed that until 1998 Corsham played its football at county level.

1990-1991: The first team were managed by Gary Lock and Rod Pratt.

1991-1992: John Bolland was the first team manager.

1992-1993: Wiltshire County League Division 2 - Runners Up.

1993-1994: John Mason was the first team manager. Off the pitch, under the guidance of Dick Brown, a new clubhouse was built and the facilities were improved to Western League standard. The new clubhouse originally belonged to the Corsham Art Students and was situated behind Beechfield House along Middlewick Lane in Pickwick! The clubhouse built in 1975/76 after the fire of 1973, is still in place behind the current clubhouse. The current clubhouse built by Club members was opened by Lord Methuen on 17 April 1993.

The photo shows Club members (left to right) helping out with erecting the current building; Edward (Ed) Brown, John Lewis, Graham Curtis, and Roland (Roly) White.

1994-1996: Gary Lock managed the first team for two seasons.

1995-1996: Addkey Senior Knock Out Cup - Champions

1996-1997: Wiltshire County League Division 1 - Runners Up. Wiltshire Senior Cup - Champions. Addkey Senior Knock Out Cup - Champions. Wiltshire Senior Cup - Champions.

1997-1998: Wiltshire County League Division 1 - Champions. Promotion was achieved after winning the county league by goal difference from Devizes Town Reserves.

1998-1999: Promoted to the Western League.
1996-1999: Pete Tripp managed the first team for three seasons.
1999-2000: Chris Jeffries managed the first team for one season.

2000-2001: Rob Humphries managed the first team for one season.

2001-2003: Mark Godley managed the first team for two seasons.

2003-2004: Wiltshire Senior Cup - Runners Up: After 5 years in the Western League Division One, Colin 'Nobby' Bush was appointed manager and in his first season in charge, the first team finished 5th and reached the final of the Wiltshire Senior Cup, losing on penalties to Trowbridge Town.

2004-2005: Western League Premier Division - Runners Up: With the restructuring of the league, Corsham Town now played in the Western League Premier Division, finishing runners up at the first attempt and also winning the Wiltshire Senior Cup by defeating Bemerton Harlequins in the final. Once again, ground improvements continued, this time under the chairmanship of Colin Hudd.

Floodlights were installed, a 112 spectator stand erected and hard standing was constructed around the pitch perimeter.

2004-2005: Wiltshire Senior Cup - Champions: Corsham once again runners up, another Wiltshire Senior Cup win, but against Melksham Town and a Les Phillips Cup Final victory over Willand Rovers.

2004: Record *home* attendance of 550 versus Newport County in the FA Cup, the same Newport County that played Tottenham in this season's FA Cup!

2005-2006: Western League Premier Division - Runners Up. Wiltshire Senior Cup - Champions.

2006-2007: Western League Premier Division - Champions. Wiltshire Senior Cup - Champions. Western League Cup (Les Phillips Cup) - Champions. Corsham Town in its last year under manager Colin Bush win the Western League Premier Division, which was hotly contested by a number of teams, including Bridgwater Town and Frome Town. The league was finally won in the second half of the clubs final fixture at home to Radstock Town. The club also added a third successive Wiltshire Senior Cup victory, again over local rivals Melksham Town. Following his success of five trophies in four years, Colin Bush moves on at the end of the season. Former Wiltshire Youth Team manager Mel Gingell was appointed as his successor, with a number of key players retiring.

2007-2008: Despite the difficulties, Corsham got off to a flying start and although the season finished without any silverware, the team pushed Truro City all the way; a poor run in the last month saw the club finish a respectful fifth.

2008-2011: Mel Gingell's next three seasons in charge were full of difficulties, both on and off the pitch, with financial pressures taking their toll on the playing budget, the club finishing 19th, 17th and 10th respectively. On the eve of his fifth season in charge, Mel Gingell parted company with the club and Trevor Rawlings was appointed his successor.

2011-2012: With little time to prepare for the new season, Corsham struggled for long spells and despite a late season mini revival the club finished bottom of the league. They were relegated to Division One for the 2012-2013 season. Trevor Rawlings was appointed first team manager.

2012-2015: After three seasons in Division One, finishing 4th, 7th and 9th respectfully; the Club agreed to part company with Trevor Rawlings.

2015-2016: Jeff Roberts was appointed as Trevor's successor. After a 'roller coaster' season, with some notable victories but also some disappointing defeats, Jeff Roberts accepted a position at Highworth and moved on at the end of the season.

2016-2017: Nigel Tripp was put in charge with a long term mandate to build for the future. Unfortunately despite some notable results, off the pitch issues derailed the club and Nigel was relieved of his duties before being reinstated three weeks later. He did a great job at rebuilding the team and managed to finish 4th from bottom. Nigel decided to move on at the end of the season.

2017-2018: Former player Jamie Harrison was appointed first team manager.

[Ed]. Many thanks go to Corsham F.C's Chairman Chris Perry and to John Cuthbertson for their help in piecing together the above history - and to John Cuthbertson for the photos.

Chapter 16. Ghost Stories - Twenty Seven Corsham stories.

1: Thomas Boulter the Corsham Highwayman:

Within two months of his execution in 1778 a strange rumour was heard to the effect that on a moonlit night a figure could be seen riding at break-neck speed over Salisbury Plain – a figure that disappeared into the mist. Witnesses swore that this was the ghost of the Corsham Highwayman, Thomas Boulter the Flying Highwayman and his horse Black Bess *(see Chapter 18).* It was a story that was to be repeated many times over the years. For many decades after his death, Boulter was the name of the *bogeyman* used to subdue unruly children in Wiltshire and Hampshire.

2. Horror on the A4:

Laurie Newman *(at that time a lorry driver from Bath),* was driving from Chippenham towards Bath along the main A4 road at 2.30 a.m. early in the morning. Just before he reached Corsham, he caught sight of a figure in his headlights walking in the middle of the road in front of him. His first impression was that it was a nun. Slowing down, he pulled out to drive around the figure but just as he was about to pass, it turned towards him. In place of a face, he saw a white blur. Suddenly, the figure leapt onto the footplate at the side of the driver's door and stared at him through the glass window.

What was particularly terrifying was that instead of a human face, he saw a grinning skull looking back at him. The figure continued to hold on to the lorry for a few moments and then completely vanished. Mr Newman was so shocked and upset by this nightmarish experience that he was unable to talk about it for next three months. Eventually however, he met a woman when delivering goods to London Airport who was a psychic. He told her about the experience and she reassured him that he would never see the *fleshless* phantom again.

3. The Flemish Weaver:

Pub landlady Dawn McHugh called in the *Ghostbusters* after she was attacked by an angry spirit haunting her 17th Century pub in 2010. Mrs McHugh, 46 says, *'The ghost tripped her up, sending her flying down the stairs',* at the Flemish Weaver in Corsham High Street. The drama happened on Easter Monday, only days after Mrs McHugh moved into the pub with her husband Mac. It meant she ended up in hospital for the day until doctors were satisfied that her suspected fractured skull was, in fact, bad bruising. Mrs McHugh said:

'The first time it happened I thought nothing of it but it happened a second time just a week later when I was putting some curtains up. I felt something strong pulling me around.'

4. The Wine Merchants:

The family home in Corsham was a very large eight-bedroomed house in the High Street, and housed my father's shop, which was a Wine Merchants. At some point, my father negotiated with the Barnett Brothers who owned the newsagents next door and he bought their cellars from them, a doorway being subsequently knocked between the two cellars to make them into one large area beneath the two properties. It was my job to bottle up the casks. I would settle myself down with the candle-light adding its warm glow until suddenly felt the temperature in the cellar drop considerably. At first I assumed that there was a change in the wind direction of something as simple as that, but the room got colder and colder until it felt icy cold. I became a little disconcerted and concentrated on the job in hand even harder. Suddenly the air seemed to get thicker, the cold became more intense, and the hairs on the back of my neck started to bristle and I could sense that I was being watched from the far corner of the cellar, just below where the trapdoor opening was that led up to the street. The feeling became more and more intense, as though somebody *or something* was willing me to leave the cellar. I finished bottling that cask as quickly as I could and then rushed upstairs, afraid to say anything to anyone for fear of appearing a fool. I never went down into that cellar again. Many years later, in discussion with my eldest brother, he told me that the same experience had happened to at least three of us, although we each felt it was not something we wished to open a discussion on!

[Colin Gordon-Farleigh]

5. Joe James:

My favourite Corsham ghost appeared in a house close to the site of our old Corsham railway station. The previous owners had always testified to a *'benign presence'*. Nevertheless, the present owners were taken aback one day when their young son observed, quite coolly, *"Who is that man sitting in the front room? He's wearing a tall black hat"*. The mystery was compounded some time later, when the younger daughter queried, *"Father Christmas is standing in our front room, but he is not dressed like Father Christmas"*. Nothing was visible to the adults. Could it have been Brunel?

6. Jaggards House: The Jaggards House ghosts are already established and famous. This historic 16th century residence in Neston claims not one but two ghosts.

Curate - Mr. Buhner's declaration of 1880: *'I was lying in bed in Jaggards House with my wife when suddenly I woke up with a start, the moon was shining brightly and I plainly saw at the end of the bed an old woman in a poke bonnet, she looked straight at me and then disappeared. Some time after I told my wife and she told our old housekeeper, who informed her that the old woman in the poke bonnet was the regular ghost and had been often seen there.*

I had lately been nominated to the Curacy of Neston or Corshamside, and Jaggards House, the property of Mr Fuller, had been assigned me for a residence - I had driven over from Bath (9 miles) with my wife, bringing with me several boxes of books, which were to be unpacked and taken back for a fresh cargo. My wife was lying down on a sofa downstairs tired out and I was in a large room on the second floor in the centre of the house. There was a maid in the room with me. I had a door open at one end of the room in order to get more light, this door opened on the stairs and there was a passage going past this door from the stairs to a room in one of the wings of the house. Suddenly as I was unpacking I heard a rustling along the passage leading from this room and looking up I saw with surprise, a lady, young looking (although I couldn't see her face) dressed in a blue gauze dress with a long train, in style I should say about 100 years ago. She wore her hair, which was brown, hanging down her back. She slowly walked down the stairs disappeared round the turn and I could see the folds of the dress gradually disappearing behind her. The maid saw nothing. This is all I ever saw. I didn't mention it to my wife till afterwards for fear of frightening her.'

The Governess's depositions: *'I am the eldest of a large family and my mother is a widow. I have a very comfortable home, and yet what I am about to relate compels me to leave. About 5p.m. one summer afternoon I was sitting in the library, Mrs Bulmer and Miss Bulmer in the garden, I observed them rise to go in, so I also rose to get ready for tea. As I was going up the winding oak stairs I observed a lady dressed in a blue dress coming down, I did not much observe her dress, though I do recollect it was very old fashioned, but I noticed her face especially, it was a pretty face, but had a look of sadness which made it dreadful to look at. Just before it reached me it turned into a chamber on the stairs which was used as Mr B's dressing room. I quickly rushed forwards shut the door and fastened the latch which was of a kind that could not be opened from the inside, and then rushed downstairs, and screamed out, the serving man came, I briefly told him what I had done and then fainted.'*

By Mr Bulmer: *'I went up and looked but could see nothing. The governess evidently was really very frightened, but then at one period, though not lately, she had, I feel bound to confess, dabbled in spiritualism.'*

[Ed - sounds like they've all had a little bit too much of Bulmer's Cider to me!']

Besides these, there are innumerable visions of the servants, but only ever mentioning a ghostly old woman and a ghostly young lady. Except once, when a groom was frightened (as he said) by a headless man walking in the garden!

Since then, the house has been done up and modernised and the ghost of neither the old woman or the young one has not so far as I can discover appeared again. The Bishop of Gloucester however tried to lay it, and has perhaps been successful. To show the ghost is authentic, I may mention that when Lord Methuen went to Court the Queen more than once asked him about the ghost at Jaggards. I will vouch myself for the accuracy of what is written here - H...y M...s L.y.

Copied from a paper written by member of the Loy family a former vicar of Neston Church who resided at Jaggards.

7. The Hidden Corpse of Corsham:

Documented in the 1895 in a Corsham house that no longer stands, a young girl staying with her grandparents witnessed an elderly man emerging from a non-existent doorway on an external wall near the staircase. Nobody else in the room saw either the man or the door. In 1895, whenever the granddaughter stayed at the house, she would sit at the bottom of the stairs waiting for the ghost's reappearance. The ghost would step out of the long-vanished door halfway up the stairs. When the building was demolished many years later, a skeleton of an elderly man was discovered in a secret recess in the exact position the girl had seen the phenomenon! The exact location of the house has been lost in time!

8. *The Rudloe Arms:*

Entry on Trip Advisor. *"We stayed in an annex building with under floor heating and a huge bathroom with separate bath and shower. The bath had a ledge for resting your legs. What disconcerted me were the three ghosts I saw in the week we spent there. I saw a very large dog bound towards me then disappear at one point. I was informed when I moved to Corsham that the house had once belonged to a family who bred St Bernard dogs. The gentleman on reception told us that some guests leave in the middle of the night, scared witless".*

9. Monks Park:

A private residence in this area is said to be haunted by a Roman ghost; though it has not been seen for some time! The ghost also stalks along the little street known as Monks Park. Common sense would indicate this ghost should be a monk, but it is not. The phantom seen here is described as being a Roman legionary. He wears steel armour and a short, skirt-like affair studded with metal plates. Although this phantom does not carry the typical oblong Roman shield, he otherwise fits the description of a Roman soldier.

10. Arnold House:

Miss Pictor lived in Arnold House on the High Street *(now the Corsham Heritage and Information Centre).* Although she hardly ever spent any money on herself, she kindly left the Arnold House property to Corsham Parish Council after she passed away in 1959...... then her ghost began to walk.

"Oh yes, old Miss Pictor," confirmed the man on duty at the Information Centre in late 2003. *"She comes through that doorway there,"* he said, pointing to the downstairs corridor and a doorway to the right of the front door. *"We've got an electronic counter thing that is supposed to tell us how many people come in and out of the information centre, but it counts her as well. Sometimes it goes off even when you don't see the ghost. But we know she is there anyway."*

Another member of staff confirmed the presence of the ghost: *"We first noticed the strange noises a few years ago, just after we opened. It is like footsteps from the room upstairs,"* this being the room in which Miss Pictor used to sit for hours at an upstairs window watching the inhabitants of Corsham going about their business along the High Street below her.

11. St Bartholomew's Church:

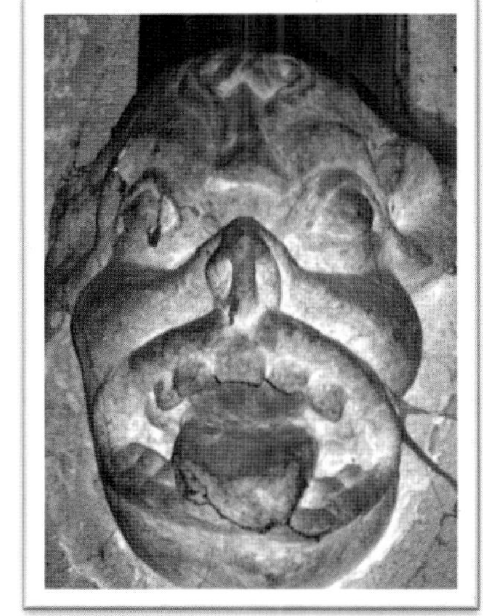

The church of St Bartholomew has a rather odd and most unpleasant ghost. The church itself dates back to Norman times, but much of the present building is the result of a major reconstruction in the 19th century.

The best recorded sighting of a ghost came in the 1930s, when Lady Winifred Pennoyer and a friend were sitting in the churchyard and chatting. Walking between the tombstones, came a very short and rather stocky man. As he came close to the two women, he turned and gave them a stare of undiluted hatred and evil.

Lady Winifred was severely shocked by the utter malevolence she felt emanating from the man. She turned to her friend, only to find that she had fainted and was now unconscious. The man promptly vanished. When the friend came to, she reported seeing the little man and then being overwhelmed by fear and dread, after which she remembered nothing. The hideous little man is not seen very often, which is probably just as well. Those who do see him usually report feelings which vary from unease to downright hostility - a strange phantom, and one best avoided. Another strange occurrence seen there is the sighting of a tiny two foot high malevolent man - some sort of goblin who appears from time to time.

12. The Ugly Fairy - Corsham - Churchyard:

This little creature, standing no taller than one metre, was seen sitting upon one of the gravestones. It was once seen by two women - one fainted, the other traumatised. A third woman with them saw nothing.

13. Box Tunnel:

A ghostly railway train haunts the track between Corsham and the Box Tunnel entrance. Painted in the bold colours of the Great Western Railway, this steam train of 1920s' vintage comes tearing out of the tunnel at high speed. Smoke billows from the funnel, steam spurts from the pistons, and the wheels spin with whirling speed. Rushing along as if every moment counts, the train pounds the line for almost a mile until it reaches the outskirts of Corsham. There it fades from view. *"Imagine you put a stone in water and let it drop,"* said one witness. *"At first you see it very clearly. Then it seems to fade and get a bit blurry. Then it is gone."*

14. Royal Oak public house:

'Twelfth Hour Investigations' offered to spend a night in this pub after a barmaid reported seeing a black figure out of the corner of her eye. In 2007, the landlady of the pub reported seeing a tall figure dressed in a dark monk's habit walk across his bedroom early one morning. Other members of staff glimpsed the figure in other parts of the building. The spiral staircase is also reputed to have the ghost of an eloquently dressed female who appears to be flicking her dress about coquettishly as she comes down the staircase. *[Ed] Could it have been something to do with too much 6X?*

15. Corsham Court: A maid scrubbing the rear stairs at the Court noticed a woman standing at the top of the steps. She moved out the way, only to see the woman had vanished.

16. Priory House owned by Simon Harcourt-Smith 1946. A child was taught the Ave Maria prayer by a *'man in white'* while being looked after by the housekeeper whilst the child's parents were out of the country. It was speculated that the *'man in white'* was a White Friar, who once used the house.

17. Priory Cottage. When I first arrived at Corsham, I shared accommodation with Sid Donkin and *'Thatch'* Leighton-Mathews at The Old Parsonage in Pickwick but soon moved to a tiny 16th Century cottage adjoining Priory Cottage in Bence's Lane, only a stone's throw from the back gates which led to the Estate Yard. This was a good short cut when late for breakfast or lectures. When the back gates were locked at night, we scaled the ten foot high stone pillars! There was a ghost, I think she was known as the Grey Lady, when I saw her, she appeared to be dressed in black and was walking near the west wing!

18. The Church Street Lady. A Grey Lady has been spotted on several occasions near the gated car park entrance at the end of Church Street, watching you as you walk towards her!

19. United Reform Church. *[By Chris Perry].* We owned the United Reform Church in the centre of town *(now Grounded)* and ran our print business there for 15 odd years. During our ownership, we experienced numerous psychic phenomena. Cold spots, floating lights, typesetting machines typing by themselves, objects moving etc. I always felt a presence was trying to communicate with us. A number of years later I returned to the building after it was converted into a bar and whilst having a drink my full pint flew across the table, remaining upright, onto the floor. This was repeated a few months later on another visit.

20. The Flemish Weaver. Many years ago, when the *Flemish Weaver* was called the *Pack Horse*, I heard a tale about the Hangman who travelling to Bath Assizes, who used to stay in the Pack Horse, which faces out to Church Street. I was told he met a sticky end in the back yard on the way to his horse that was stabled at the rear. Did someone get their revenge? The hangman's ghost haunts Church Street to this day.

21. Corsham - Hilly Road. In September 1968, a Lacock W.I. member reported driving past a large American-style car heading in the opposite direction up the hill near Pickwick. The car had no driver and its lights were full on.

22. The 1959 Potley Warm Spot! *(from an anonymous story found on the internet some years ago):* About 32 years ago I lived in the Corsham area, first in a place called *'The Ridge'* which is close to Neston, and later in Corsham itself. Having made friends in Neston whilst at *'The Ridge'*, it was my practice to spend evenings in Neston at the local pub with friends and go home either by car or motorcycle, travelling the easiest route which is through Neston, down Rough Street, through Pound Pill into Corsham itself and on to my home in Pickwick Road. At one point I was without a car or motorcycle and needed to take the shortest way home, which is from Neston to Moor Green, taking the road right and up a short hill to join the road that runs from Westwells to Potley.

The first night that I made this walk was in winter, a night cold enough to encourage one to get home as soon as possible. Walking along from Westwells to Potley, on the Potley road, "I was surprised to find myself in an area which appeared to be much warmer," and walking a few yards further on I came out into the cold again. I turned around and walked back again, to find myself once again in this band of what appeared to be warm air. I mentioned this to a few people in the area but nobody had come across this.

A couple of nights later I pressed a couple of friends to walk this route with me and they too noticed the seeming temperature difference. It later became our practice to pause here in winter to have a smoke and "warm-up" before completing our walk through Potley and up into Corsham. In 1967 I left Corsham and took up employment in Swaziland, an environment far different to the mists and frosts of Wiltshire.

I met and married my present wife and when the finances and opportunity presented itself, we decided that we would come over to England to visit relatives and travel around, mostly in the South West. One day, I was reading an excellent book on strange phenomena called 'Mysteries of Time and Space' by Brad Steiger and I was reminded of this strange effect that I had experienced on that road.

As we were soon to be making the trip over to England I asked my wife if she would like to be a kind of guinea pig and take that walk with me to see if she also felt the warmth. So when we were in England the next month I set out with my wife and daughter to walk a circular route to see if she could detect anything. I gave her no inkling as to where she might feel something. Our route took us from a pub at the bottom of Pound Pill, over the railway bridge, (towards Gastard-turning right at Monks park and then right) into Rough Street, then left past Lypiatt Camp, down into Neston, turning right in Moor Green to go up the hill to join the Westwells/Potley road, down through Potley and back past the old railway station to complete our walk. It was a pleasant summer evening and the air was still and warm, what I considered to be ideal conditions for phenomena hunting!!!! We strolled along, enjoying the evening and never mentioning the reason for our walk. As we approached the warm-spot area I made sure that I walked ahead and passed through the place about 20 yards ahead of my wife. I was careful not to look back or pause and as she reached the spot she called out to me, *"It's here, isn't it!!"* I walked back into the warm region and she was exactly right. It feels as though one has walked from the cold outdoors into a warm room and then out through another door again. The band is about six to eight paces wide and has in fact moved somewhat from when I first experienced this in about 1959. We came back in a car and one can feel the effect even inside a car. It is weaker now and the last time we were there it was hard to detect, but I do know that the strength of the effect varies.

Where is it? At the end of Park Lane when you get to Hawthorn roundabout, turn left down the hill to Westwells. Turn left at the very bottom and up the hill towards Potley, you pass a riding stable at the top of the hill, then look out for a sharp bend to the right, you can park safely there under the trees. This is where the "band" used to be. If you now walk towards Potley on that road you will find that it dips opposite some houses on the right and then goes uphill again. The band is now in that dip and it is almost opposite a gap in the hedge which is the beginning of an old footpath down through a field into a wood. I am an electronics engineer and a great believer in statistics .... if I hold a wire and get a shock once, I strongly believe that it could happen again, but there are no statistics unless I either repeat the stupidity or measure it with a meter. Most paranormal effects seem to be temporary, but this one seems to be more permanent. Certainly it has lasted over 40 years and is still detectable. As to what it is caused by I cannot say.

I work with high powered radio frequency machines and it certainly feels like the radiation from a *mistuned* radio frequency generator. I have looked for other possible causes... ventilation shafts from one of the many underground workings in the area perhaps, but I could find none there. Ley lines? I have never heard of this effect described for the presence of ley lines. Yes, I do have some ideas about it but I have as yet no evidence to support them, it would need some instruments to check. I believe the effect to be electromagnetic.

It is known that the earth's magnetic field becomes more concentrated in some areas than others and I think this place on the road to be one of them. I have not as yet visited the area with a sensitive compass, electrostatic detector or RF monitor, but I hope to do so. That the effect feels the same as walking into an extremely strong electromagnetic field from a high frequency generator leads me to believe that it is to do with the earth's magnetic field, after all it is believed that ley lines are magnetic in nature. Strange too that many public footpaths follow ley lines and bend and go straight again for no apparent reason. **Note:** [Ed]. An old 'tramline' used to transport the local quarried limestone to Corsham Station ran right alongside this *(warm spot)* area!

23: IN CORSHAM: *The following appeared in the Wiltshire Independent in 1862 on Thursday 27 November:*

For some days past not a little commotion has existed in the Corsham neighbourhood of a certain gallant Captain's residence by reports that the house had suddenly become haunted; and a suredly evidence was not wanting to establish the fact of its being nightly troubled by some mischievous corporeal or incorporeal assistant. Like others of the same fraternity, this ghost intimated its presence by sundry knockings upon the walls and windows and shutters, floors and ceilings, occasionally so violent as to shake the whole building, frightening the Captain and his Lady out of their proprieties, and causing considerable annoyance to the occupiers of the adjoining houses.

None seemed more terrified than the servant girl, whose agitation appeared excessive. To allay her fears, the gallant Captain paced the house with loaded firearms, declaring his determination to take summery vengeance upon their nocturnal disturber.

Presently, a thundering knock was heard at the front door, followed by the report of a pistol fired into the midnight air, fortunately with no more serious result than startling the policeman, who had stationed himself so as to command a view of that part of the building. Feeling convinced that the disturbance originated from within, the police officer intimated his suspicions that the girl was at the bottom of the mystery, thereby provoking a storm of indignation from her confiding employer. Unlimitedly however, he was admitted into the house and the family retired to bed.

The knocking still continued at intervals as before but was now confined to the upstairs apartments. Divulging himself of his boots and creeping softly up the upstairs into the girl's bedroom, the officer caught her in the act of banging the window frames with all her might. Of course, the annoyance was suddenly terminated and the girl being dispatched to her home it has not been renewed.

24: Owl Ghost in Pickwick 1923. *From the Saturday 10 March 1923 Wiltshire Times and Trowbridge Advertiser :* An amusing incident happened. The occupants of one of the houses in Pickwick Road were disturbed by ghostly sounds and for four nights very little sleep could be had.

The trouble was brought to a climax by the plumbers' men coming with a set of rods and these being put up the chimney brought down the *'ghost'* in the shape of a common brown owl which must have got stuck in the chimney and was unable to get out until assisted. Peace was once again restored and the ghost laid!

25: The Witch (man) of Corsham! In 1756 the church plate was stolen from Broad Hinton (about 5 miles (8 km) southwest of Swindon). A reward of ten guineas was offered for its recovery. One of the church wardens went to see the Witch of Corsham.

The witch told the warden to leave the plate chest open for three consecutive nights and if the thief failed to return the silver, the witch would take action in his own way.

Before the time was up, the silver had been returned.

[Ed] I think it was the warden don't you?

26: Almshouse: The following is a strange story concerning Lady Margaret Hungerford of Corsham, related by Sharington Talbot, a squire of Lacock who in a letter dated 1666, tells of a Corsham mystery or wonder.

'In Lady Margaret's house there, a certain room had been cleaned and shut up for the night. Morning came, and there on the bare floor was painted a picture in colours of my Lady, drawn to life. What this might betoken none could say, but my lady would not have the same rubbed out, slighting the portent. Be it noted however, that she had since fallen into a hectic fever.'

27: 'Grandpa' Cawte's Escape. At the end of the High Street next to the Methuen Arms was *'Cawte Bros'*, later called 'Cawte *and Son, Plumbers Decorators'*. Some of you may remember the two grandsons who ran Cawte Bros, Motor Engineers on this site. 'Grandpa' Charles Cawte founded the business in the late 1800s and had spent much time in Canada and America in his youth.

Before the outbreak of World War he decided to visit the USA again to look up some old friends. He booked his passage and went down to Southampton the night before his ship sailed, to stay in a local hotel. Whilst there he met an America who was distraught at not being able to get a ticket on the ship sailing next day.

As soon as he heard that 'Grandpa' Cawte had a berth, the American offered him an enormous price for his ticket. Well, Grandpa thought, at that price my holiday will cost me very little and it doesn't matter if I delay my crossing by a few days, under the circumstances.

So Grandpa sold his ticket, and the next morning on 10 April 1912, an ebullient American dashed up the gangway to claim his cabin.

And the name of the liner was...'The Titanic'.

Chapter 17. HaHa Wall / Sunken Fence - Corsham Park.

What is a HaHa wall? A HaHa wall consists of a sunken stone wall, its top being level with the garden and a deep ditch on the far side. The construction is such that it allows stray Deer to leave the garden but not to enter.

In the 1976 booklet on page 26, *'Corsham Court - A Gothic Dream'*, written by ex-Corsham art student Leslie Harcourt, Leslie notes that it was actually Humphry Repton in 1798 who realised Lancelot Brown's original proposal to introduce the HaHa, a sunken trough in the land that separates the garden from the Park.

By the third quarter of the 18th century the cost for building a Park wall averaged around £1,000 a mile, whilst the rate for digging a HaHa was 7s.11p per yard, almost a third less expensive at about £656 per mile.

There is a *HaHa wall* that acts as a hidden boundary between the gardens of Corsham Court and the Park, running south to north. The wall was constructed so as to be invisible from the house. It allowed the old iron garden boundary fence to be removed. It also acted as an efficient deterrent to keep out the deer that roamed in the nearby Deer park. The first part by the Church (that can be seen in the photo above) was built later by John Methuen, 6th Baron Methuen in 1994. The HaHa design was invented by Charles Bridgeman in about 1710, and the idea was incorporated in Lancelot Brown's design for the major works carried out in the grounds of Corsham Court and Corsham Park 1760.

"To wit, the making the great walks and sunke fence between the house and Chippenham road".

In addition to the HaHa wall, Capability Brown sank all the boundary hedges within the park to create a view across the estate giving a view of gently undulating ground, falling away towards the distant lake. Iron fences were also sunk and hidden at the bottom of ditches on the far side of the rolling ground to the east of the house so that they could not be seen. The sunken iron-railing fence in Corsham Park, starts at the corner alongside the very back of Saint Bartholomew's churchyard wall and travels north/east, firstly towards the lake and then veers off left to finish up at the south edge of the Mynte Wood near the Dry Arch. The public footpath runs all the way alongside.

In September of 1941 the Ministry of Supply decided to requisition all unnecessary **iron** gates and railings to be cut down and used for scrap in the iron and steel factories, as part of the war effort. Faced with an oversupply, rather than halt the collection, the government allowed it to continue as it was of great propaganda value. The ironwork collected was stockpiled away from public view in depots, quarries, railway sidings. It was said that only about 26% of the iron work collected was ever used for munitions and by 1944 much of it was rusting away in hidden stockpiles. Meanwhile the country was left littered with the stumps of removed railings which can still be seen in any town (including Corsham) today, as many were never replaced. Thankfully, the District Council's interpretation of *'railings not to be included'*, i.e. those necessary to prevent cattle etc. from staying, and railings of a historic interest, referred to the sunken railings in Corsham Park. Hence they are still here today, rusting away with dignity these past few centuries and not rusting away in some backwater! One suspects that Anthony Paul Methuen (1891–1975), 5th Baron Methuen (British soldier, architect and peer) at the time, may also have had some influence on whether his railings should be cut down or not. Or perhaps they survived because nobody knew they were there; hence proving the efficiency of the *hidden* sunken fence design!

The final stretch of the sunken fence near to the Dry Arch is a haven for grass snakes, slow worms and also adders! The sheep still use the shrubbery alongside the sunken fence for cover in hot summers and it is the home for a wealth of other wild life. Here, the trough/ditch also acts as an efficient drainage system, with water cascading down in the winter months from the top end of the park, into the culvert by the first Kissing Gate, and thence through a channel into the nearby lake.

'As young lads in the 1960's, we used to dare each other, to see who could jump over the fence at the deepest, widest parts of the trench.' *[Ed]*

If you look carefully along the last long stretch of the sunken fence near the Dry Arch, you can clearly see the ridge of soil that was excavated when the trench was originally dug out. The soil was thrown out each side by the men who physically dug out the trench. This would have been very hard work that can only be admired when you see the long deep trenches. The ground beneath, is not just soft soil, but full of stones. There were no mechanical diggers then. Give those men a thought when you next walk by; and if you look a little closer, there's always something new to see along Corsham Park's footpaths each season.

In 1952 Prince Margaret visited Wiltshire to inspect Youth Organisations. When she was in Corsham, she visited the Scouts and Guides at Corsham Park, with the 1st Corsham Senior Scouts under Assistant Senior Scoutmaster John Methuen and Assistant Ryan Aust. To reach the house (Corsham Court) for tea, they had to pass over a bridge erected over the HaHa wall. At the bridge, several photographs were taken and *'three cheers'* for H.R.H. were lustily given before the Princess was escorted off for tea.

Chapter 18. Highwayman, James Boulter 1748-1778 (alias Baxter) The Flying Highwayman.

Thomas Boulter, 'The Flying Highwayman' from Wiltshire.

In the early days of King George III, Wiltshire the county of the *'Moonrakers'* was largely favoured in the Georgian era by several *'Gentlemen of the Road'*, many of whom were regarded by the local peasants as little short of heroes.

There is a legend in Corsham, that Dick Turpin (1705 –1739) once held up the mail coach at the Dry Arch in Mynte Wood, in the north-east corner of Corsham Park, but this is romantic supposition by the locals, for the Dry Arch is an original feature of Corsham Court's two-mile 'Great Walk' now called the 'North Walk', originally designed by Lancelot Brown in the latter 1700's. [Note: Mynte is the Danish word for mint].

Nevertheless, we did have a local highwayman who frequented the old roads of Corsham!

Of the *bold riders*, Wiltshire's Thomas Boulter, alias Baxter also known as the *Flying Highwayman of Wiltshire*, was by far the most prominent figure of the easy-going thieves who preyed with impunity on the travelling public of those days. It was at Poulshot, a village near Devizes that this famous highwayman was born. The lonely turnpike road leading out of Corsham and past Chapel Plaister towards Bath was one of his favoured haunts! The good name of Boulter or Bolter are, or have been numerous in Wiltshire, especially at Lavington and Cheverell. It's a shame that one of them ends up on the gallows. Doubtless, one would like to think that most of Boulter's descendants were as good citizens as their neighbours. A memorial of one of them survives where few would think of looking for it, viz, in the belfry of Rowde Church; where on Bell number III, hung in the time of Oliver Cromwell (1599-1658), are cast the words, *'Nathaniel Bolter made me. 1654'.*

Thomas Boulter, whose very appearance was terrifying, was a tall swarthy man with a thick scar on his cheek, the result of bullet wound which tore the skin off his forehead and burned his left eye during a thwarted robbery in Gloucester. He held up coaches in broad day-light, threatening the occupants with pistols and taking not only their money but also jewellery, wedding rings, watches, clothes and anything else of value. He liked to play the *gallant* with the ladies and was not above returning some trifle of sentimental value, providing he was asked in the right tone of voice.

Boulter's father had contempt for the Law of the Land. He once rented a gristmill (for grinding grain into flour) at Poulshot near West Lavington. He was sentenced to death which was later commuted to a term of fourteen years transportation for stealing a horse from Mr. Hall of Trowbridge in 1775 and then riding it to Andover to sell for £6. His neighbours, not without reason, thought that he was *a rogue in grain,* and he was once whipped in the Market Place for stealing honey from an old woman. Thomas's mother was not much better, and was once publicly flogged in Devizes Market Place for some criminal misdemeanour.

Thomas Boulter's Uncle Isaac Blagden was shot with a brace of slugs in the leg and crippled for life while attempting a highway robbery against Colonel Hanger near Market Lavington and ended his life as a cripple in the Lavington Workhouse. The gentleman who shot him, deemed him sufficiently punished for his crime and prosecuted him no further. With a family history like that, it's no wonder young Boulter eventually turned to robbery as a career.

As a young man, Thomas Boulter worked in his father's mill until 1774. After his father was transported, Thomas used the small capital accrued from the mill to set himself up as a grocer in Newport on the Isle of White, in his sister's house where she already ran a milliner's shop. But he was high-spirited young man and within a year the grocery business was making a loss and had *'bored him to tears'*; so in the summer of 1775 he left his sister's abode to become a Highwayman.

Boulter, was once described, '*At about five feet nine inches high, of a fresh complexion, and wore his own black curled hair, and a round narrow brim'd hat, was dressed in a claret coloured Bath beaver surtout coat, black waistcoat, leather breeches, and light coloured ribb'd stockings, but had neither boots nor spurs on.*'

His first criminal act was committed on the western road between Stockbridge and Sutton where he met the *Salisbury Diligence* coach containing two passengers. He had to ride past the coach two or three times to build up his courage before eventually shouting out *'Stand'* and ordering the driver to stop. In less than two minutes, he had robbed the passengers of their watches and money, saying that he was *much obliged to them, for he was in great want*, and then *wished them a pleasant journey!* Finding this new vocation much easier than expected, he robbed everyone else that he met on his journey to Salisbury. By the time that he reached his mother's house in Poulshot, he had bagged seven watches and £40 (about £2,500 in today's money).

On a later occasion, after going through Somerset, Dorset and Wiltshire he amassed a sum of £500 (£30,000 in today's money). He then spent some time again with his mother who was now living alone back at Poulshot, as her husband was already on his way to the plantations........ goodness knows what his mother must have thought of her thieving son! More likely she encouraged him!

'Boulter used to feed his horse with bread soaked in wine.'

In the spring of 1776 Boulter stole a horse from Peter Delme of Stokes Marsh near Erlestoke, undoubtedly the best horse he had ever rode, either as an honest man or as a highwayman. Black Bess, she was called – named after the famous horse of that other notorious *'Gentleman',* Dick Turpin. It was also said Boulter used to feed his horse with bread soaked in wine.

Later in 1776 after fleeing from Windsor and Maidenhead, Boulter moved ground to Bath and Bristol, and then made his base in Poulshot where his mother lived.

In the summer of 1777 when Boulter was en route to visit his mother at Poulshot, he came across two ladies in a post-chaise travelling towards Bath. The terrible pistol was once more drawn from its hiding place. This resulted in a handful of guineas and the daintiest of gold watches being handed over. In fear of being caught for his many crimes in the area, he fled north where he was later captured and committed to York Castle in irons to await trial. After being sentenced to death at the March Assizes, Boulter was granted the option of execution or entering the army by *'taking the King's Shilling'* in consideration for reforming his life. Needless to say, Boulter took the shilling.

Boulter enlisted in a marching regiment that was temporarily based in York and for the next four *days promised fair to make a good soldier of himself.* But no sooner was he called upon to keep good hours and to preserve the stiff postures of the parade ground, he realised that the new profession of arms would never square with his tastes. On the sixth day he was ordered to prepare himself for the field by seven o'clock the next morning in uniform. But by this time he had already had enough of the soldier's life. He deserted the following night from his quarters and made his way to Nottingham where he persuaded a coachman to *take him up* and deliver him to Bristol. Here, by chance, he met twenty-five year old James Caldwell (who was already a notorious cold-blooded killer), the landlord of 'The Ship' in Milkstreet (later the 'Armada') pulled down later during the 1950s, near the corner of Old King Street. During the winter of 1777 and the spring of 1778, Boulter and Caldwell scoured Salisbury Plain and the neighbouring countryside for easy pickings!

Boulter had a dashing off-handedness, his bonhomie encinctured with a quiet humour which fascinated and disarmed his victims, who felt that had he been so disposed, could have descended on them like the *Hammer of Thor*. His newly acquired companion Caldwell, was a somewhat smaller man but of a ferocious and unrelenting cast of mind and it was often with the greatest difficulty that Boulter restrained him from the wanton crime of blood-lettering. Boulter had light hair and the fresh colour of the Saxon. Caldwell's dark and lengthened visage was stamped with that lowest order of wickedness, Bristol -villainy.

The stretch of the London to Bath Turnpike road which ran past Chapel Plaister (then the *Bell Inn* ale house until it was restored as a chapel in 1893) and up over Kingsdown, was trurnpiked in 1713 and was the main route into Bath, long before the A4 and the 'Fiveways to Box' routes were established. The Bell Inn consisted of a pair of cottages, a chicken house and a store. It was here, and along the top of Kingsdown that Highwayman Thomas Boulter and his compatriot James Caldwell once plied their trade for a while.

This stretch of road was the ideal place to hold-up mail coaches, as there were numerous places to hide, very few inhabitants, was completely dark at night and the coach horses would labour very slowly up the long incline towards Kingsdown making robbery much easier. This became a notoriously dangerous place to travel at night. In 1737 the *'Horse and Jockey Inn'* (now a large private house known as the Old Jockey) was built at 'Cuffs Corner' on the hill towards Kingsdown. In its prime, the Old Jockey Inn was a safe haven on the eastern side of Kingsdown. Private travellers would be urged to stay overnight in the Inn, until they could be met and escorted safely down into Bath the next morning in daylight. Originally, it took three days to get from London to Bath on a coach along the Turnpike's muddy roads!

'I'm not going to stop for you or any man living'.

CHAPEL PLAISTER IN 1790
From a drawing in the British Museum by L. H. Grimm

Boulter operated for a while, from the small *Bell Inn's* adjoining building used as a chicken roost. In the dark evenings, Boulter kept watch from the chicken roost's small window, on the look-out for horse-drawn coaches to appear on the long downward stretch of road from Rudloe (B3109) between the two Fiveways junctions. From thence, he made his way to the top of Kingsdown where armed robbery would ensue. The Chapel Plaister location was a well suited look-out post for his purposes, as from there, one can command the long stretch of road in both directions, along what was then the *high road* from London to Bath.

On one occasion at Roundway Hill in Devizes, Boulter encountered a butcher on horseback, who proved to be less compliant than was expected. When ordered to stop, the butcher simply replied, *'I'm not going to stop for you or any man living'.* Whence Boulter tried his usual experiment of holding a pistol to the butcher's head. The butcher replied, *"I don't get my money so easy as to part with it in that foolish manner. If you rob me, I must go upon the highway myself, before I durst go home, and that, I'd rather not do".*

'Good night,' rejoined the highwayman, 'and remember that Boulter is your friend'.

On 24 December 1777 Thomas Fowle of Devizes, issued a poster offering a reward of £40 for the capture of one or both highwaymen who had robbed him the previous Monday of five guineas and a half and his watch. This is the text from the advert that appeared in the *Salisbury Journal in 1777*, written by a Thomas Fowle about his unfortunate encounter with Boulter: *'HIGHWAY ROBBERY Whereas Thomas Fowle of Devizes in the County of Wilts was attacked on Monday afternoon on the Plain near the 11 mile stone by two highwaymen, who robbed him of five guineas and a half and his watch (maker's name – Grand, London, the dial plate is remarkable by having dots of gold between the hours; and the outside case has a small squat). The two men were well mounted on dark-brown horses, one of the horses has both hinder heels white; they both had surtout coats on [a man's frock coat, of the kind worn by cavalry officers over their uniforms] and appeared to be lusty men. He who robbed Mr. Fowle was about five feet ten inches high and was booted and spurred. Whoever will give notice so as one or more of the above highwaymen may be apprehended, shall on conviction receive five guineas reward over and above the £40 allowed by Act of Parliament, to be paid by me: THOMAS FOWLE.'*

Fearing capture, Boulter and Caldwell fled to Birmingham where they were both apprehended when trying to dispose of a valuable watch to a Jew, and subsequently sent for trial to London.

On the 30th May 1778 Boulter made a remarkable escape from Clerkenwell Prison by pulling away a piece of bond timber and using it to loosen some bricks sufficiently enough to escape through a hole in the wall to the outside and then hid behind two doors to evade capture. He had previously managed to escape from his irons by using a watchmaker's saw smuggled in to him by a woman who was allowed to visit him inside. He reached Dover in the hope of escaping, but the port was closed due to hostilities with France. He eventually made his way to the Castle Inn at Bridport, where a suspicious landlord spotted him. He was arrested again on 31 July 1778 on the charge of robbing Mr. William Embry of Portsmouth Dockyard on the previous 10 May of 10 shillings and a silver watch near Horndean just outside of Portsmouth. Boulter was detained and taken to Dorchester jail, and then to the safer strongholds at Newgate, then Winchester Castle where his partner in crime Caldwell was already imprisoned!

'Boulter was the bogeyman name used to subdue unruly children in Wiltshire and Hampshire'.

Boulter (now aged 30) and Caldwell (26) were tried and found guilty at Winchester Assizes on the 31st July 1778, but their execution was delayed in the hope that they would divulge the whereabouts of their numerous stashes of swag! The four men who had apprehended Boulter in the Castle Inn at Bridport shared the reward money. At the trial, the landlady of Corsham's *'The Bell Inn'* gave evidence. When asked if she was afraid when she saw Poulter's pistols, she laughed and said that his were by no means the first pistols that she had seen loaded in her kitchen! Boulter and Baxter did eventually complete a full confession before they were both hanged at Winchester Castle on Wednesday 19th August 1778. Boulter pleaded with the trial Judge, asking him to intercede with the goodness of his heart, not to hang him but instead, to transport him abroad where he would willingly serve his Majesty in any situation abroad for life. The Judge replied that he (Boulter) must apply to another quarter, for his offences were so bad, that he (the Judge) could not look upon him as a fit object of mercy.

On Wednesday 19th August 1778 at 12 o'clock noon, a dismal cart passed out of Winchester Castle, and proceeded to the gallows outside the city bearing Thomas Poulter, James Caldwell, Mr. Read their executioner and two coffins. A noose was placed around their necks and the cart driven away from beneath them. Caldwell behaved throughout with great dignity and did not appear much concerned with his approaching fate. Boulter was very penitent and even managed to find something humorous to say to the crowd gathered for the hanging. Although Boulter held a pistol at the heads of travellers, he never really meant to use it, and it was his boast, at his last hour on earth, that he had never taken life. Within two months of the execution, a strange rumour was heard to the effect that on a moonlight night a figure was seen riding at break-neck speed over Salisbury Plain – a figure that disappeared into the mist. Witnesses swore that this was the ghost of Thomas Boulter, the Flying Highwayman, and his horse Black Bess. It was a story that was to be repeated many times over the years. For many decades after his death, Boulter was the name of the bogeyman that used to subdue unruly children in Wiltshire and Hampshire.

In the late 1770s Mary Abraham, alias Mary Sandall of Baverstock near Salisbury, actually assumed the dress and equipment of a mounted highwayman. She practised the *'stand and deliver'* business in that neighbourhood once too often and was caught and tried at the Assizes in 1779. What rendered her daring the more remarkable was that she took up the calling of a highway-woman just after the execution of Thomas Boulter.

Chapter 19. Horsey Tree - R.I.P Corsham Park.

In 2015 one of Corsham Park's beautiful oak trees was felled. She was known by some locals as the 'Horsey Tree'. Over the years, this tree with its perfect wooden saddle has given joy to most of Corsham's children, as they rode to..............................

'Banbury Cross to see a fine lady upon a white horse, with rings on her fingers and bells on her toes, she shall have music wherever she goes'.

The 'Horsey Tree' was one of the most favourite trees in Corsham Park, but thankfully we have kept several old photos to remember her by. Below - you can see her dismembered oak saddle and her face inside the trunk's bottom! ***R.I.P Corsham Park***

Chapter 20. Hospital - WWI Red Cross V.A.D. Hospital - Corsham Town Hall.

Sir John Tankeville Goldney's wife Lady Alice Frances Holbrow Goldney O.B.E., from Monks House was the inspirational Commandant of the Corsham Red Cross Hospital from 23 June 1915. She was one of many locals to work there. Alice was born in India in 1878 – the daughter of Frederick Charles Napier Goldney who was a Major in the Indian Army.

After returning from India, the family lived in Middlesex and was still there at the time of the 1911 census. Alice was 32 and was living at home with her parents and younger sisters Vera and Marjorie.

Photo © National Portrait Gallery, London.

In 1913 Alice married Sir John Tankeville Goldney in Ealing where she had lived. Sir John was the brother of Sir Frederick Goldney and had previously been married to Jane McGregor who died as Lady Goldney in 1911.

They lived in Monks House, Monks Park in Corsham. Sir John was a Bank Director of the Capital and Counties Bank but had also been Attorney-General and Admiralty advocate of the Leeward Islands, Judge of British Guiana and Chief Justice of Trinidad. He was knighted in 1893. He was also a J.P. for Wilts and High Sheriff for Wiltshire.

From 26 October 1914 Alice, now Lady Goldney, was a Nurse, volunteer worker at the Corsham Hospital, later becoming the Assistant Commandant of the Hospital and then Commandant in her own right from 25 June 1915. Lady Christian Methuen was the First Commandant.

Lady Alice Goldney remained as Commandant until the Hospital closed in 1919, supported by Sir John. Lady Alice's sister Marjorie also served as a nurse at the Corsham Hospital. Sir John Goldney died in 1920 and Lady Goldney is known to have sailed back to India soon after. She re-married in 1943 to Harold Robinson. She died in 1957 aged 79.

On 6 August 1914, two days after the start of WWI, Field Marshal Lord Methuen called a meeting at the Town Hall where the following was agreed.

- Allocate the Corsham Town Hall as a V.A.D. Red Cross Hospital with a resident fireman.
- Use the Almshouses as a temporary replacement Town Hall and Parish Room.
- Fully support the work of the local Red Cross Society Ladies' Committee in co-ordinating local effort in aid of the War.

It seems difficult these days to imagine the Corsham Town Hall building being used as a major 90-bed hospital for treating seriously wounded soldiers returning from battle on Hospital Ships - yet that was its function in WWI between its opening on 26th October 1914 to when it closed on 30 August 1919. A total of 875 soldiers were treated there by 75 nurses - at an annual cost of £2,500. Officers stayed in a house opposite. It also became the centre of the Red Cross in the area. As early as August 1914, the people of Corsham were making plans to establish a hospital in the town. Over 300 local people directly supported the Hospital. Voluntary Aid Detachment V.A.D hospitals were set up all around the country. They were staffed by voluntary civilians (who were not under the control of the military) to provide nursing care for injured military personnel. The V.A.D. system was founded in 1909 with the help of the Red Cross and Order of St. John. By the summer of 1914 there were over 2,500 Voluntary Aid Detachments in Britain. Of the 74,000 V.A.D. members in 1914, two-thirds were women and girls. Initially, they lacked the advanced skills and discipline of trained professional nurses but as time went on, they increased their skill and efficiency, and without them many soldiers would have suffered.

Lady Christian Methuen was appointed as the first Corsham Hospital Commandant on 26 August 1914, with 30 beds being quickly prepared; 24 in the large upstairs ward and 6 in the small. Prior to its use, visitors were allowed in for a small charge.

The first casualty at the hospital was Private William Taylor 7288 of the Lancashire Fusiliers. The injured men came from various battlegrounds such as Aisne, Ypres, Lille, Bathune, Labassee, Armentiers, Plugsteers and India. And their regiments were English, Welsh, Scots and Irish. There are many instances of frostbite as well as rheumatism, influenza and gun shot wounds.

Those being treated wore a blue uniform with a red tie, known as 'Hospital Blues'. Those who did not recover sufficiently to return to active service were issued with a Silver War Badge 'SWB' (also issued to soldiers who had completed the length of service), to wear on their lapel, signifying that they had completed their war service. Those deemed fit enough to leave convalescence, returned to one of the Command Depots for rehabilitative training. And some of those who were not so lucky were buried on the right hand side of Corsham's Ladbrook cemetery. One of those unfortunate souls was 25 year old Private Robert Brown from Midlothian in Scotland, who sadly died on the 21st October 1915 and was buried at Ladbrook following a funeral procession through the Corsham High Street.

In 1915 the Parish Council arranged to remove the fixed seating around the perimeter of the Council Chamber to make room for more beds; another stove was also installed in the large ward upstairs. The nurses were likely to have all been recruited from the local area and they were crucial to the running of this well respected and successful hospital in Corsham. A Nurses Home was established for a time at 91 Pickwick Road which was built in 1909.

There is a large plaque in the large upstairs room of the Town Hall, listing many of those who worked at the Hospital as nurses and volunteers, including those from the local village V.A.D. Groups in Biddestone and Box. Corsham received amazing help from these groups and from volunteers in the villages. The townspeople contributed to the war effort, with ladies knitting and sewing. Events were also held throughout Corsham and in the local villages to entertain the soldiers.

A list of those who worked at Corsham follows. No doubt there were many others who helped out, such as Miss Gidden for instance, who met and married one of the wounded soldiers, William Alford.

RED CROSS HOSPITAL CORSHAM ROLL-CALL October 26th 1914 - August 30th 1919. Commandants of the Hospital and of Wilts 30, Corsham: Honourable Christian Methuen, October 26th 1914 to June 22nd 1915. Lady [Alice] Goldney O.B.E., June 23rd 1915 to August 30th 1919. **Medical Officers:** A. G. Wood, J. E. Crisp, J. H. Nixon, S. Taylor, J. P. Martin, Lieutenant-Colonel R. Simmons. **Chaplains:** Rev. H. B. Ellison, Rev. A. J. Winnington-Ingram, Rev. W. P. Tucker.

Voluntary Aid Detachments (V.A.D.) WILTS 30, CORSHAM.

Assistant Commandant: Margaret Fitz-Adam Ormiston.

Quartermasters: Dorothy Brinkworth, Irene Parkinson. **Assistant Quartermaster:** Gladys Rogers.

Nurses: Beatrice Bayliffe, Elsie Bayliffe, Florence Bishop, May Blake, Lilian Brakspear, Ethel Brinkworth, Christine Butt, Frances Clarke, Ellen Coates, Emmie Cole, Florence Crisp, Kathleen Crisp, Katherine Duncan, Phyllis Flower, Norah Fuller, Louisa Gale, Edith Gane, Katherine Goldney, Lucy Goldney, Marjorie Goldney, Ivy Gough, Ada King, Irene Parkinson, Joan Pictor, Clara Spackman, Augusta Taylor, Cissie Willis and Ellen Hardiman, who served in the Corsham VAD until Oct 1915, when she joined Chippenham VAD (awarded RRC).

Mr. Percy Gane M.B.E. the Commandant of the 3rd Wiltshire V.A.D. was the transport officer for the Corsham Hospital. He died aged 69 in January 1935.

The following is a testament to the ordinary people in Corsham for their support of the wounded in the Corsham Red Cross Hospital during WWI. The examples shown below are just a few of many stories of how the people of Corsham pulled together in the most difficult of times during WWI (28 July 1914 to 11 November 1918) and beyond. They did the best that they could for the injured men, to get them well and strong so that they might be sent back to their homes to convalesce or back to their places in the fighting line.

Corsham was one of the first towns in the district to open a Red Cross Hospital in 1914. It did not take very long for the Hospital to be in full working order. The patients were warm in the praise of the nurses. The staff number was originally about twenty, including Commandants the Hon. Christian Methuen and Lady Goldney, Matron Nurse Pedley and Quarter Master Nurse Rodgers with help given by Mrs. Hedworth Williamson and Mrs. J.S. Corbett. Mrs. J. Gane was later in charge of the cooking arrangements - a department that worked very well once it was set up!

It was not just Corsham; all the local villages were involved, but the contributions of Biddestone and Box in particular stood out. Both villages had their own Voluntary Aid Detachments (V.A.D.) comprising of local women trained in basic first aid and hospital support skills. The Biddestone V.A.D. (Wilts 40) Commandant was Mrs. Charlotte Hedworth-Williamson and consisted of 31 women from Biddestone and Slaughterford. Mrs Alice Wait, a laundress, took on the responsibility of collecting and returning the washing from the Corsham hospital. Hospital records show her contribution as 1,560 hours of unpaid voluntary work!

The Box V.A.D. (Wilts 56) Commandant Mrs Stephen Langton, had 17 nurses who regularly attended the Hospital and 35 men who acted as orderlies. One of these was the Reverend De Vere Awdry who recorded over 1,100 volunteer hours in just over a year at the Corsham Hospital, Bowood and Chippenham. He was also the father of the Reverend W. Awdry who went on to write the famous *Thomas the Tank Engine* children's stories!

At the beginning, the 36 beds were regularly kept full by wounded men sent from the Bristol Hospitals. The first telegram came in October 1914, saying that twenty wounded men would be arriving on the 6.11 at Corsham Station. A large crowd waited on the station platform and at the Town Hall. A small fleet of motor cars belonging to Field Marshal Lord Methuen, Hon. Cecil Parker, Mrs. Chappell and Mr. F.A. FitzAdam Ormiston were used to convey the wounded to the hospital. Most of these early patients were sick cases from the Codford training camp on Salisbury Plain but some had been through Mons and the Aisne.

They also included six gallant wounded Belgium soldiers who looked a little war-worn and weary amidst their bandages. But they seemed to be quite happy amid their strange surroundings. One of them, an Army cyclist scout, brought his bicycle with him! Lord Methuen paid the men a visit and invited them to the gardens and grounds of Corsham Court. On Wednesday, he sent a car around and took those who were able, to Monks House where they were hospitably entertained to tea by Lady Goldney. On the following Thursday, the Vicar's wife, Mrs. H.B. Ellison took two of the wounded Belgians on a bike ride around Corsham! The doctors in charge were Dr. J. Ellis, Crisp and A.G. Wood (Corsham), Dr. Nixon (Chippenham) and Dr. Taylor (Lacock); the Corsham Boy Scouts also helped move the wounded.

There was no place yet for a proper kitchen so the meals were first cooked in the two bedrooms of a small house opposite, and carried over, with 30 evening meals being required immediately for the *newcomers* and full English breakfasts being 'knocked up' early the next day, all under the supervision at short notice of Matilda Talbot from Lacock Abbey (who stayed on helping out at the Hospital for 9 months before going out to France to help run a canteen for French soldiers). One of the Corsham bakers proved to be a tower of strength by providing bread, butter, tea, sugar, milk bacon and eggs for the wounded. There were men's meals, nurse's meals and the Matron's meals to be planned, including any special diets that were needed. It must have been an enormous task with so little notice and with only two frying pans! On one occasion, two soldiers made a mess of skinning some rabbits that had been caught.

In March 1915 one of the wounded soldiers in the WWI Town Hall Hospital who had been transferred in from one of the Bristol Hospitals was discovered to have the *spotted fever* (later found to be meningitis) and was removed to the isolation hospital at Combe Down in Bath. In January 1915 the three Town Hall Wards were renamed George, Nicolas and Albert instead of numbers! By 1916 the Corsham Hospital was working at maximum capacity. Extensive alterations were carried out to increase capacity. Mrs. H.J. Hulbert's house in the High Street was taken over and converted into a Nurses' Home; the kitchen was rearranged and the larger rooms were fitted as wards making extra accommodation for 18 beds. The Matron's room in the Hospital was converted into a ward and the Commandant's Office moved into Mrs. Hulbert's house.

Photo above shows patients outside No. 1 Church Street, the house on the corner (now Coppins).

Public visiting times were tightened up and a specific day agreed when donors and subscribers could visit. A new ward called the 'Box Ward' was opened after being equipped by the inhabitants of Box village, under the leadership of Mrs. Stephen Langton the Box V.A.D. Commandant. By July 1916, three-hundred and ninety-four patients had been treated at the Corsham Hospital, plus 59 outpatients and remarkably, the Corsham Hospital was still free from any debts. It soon became necessary to find even more additional beds and this was achieved by acquiring the nearby premises formerly used as a Liberal Club (to be used as a day room for the men) on the other side of the street and the old Bank premises near the Town Hall. Alterations were made to these additional buildings and to administration procedures to allow an increase in beds from 50 to 60. The Hospital headquarters were moved into the nearby old Bank House at 61 High Street.

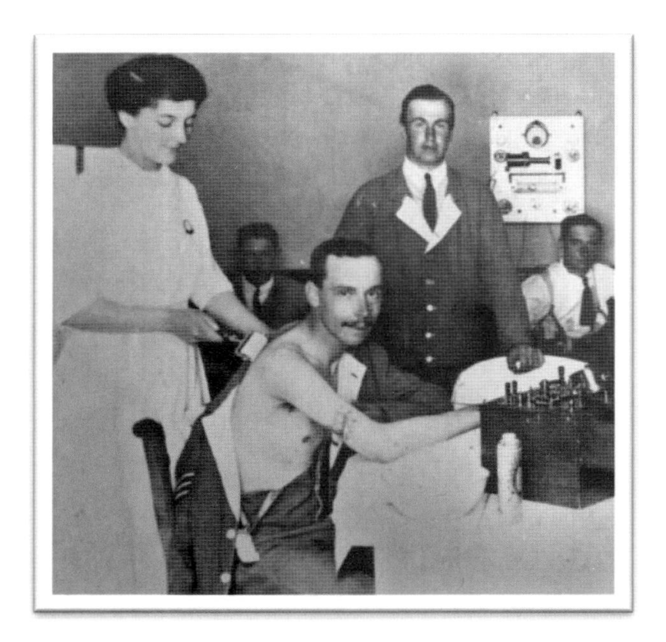

An 'electrotherapy room' was later created as part of the hospital's treatment facilities, in one of the houses opposite in Church Street. This involved applying an electrical stimulation to retard and prevent atrophy and to restore muscle mass and strength, following surgery upon a wound. The photo shows a soldier being treaded there in July 1918.

It became a regular sight at the little Corsham Station; a fleet of vehicles of all descriptions waiting for the wounded to arrive. There were no gleaming sterilised ambulances in those days, rather it was Messrs. Hiscock's light motor lorry that was used to convey the stretcher cases up Station Road hill and along the High Street to the Town Hall Hospital; whilst the less serious cases were chaperoned to the hospital in Mr. Harold Brakspear and Mr. R.C. Mattick's posh automobiles. On other occasions the vehicles were provided by Lord Methuen, the Hon. M.G. Talbot, Mr. E.A. FitzAdam Ormiston, Mr. J.G. Talbot, with Mr. Hancock's large van being used to convey the stretcher cases! On other occasions, the motor charabanc lent by Messrs. S. and R. Hiscocks was used for the stretcher cases along with a large horse drawn ambulance belonging to the local stone firms. The relief station master Mr. A. Sparey played his part admirably, by not allowing anyone onto the platform who should not be there. The trains were backed into the goods station entrance to allow the wounded some dignity whilst they were taken off the train and into the goods shed. Most of the men who came in were from the front, some suffering from frostbite. One local soldier, Rifleman E. Gifford, from Walcot in Bath was blown off his motorcycle and into a ditch by a shell. He covered himself with leaves until he could hear English voices passing by five hours later. He spent 11 weeks in Cambridge Hospital after being operated on.

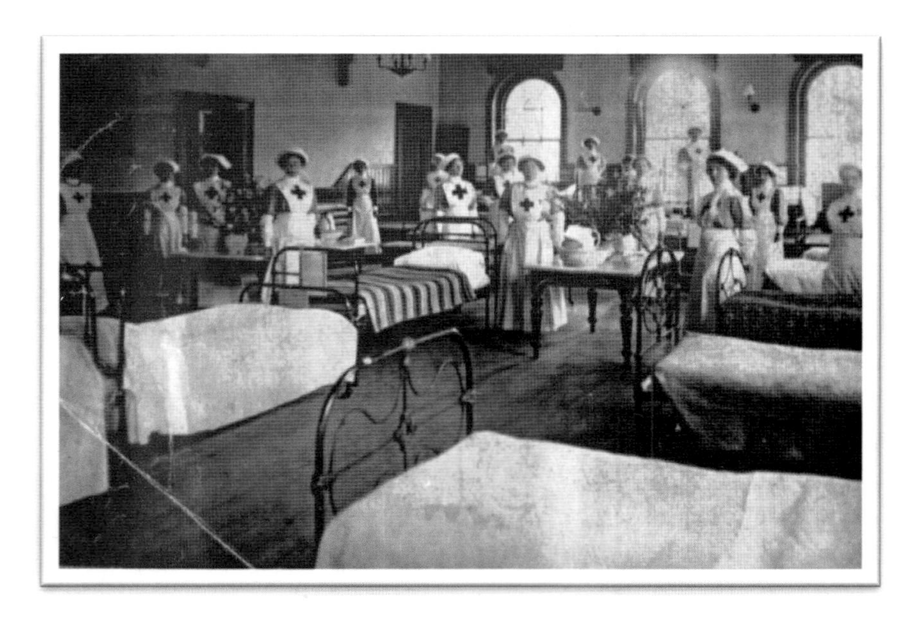

Wounded soldiers were regularly transferred from other hospitals; below is an example of the type of injuries that these men had. Among the wounded transferred to Corsham from the Second Southern General Hospital at Bristol in June 1915 were:

Corporal T. Barrable, 8th City of London, bomb wound in the thigh.
Corporal J. Mellrose, 3rd East Lancs, serious shrapnel wounds in legs and arms.
Private W.H. Sanders, 3rd Wilts, bullet wounds in legs and head.
Rifleman G. Hancock, Kings Royal Rifles, gunshot wound in foot.
Rifleman J. Thorpe, 2nd Rifle Brigade, gunshot wound in thigh.
Private J. Elwood, Duke of Cambridge's L.I. gunshot wound in leg.

Several of the men were engaged in the second battle of Ypres and the assault on Hill 60 which was in fact man-made. It was created in the 1860's from what was dug out from a nearby railway line. However, with a height of 150 feet any elevation within the Ypres Salient was advantageous to whoever held it and for this reason Hill 60 became a prime target for both Allies and Germans. It was at Hill 60 that the Germans first used poisonous gas against Allied troops on April 21st 1915. A second attack using poisonous gas took place on April 22nd.

The cartoon above, was drawn by Private J Kerr (55626) 198th Machine Gun Corps from London, when he was recovering in Corsham Hospital. In 1922 now in the 207th COY Machine Gun Corps (Infantry) he was awarded a Military Medal for bravery in battle.

Private Fred Wheeler, who was seriously wounded whilst in the trenches at Landrecies (a commune in the Nord department in northern France) said that it was treachery by the German Army Corps that resulted in many deaths. Whilst they were in the trenches an aeroplane flying the French colours flew down their lines and back again, thus enabling the enemy to get the range. It flew away out of their reach and back to the German lines. For four hours they were shelled and unable to fire back a single shell in return. Over 600 casualties occurred to the gallant *Gloster* Regiment. Private Fred Wheeler received shrapnel wounds to the thighs. As he lay in the trench, Private Fred Wheeler was jumped on by a colleague who thought he was the enemy! This is how Fred expressed the situation written as a poem in the Corsham Hospital:

It was in the month of August,
When I was called up to the front,
To help fight for France and Belgium,
Against the German Huns.

It was at the town of Landrecies,
Where the trenches we had were close by,
That some comrade in the darkness,
Took me for a German spy.

In Corsham I am stranded,
Where nothing but kindness is shown,
To rest and think of our laurels,
Which history has always made known.

News was received in Corsham on a regular basis concerning the fate of its men. For example, in November 1914 news reached the home of Pte. Pearce, a reservist of the Wiltshire Regiment who died in a French Hospital. Before joining up, he was employed by Mr. W. Miller of Thingley Farm. News was also received on the same day that Gunner Oscar Bush who was a Reservist who had worked in Lord Islington's gardens at Hartham Park had been killed in action. He left a wife and two children. A funeral service was held where he fell, conducted by the Army Chaplain - a former Corsham Vicar from 1902-1908, the Rev. Edward Anthony Sydney Gell.

In July 1915 for the second year, the workmen employed by the Chippenham Rural District Council abstained from their annual outing, which under the present conditions, they felt they could not take. The funds collected were donated to the Marquis of Lansdowne's county fund, of which £10 (£700 in today's money) was sent to aid the Corsham Hospital. They asked for the money to be spent towards a new bed called, 'The Roadmen's Bed'. The bed was put up and the reminder of the fund was applied to the *wants* of the hospital.

A sigh of relief must have been given in June 1916, when at the *Rural Tribunal Grant Exemption Appeals* sitting, an exemption was granted to Ernest Merritt the Corsham Undertaker and Coffin maker. The Recruiting Officer stated that the Commandant of the Corsham Hospital had *wired* that. *'If Merritt was taken away they would all have to make their own coffins'.* Other Corsham exemptions were given to John Butler (shoeing smith), William Fredrick Hancock, coal merchant and Thomas Arthur Ives the butcher, all of them playing their part in the *war effort*. In 1916, a number of soldiers from Chippenham were sent to the Corsham hospital, after they had contracted measles.

Funds provided by the Government *only* covered the cost of food and medical requirements for the wounded. This meant that an enormous amount of extra money had to be raised locally by the Corsham (and other local town) inhabitants, by staging regular events and via generous donations. For example, the Wiltshire Farmers' Ltd. donated £50 (£3,000 in today's money), the Nurses Penny Fund collected 19,200 pennies from the various Parishes, amounting to £80 (£5,000 in today's money!) Local people went **Above and Beyond** in their support while their fathers, sons and brothers were away from home fighting for their country. Fetes and music concerts (many organised by the Spackman family) were held regularly to boost the Hospital funds.

The Corsham Red Cross Hospital also relied on the Corsham public to play their part - and they certainly did. Gifts were provided almost on a daily basis, such as vegetables and salad from Lady Methuen, eggs from Mrs. Rogers, egg cups and walking sticks from Mesdames Crook, Powell and the Misses W. Rodgers and Sawyer, invalid delicacies Mesdames Blake and Eastmond, potted meat from Mrs. Garne, trout from Mrs. Butt, cakes from Daymond's the baker, slippers from Mr. Moody, blankets from Lady Margaret Spicer, jellies from Miss Brinkworth, stationery, Miss Bishop, towels, Mrs. Elliott, papers, Mrs.Cruttwell, mending by the Misses Halhed and Sainsbury, pillow cases, soap, coal scuttle, knives and forks from the Corsham Liberal Club, gas cooker from Messrs. Moody, Gooding and Oatly the auctioneers house and estate agent, sugar and lemon squeezer from Miss Lucy Goldney, and cigarettes from Mr. Jennings and Mrs. Oxley!!!. etc. etc. etc. The injured men who were able, were regularly invited home to tea by the Corsham locals.

In July 1915 at the Petty Session, Sir John T. Goldney said that complaints had reached him of wounded soldiers from the hospital being constantly seen going in and out of licensed houses in a state of intoxication, when they should recuperating be in the hospital!

In December 1915 Claremont College the high-class boarding school for girls, gave two Shakespearean performances of "Love's Labour Lost" in the Parish Room. The first performance was devoted for the recreation of the soldiers in the Corsham Hospital and the second to the general public. All funds were given to the Red Cross Blanket Fund. The performance included two solo dancers Miss Sylvia Norton and Mary Berry accompanied by Miss Pearce who provided the music. The dresses were charming and the very best was made of the limited stage accommodation.

AUXILIARY POSTMAN'S DEATH OUTSIDE THE CORSHAM HOSPITAL.

George Mansfield, a 52 year old Postman from Chippenham died as the result of injuries received on the evening of 1 August 1916 when he fell off his bicycle outside the Corsham Red Cross Hospital.

At a quarter to six in the evening, Mansfield, was slowly peddling his son's bicycle on the wrong side of the road along Corsham High Street on his way home after an evening ride. As he approached the Town Hall and prior to the collision, he whistled to attract the attention of two Corsham nurses (driver) Miss Daisy Evelyn Large (of Belmont House Corsham) and Miss Mitchell who were sat in a governess car (a lightweight two-wheeled carriage, with seats positioned along the two sides, drawn by a pony).

Whilst the two nurses who had just finished their shift were waving farewell to their colleagues at the hospital, Mansfield collided with the near shaft of the car which struck his stomach. The ladies were driving south towards the direction of the Station and crossing the road in a slanting direction to get to the proper side of the street. A witness said that Mansfield saw the vehicle and moved onto the wrong side of the road to avoid it.

Another witness (tailor Alfred W. Butt) said that there was plenty of room for the cyclist to have passed the vehicle on his side of the road. Mansfield was quickly taken into the Red Cross Hospital where everything possible was done for him.

Being very ill and getting worse, he was moved to the Chippenham Cottage Hospital the next day suffering from a cut to the left side of his head and a contusion (bruising) of the stomach. An operation was performed for an internal abscess and other internal injuries, but death occurred due to blood poisoning from the abscess.

The deceased's son Albert Edward Mansfield stated that, *"His father had previously lost the sight of his right eye, but otherwise suffered from no infirmity and was accustomed to cycling".* He went on to say that; *"On a previous occasion his father had met with an accident when cycling from Corsham to Chippenham, having collided with some cows which were driven from a field onto the road in the dark".* **R.I.P.**

An inquest into the accident gave a verdict of 'Accidental Death' but were of the opinion that the accident would not have happened if Miss Large had exercised more care in keeping a look out in the direction that she was driving.

On 4 August 1923 on the seventh anniversary of George Mansfield's death, his wife (now living in Pickwick) Mrs. Louisa Mansfield aged 60, suffered a broken thigh when a motor cyclist ran into her as she was crossing the road at Pickwick. She was removed in the Corsham Motor Ambulance and taken to the Bath Royal United Hospital.

On the afternoon of 8 September 1917 an enjoyable cricket match was played on the Box cricket ground between a party of convalescent soldiers from the Corsham Hospital and a local team selected by Mr. B. Vazey. The weather was fine and but for the absence of so many old familiar faces of the 1913-14 Box team, one was reminded of old times. Out of the regular playing members of the Box Cricket Club, all but the two who were under age, were on active service in various parts of the world. During the interval the teams were entertained by the Box Nurses and their friends.

The photo shows a Motor Ambulance being presented to the Corsham Hospital by Col. Spencely.

The above photo shows the last day of the V.A.D. Corsham Hospital. Mr. Daymond's father Joe is standing second from right. The gentleman in the wheelchair far left is Mr. Jennings who lived at Ashford Cottages in Priory Street. He was injured in the war and looked after by the milliner who ran the Gables shop at the other corner end of the High Street.

Recognition of the Red Cross Work in Corsham.

Six years to the day after the Corsham Hospital was opened in 1914, a gathering took place in the Town Hall on Tuesday 26 October 1920, when a marble tablet was presented by the inhabitants of Corsham to Lady Goldney to commemorate the use of the Corsham Town Hall as a Red Cross Hospital and for the patriotic service rendered by her ladyship and her staff for the benefit of the country's sick and wounded soldiers during the war. The tablet was unveiled by Lord Methuen. Other presentations were made in connection with Red Cross work in Corsham. On the outbreak of war, Corsham rose nobly to the occasion, by providing for the sick and wounded. The hospital's capacity was extended as necessity arose.

It became one of the best equipped and most efficiently managed in the county. For the greater part of the time, Lady Goldney was the Commandant and she was successful in gathering around her a willing and efficient band of workers. It was this service that the Corsham inhabitants desired to recognise and the large gathering which filled the Town Hall that Tuesday evening bore testimony to the feelings of appreciation of the residents. Lord Methuen unveiled the tablet, which is placed on the wall of the upstairs hall near the entrance. Although Lady Goldney said that the decoration that she had gained for her work in Corsham (she was awarded an O.B.E. for her service) was in recognition to her staff, there were few like her who could have combined the power of organisation necessary to make everyone around her work so efficiently during those very difficult times.

Lady Goldney had not only brought honour to herself but honour to Corsham and its people.

Lady Goldney who spoke warmly of the ordinary people of Corsham said, *"There had never been a thing that she had asked for but what they had given her, money, houses in fact"*. She thought they suspected that every time that a Corsham person saw her looking at their house that she was going to take it! They had given her everything she had wanted, even down to onions! She was presented with an album containing the names of all the Hospital donors, 507 in number.

Mr. W. Field, the Chairman of the Corsham Parish Council was presented with the Army Council's framed certificate - the wording being :

'DURING THE GREAT WAR of 1914-1919 this building was established and maintained as a Hospital for British Sick and Wounded. The Army Council, in the name of the Nation thank those who have rendered to it this valuable and patriotic assistance in the hour of its emergency, and they desire also to express their deep appreciation of the whole-hearted attention which the Staff of this Hospital gave to the patients who were under their care. The War has once again called upon the devotion and self-sacrifice of British men and women, and the Nation will remember with pride and gratitude their willing and inestimable service.'

A similar certificate was presented to Mr. C.W. Churchill on behalf of the Liberal Club who had gratuitously lent the whole of their Club building to the Red Cross Hospital for the purpose of extending the Hospital's capacity. A singing of the National Anthem closed the proceedings.

On Friday 21 October 2016 the Corsham WWI hospital ward was recreated and filmed by the BBC.

Corsham lost 115 men in the First World War, all of whom are remembered on the Memorial opposite the Almshouses alongside the Corsham Park gates and on the memorial to the right of the entrance porch at St. Bartholomew's Church. Stories of many of the Corsham men who went to war, can be found online here: http://corshamcommemorates.weebly.com/corsham-stories.html

Below is the Corsham Town Hall in 2016; changed very little since it was used as a ward during WWI.

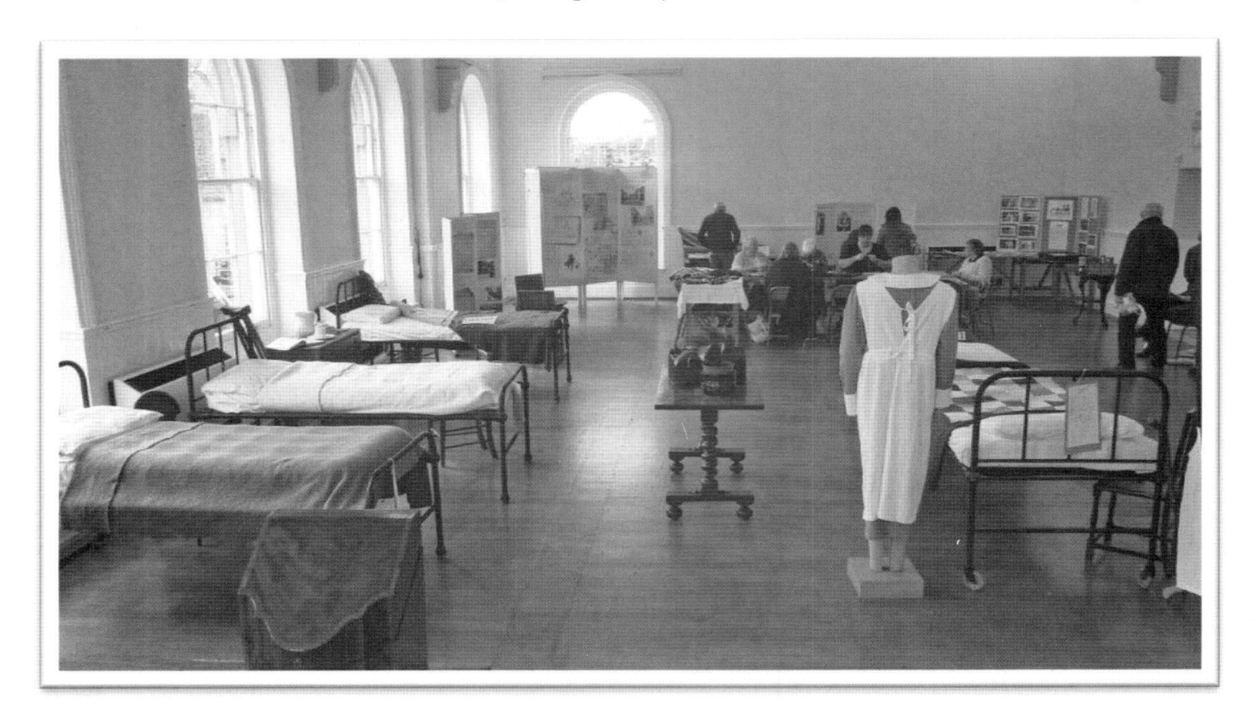

'A big thank you goes to all of those who worked in our WWI hospitals and local V.A.D. Groups.'

And many thanks to Kevin Gaskin for his help in compiling this chapter.

Chapter 21. Ice Houses.

An ice house is a structure built partly underground, for the preservation of ice for use during warmer weather.

For centuries, the only way that people could preserve and store their food in Corsham, especially milk and butter, was to place them inside cool cellars, outdoor window boxes or even underwater in nearby ponds, lakes, streams or wells. There was little use then for refrigeration, as food preservation used *time-tested methods* such as, salting, spicing, smoking, pickling and drying. For those who could not afford the luxury of delivered ice, they had to make do with the aforementioned methods.

The delivery of ice to customers using factory made ice, continued well into the twentieth century. Ice was also harvested from lakes and rivers every winter and stored in large commercial ice houses, the proprietors of which sold the ice to the local *'Ice Man'* or direct to customers in the summer months when it was required. Ice started to be imported from the United States in the 1840's and from Norway.

Each spring, as the weather turned warmer, the delivery of ice began. The local *'Ice Man'*, along with his horse and wagon became part of the summer street scene of every town. Those who could afford it obtained their ice from him. Each morning, he would collect the blocks of ice from a local supplier and then load them onto a large truck or horse drawn wagon. The blocks would be grabbed using huge sharp tongs and then swung into the cart's ice box. Scales for measuring the large the blocks of ice were attached to the ice wagon's side.

When the 'Ice Man' arrived in your street, he would chip off what you needed with a super sharp pick, called appropriately an ice pick! The purchased ice would then stored indoors, inside wooden ice boxes with hollowed out walls insulated with sawdust, cork or dried seaweed and lined with tin, zinc, porcelain tile or opal glass. The Ice Man would also supply the local shops, carrying the blocks of ice into the shops using a padded sack over his shoulder to protect him.

But in general, most perishable food was stored in a cool cellar or in a small room called the pantry which was often located on the coldest (North) facing wall of the house/cottage. The pantries often had a tiny window high up and protected by a sort of metal sieved screen to keep the flies out. The cooler temperatures in a pantry would only have been enough to keep the food cool for a few days; but houses were also much cooler in those days as not many people had central heating. Milk and other dairy products were stored in containers that were packed in shaved ice and then delivered to your door by horse and wagon.

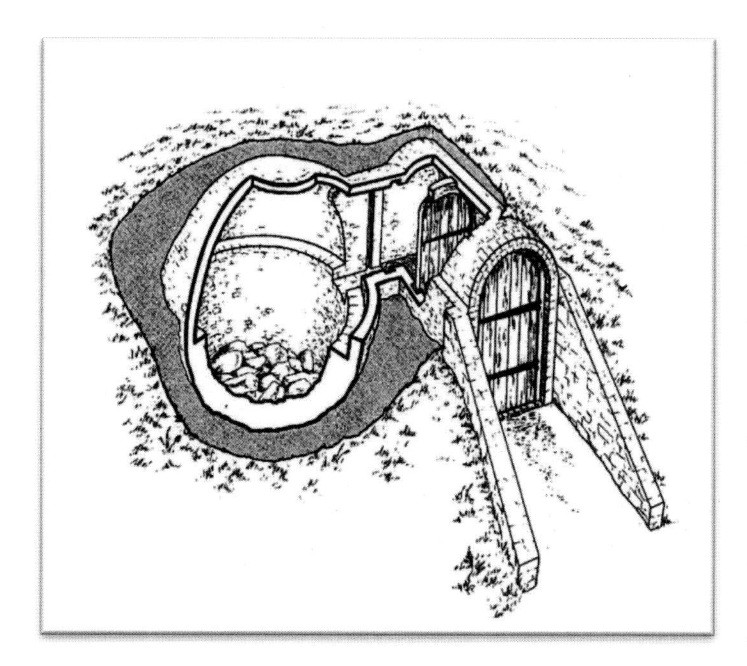

Although artificial refrigeration began in the mid-1750s and developed in the early 1800s, it wasn't until 1913 (when there was growing need to keep food and drinks longer) before refrigerators for domestic use were invented by Fred W. Wolf of Fort Wayne, Indiana. Prior to this, large estates such as Corsham Court and Hartham House relied on an Ice House to store ice throughout the year. Some ice houses were built as underground chambers, usually man-made and close to natural sources of winter ice such as freshwater lakes. But many were simple buildings lined with various types of insulation.

The Romans were the first to build ice houses, though not very widely here in the UK. In the 17th century, grand country houses followed the fashion of having one built. Ice houses then fell out of fashion until about the late 18th century.

During the winter, ice and snow would be cut from lakes or rivers and taken into the ice house and packed around with insulation, often straw or sawdust. The ice would remain frozen for many months, often until the following winter, and could be used as a source of ice during summer months. The main application of the ice was for the storage of foods, but it could also be used simply to cool drinks, or to allow ice-cream and sorbet desserts to be prepared.

When James 1 was king, he commissioned the construction of the first modern ice house in Greenwich Park in 1619. And we have some fine examples right here on our Corsham doorstep!

There are at least two ice houses remaining in Corsham; one in Corsham Park, and one in Hartham Park. The Corsham Park ice house is sunk into an embankment beside an iron boundary fence separating two fields *(note - these fields are not a public right of way!)*. The top part of the brick dome actually rises above normal ground level but was disguised with earth, clumps of hawthorn trees and bracken. Hiding it below an earth covered mound was part of the design to keep the temperature down. The Corsham Park ice house opening is now protected with a strong iron grate to prevent entry, as it has become a danger to inquisitive children and to the sheep.

The ice house in Corsham Park is designed with a few steps leading down into a small barrel vaulted brick passage which would originally have been sealed with a wooden door. At the far end of the vaulted passage is the ice chamber that is partly sunk into the hillside and lined with brick. The chamber is around 3m deep and the total interior height from the funnel shaped domed roof is around 5m. In the brick floor of the chamber is a circular basin with an adjoining drain originally covered with a stone slab. Melting water would fill the basin before overflowing into the drain, thus allowing the slow-melting ice to escape. Both the ice chamber and the passage have an inner shell of brick, but unlike some ice houses there is no insulating gap between the layers. Clay was piled around the outside of the passage and the chamber to increase insulation.

Because of their temperature control efficiency, a full ice house (packed with ice and straw) could take up to 18 months to thaw. They were brick-lined and their cylindrical shape and roof was engineered for temperature regulation and strength. The ice house in Corsham Park is very much like Buonarotti Papworth's 1818 plan for one of his early designs.

Everything about the design of an ice house is focused on minimizing the amount of ice that melted during warm weather. There are no windows; there are drain holes at ground level for water from melting ice to leave the building and the ice blocks (also called cakes) were packed tightly together. On top of each layer of ice blocks there was a thin layer straw or sawdust to keep the layers of ice from freezing together.

When the Corsham Park Ice House was built in the *Icehouse Covert*, several small 'Stew' ponds were combined to form a large pear-shaped lake alongside. If you look carefully, you can see the hollow in the field where the north/east lake was. This was filled in 1798 before the eleven acre east lake as we know it today was built. Hence, that is why the ice house is where it is. In those days, the ice house would have been right next to the original lakeside.

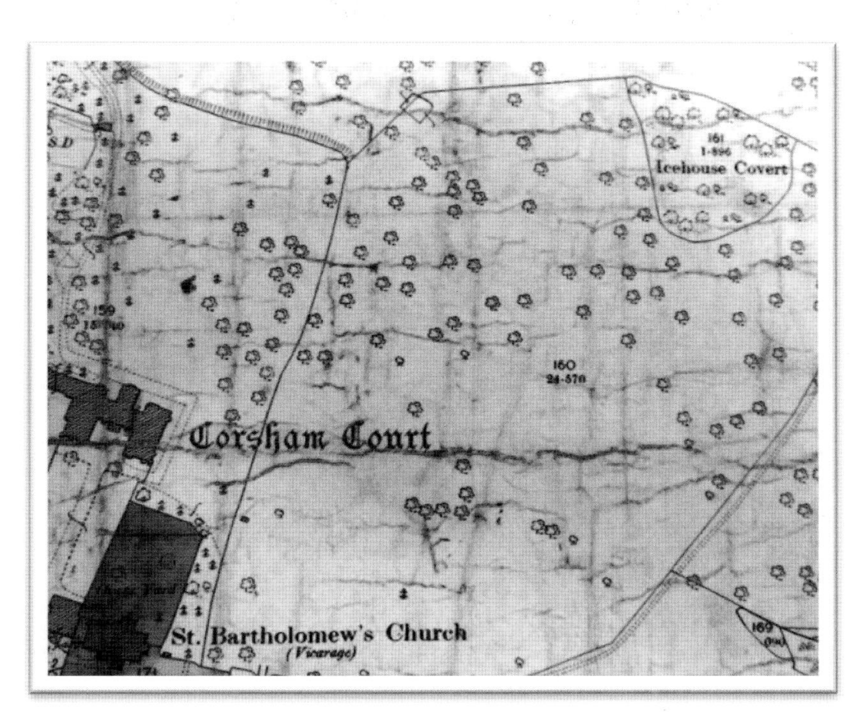

The ice house is recorded as Wiltshire Buildings Record Number, 00724.2. Grid reference ST 87705 70905.

Whilst some ice may have been collected from frozen lakes, some probably came from the local Ice Man. But the nearby Corsham Lake provided most of the ice required. In the winter, when Corsham Lake had frozen over, an ice auger would have been used to drill holes into the icy surface. A metal ruler with a hook at the bottom end was inserted into each auger hole to measure the thickness of the ice.

The *ice cutter* would read the number on the ruler that was even with the surface. This allowed the ice cutters to know the thickness of the ice in different places and decide where to begin harvesting. Blocks of ice were then cut out from the lake, using a long handled pond ice saw to cut through ice that might be 18 inches thick.

A good ice cutter would have been able to pull the saw almost out of the ice then lean far over to push the saw almost to the surface of the lake. Pike poles were then used to guide floating ice blocks toward the edge of the lake near the ice house. The pointed end could be used to push the ice, while the hook could be used to pull a block closer.

The long pike pole was also used to move ice blocks into place inside the ice house. Some pike poles were 16 feet long to allow a man to reach an ice block that was floating too far away.

Large blocks of ice that weighed several hundred pounds could be moved over ice or frozen ground on a wooden sled. To prevent both men and horses from slipping on the ice, the horses wore special horseshoes with long cleats; the men wore *'creepers'* a metal plate with short cleats that strapped onto the heel of their boots.

The winter ice from the lake would have been used to pack meat, and for storage of other perishable foods. Ice was also used for medicinal purposes: to treat fever and inflammation. At one time, a common prescription for indigestion was being told to suck on ice.

In some cases, large meat and fish stocks did not necessarily need to be preserved on a large estate because they could simply be caught from estate lakes and ponds when needed. Nevertheless, a hundred years or more ago some meat was probably stored in the Corsham ice houses, as this was the only way that it could be refrigerated in reasonable amounts over a long period.

One can imagine the Corsham Court estate staff retrieving meat from the ice house. Bursting open the wooden doors (into the underground cellar stuffed with straw for insulation) they would have encountered a dark and bitterly cold place. A side of beef, pig, sheep or lamb would have been man-handled from out of this hostile environment and carted over the fields for culinary ministrations in the Court.

Between 1939 and 1945 when the ice houses in England fell into disuse, they found a new purpose. Some were reinstated as ice and food stores, as garden sheds, fruit stores and wine cellars, but many, by virtue of being subterranean and strongly built, became air raid shelters.

In 1816 the Hartham estate was purchased from the Goddard family trust by American exile Michael Joy who added an ice house (see photo), which subsequently served as an air raid shelter during the Second World War.

Chapter 22. Libraries in Corsham.

The photo shows the purpose built library when it was located next to the Mansion House.

1839: A 'Corsham Literary and Scientific Institution' was established with Mr. Strong voted in as its first president. Meetings were held in the long room at the Methuen Arms and in the Methuen School opposite.

1839: On 1 November the members of the Corsham Literary and Scientific Institution received a valuable addition to their library, from H.F. Talbot Esq., of Lacock Abbey, consisting of a series of Voyages and Travels, in 9 volumes.

1882: When the Corsham Town Hall was rebuilt, a library/reading room was created on the bottom floor called the *Mechanics Institute Library*, which over the ensuing years gradually became defunct.

1888: A library containing 83 volumes provided by many friends, including Mrs. Mayo, Mr.T.B. Potter, M.P., Mr. Handel Cossham, M.P., Mr. A.G. Westby and others, is established in the Corsham Liberal Club at the end of the High Street (where Barber's the Newsagent resided later).

1894: At the Parish Council Meeting 25 June, Mr. G.P. Fuller told the members that they had the power of starting a proper public library, and he did not see why the Parish should not take this matter seriously into consideration in the future. It would only require a bare majority of the electors of the Parish to pass a resolution to the effect that they were in favour of a public library. They were precluded from spending more than a penny rate, which would produce £100 (about £9,000 in today's money) and go a long way towards making a very good library if they wished it.

1897: The Parish Council spend £10 for the provision of new books for the library.

1902: In October Mr. J Sheppard, Chairman of the Methuen School managers, sanctioned the formation of a school library, provided the managers made themselves responsible for the character of the books circulated and to provide cupboard accommodation.

1912: Mr. Lewin Spackman of the Caxton Printing Works, opens a library at his new offices in Caxton House opposite the Flemish Buildings at the very end of the High Street, with 150 volumes of up-to-date fiction available on the shelves.

Caxton House, which originally formed part of the Corsham Temperance Hotel *(see Chapter 50),* is a fine example of a Grade II listed three bedroom house on the High Street in Corsham. The first document record of Caxton House was in c.1805. The building was once home to several historical families such as; Mr Harrison, Taylor, Bradbury and Spackman. This property has had many uses over the years, including a livery supplier, stationer, printer and a dry cleaning business, after which the building returned to residential use. To the rear of the property is a lovely high walled courtyard with raised flower beds, a summerhouse and an old privy which is used for storage.

The photo above, shows the inside of the old black hut library in Brunel Avenue / Pickwick Road.

1921: The Rev. J. Chugg suggested at a Council Meeting that a room in the Town Hall could be used as a *good* library in splendid memory of the 19 fallen. Mrs H.G. Mansfield replied that she had already applied to the County Librarian and he had agreed to make the Corsham hall one of Wiltshire's County Library Centres. The County Librarian sent the Corsham Library a box of seventy books in January.

1926: A letter from the Wiltshire County Librarian was received by the Parish Council early in the year, offering to supply the necessary books to form a Free Library at Corsham. It was agreed to accept the offer and a committee was formed to make the necessary arrangements. Wiltshire County Council provided 300 books for the public library to be set up in the *Card Room* of the Corsham Town Hall. In December, the Free Library was opened in the Town Hall by Mr. H. Burgess, chairman of the Corsham Parish Council. Others present where, Mrs. J.E. Crisp, Mrs. J. Cowley, Rev. W.E. Bryant, Messrs. C.W. Churchill, A. Bird, J. Daymond, H.B. Coates and several others. Mr. Burgess hoped that both the young and the old of Corsham would make good use of it. The library which is being run by a number of local residents will open every Friday. Fifty people joined up on the opening day. It was run by volunteers and it was not long before 140 people had taken advantage of the 2p. *Joining Fee* for the library card; after which books could be secured free every week. But it cost 1p. per week if the book was kept out over one week.

1927: In May, the Library Committee re-elected the Chairman Mr. C.J. Fortune. There were now 273 library members enrolled. The Committee suggested small improvements and that the library should be opened on Fridays during summertime from 3 to 4p.m. and 6:30 to 7p.m. and a rota of assistant librarians be obtained.

1930: Due to the number of books that had gone missing, Mr. Hamilton the County Librarian introduced a new scheme to be established in the County, to keep a tighter hold on the books. A great number had been lost under the old system. A consideration was made to open the library on two evenings per week.

1931: There seems to be slackness with regards to borrowers, as books were not always being returned promptly. New rules and suggestions were adopted to try and alleviate this problem.

1932: A notice was printed and displayed in the library, forbidding dogs entry during library days. Miss Freeth and Mr. Alan are appointed as assistant librarians.

1933: The Town Hall is refurbished. The *Mechanics Institute* takes charge of a new library room and a new coffee bar is opened in the Town Hall.

A National Central Library was set up and the national indexing of books commences, incorporating all the libraries in the country. It also acted as a point of contact between British and foreign libraries. This lead to a rapidly growing affiliation of libraries (at present 132) containing over five million volumes. All of the libraries agreed to lend books to others whenever possible. Books were now being lent to readers outside of Wiltshire through the auspices of the National Central Library.

1934: The County Librarian wanted to provide Corsham with more books and a better display. The Parish Council did not wish to give up the Council Chamber in the Town Hall for books!

1943: The library moves into the Town Hall's Council Chamber and Mr. Bird hands over his duties to a paid librarian, assisted by a team of volunteers.

The photo shows the coal stove in the old black hut library in Pickwick Road.

1944: The multiple use of the Council Chamber and its limited size made it unsatisfactory for continued use as a library. The library was transferred into the large black hut between Brunel Avenue and Pickwick Road (in the cutting along Pickwick Road directly opposite the junction with Oliver Avenue). In cold weather, the windows of the black wooden hut would be covered with the condensation produced by a small coal-fired stove which barely kept the building warm.

The books were crammed onto the shelves which you had to squeeze between when making a selection. The musty smell of the old books combined with the damp, was a odour that would be remembered for life - for those of us who visited there! Add into that mix, the aroma from the tiny (single pan) toilet, which was immediately to the left as you entered the building. There was no computerised system in those days, the little cards inside each cover were taken out, meticulously stored and retained in the library to show who had borrowed the book and when it should be returned.

A job advert was released seeking a Library Assistant for Branch work. On occasions, the person appointed would be required to travel between Chippenham, Corsham, Devizes and Trowbridge, but the main work was in the Chippenham-Corsham area. Salary Scale, £60-90 per annum if under 18 years of age, £105-210 if over 18.

1951: From 1 May fines were introduced for the undue retention of books. The charge was 3d. per week or portion of week for the time that the book is retained after the date that it was due to be returned. Readers were now able to renew books personally or by post, provided no other person had requested the book.

1955: Miss Celia Burton, daughter of Police Sgt. Burton, was appointed assistant librarian at the Corsham Free Library.

1956: Mr. Parfitt was the Corsham Librarian. Lynette Bowman later became the Chief Librarian. She lived in the old Westrop Lodge house on the left, just past Corsham Football Club along Lacock Road. If you made a noise in the old library, Lynette would glare at you through her large framed spectacles (even if you accidentally stepped on one of the old squeaky rotten floorboards)!

1960: It was decided to move the library into a purpose fit building to be built next to the Mansion House lower down Pickwick Road.

1966: There was no sign yet of a new library being built next to the Mansion House. Mrs Hoare asked for a signpost to be made pointing to the existing library in the black hut to help newcomers find it.

1969: A purpose-built new library opens in town, next to the Mansion House at the bottom of Pickwick Road.

Photo shows Lynette Bowman the Chief Librarian in the new library alongside the Mansion House.

1980: The library was no longer opened on Saturday afternoons and it was proposed to shut it on Saturday morning as well.

2013: Corsham residents were asked to say what type of facilities they would like to see in the town's new library.

The library would be part of the new Springfield Campus, in Beechfield Road, which was expected to open in 2015.

The survey responses had to be completed by Saturday, 9 November.

Some of the survey questions were:

Q1. Please tell us what you think of this Library?
Q2. What was your primary method of travel to this area / library today?
Q3. Did you come to this library today intending to borrow book(s)?
Q5. What do you think of the choice and physical condition of the books in this library?
Q6. Did you intend to use a computer during your visit to this library today?
There were 22 questions overall.

The survey was one of the largest surveys of its kind in Wiltshire and provided a wealth of information for the Library Service and individual libraries to help plan service improvement and development.

Photo above shows left to right, Sarah Harding, Christine Lines and Susan Duparcq in the Pickwick Road library when it was next to the Mansion House.

2014: After nearly 45 years, the old purpose built library next to the Mansion House closed on 25 July and was demolished in 2017. Corsham library looked to recruit book-loving volunteers as it prepared to move into the new modern home as part of the town's new community campus.

2015: The new Library in Beechfield Road, opened on 7 August as part of the modern Corsham Campus attracting 700 visitors that day. By the end of December, the Campus library had a total of 7,400 registered members. The Library now stocks some 15,000 items (books, DVDs, videos, etc.) plus 3,000 ebooks. Bookable computers are also available with free access to the internet.

The photo shows the 1950/1960s black library hut between Brunel Avenue and Pickwick Road.

Chapter 23. Lime/Pottery/Brick Kilns and the remarkable Angell Family.

There is a large hidden Lime/Pottery/Brick Kiln near the bottom of Chequers Hill.

Please do not visit the quarry. It is on private land and the deep pools and undergrowth are dangerous. And please do not disturb the No. 10 Chequers, Brick Kiln Cottage occupants.

WHERE IS IT? As you go towards Chippenham on the Corsham to Chippenham main A4 road, turn right at the bottom of Chequers Hill. Head half-a-mile southwards along the wide road towards Easton and Thingley (pass the old large North Walk's Carriage Drive columned gates at the top of the rise), until you will come to the third house, Brick Kiln Cottage No.10 Chequers (which belongs to the Corsham Estate - postcode SN13 0QH).

The old quarry lies completely hidden beneath the copse of trees on the rise behind the cottage. Access to the working quarry would have been along a track which ran just in front of the cottage which is occupied and part of the Corsham Estate.

The cottage, now known as 10 Chequers was originally called Brick Kiln Cottage (and is still known by that name by the current Electricity Board). Brick Kiln Cottage was also once known as 10 Chippenham Road - a strange name, considering that the road itself does not actually lead to Chippenham!

The Angell family lived there from the time of the First World War until the early 1950s. Their nearest neighbours were the Mizen family, who lived at 8, Chequers, this being the cottage at the end of Green Lane, directly opposite the large gates that guard the entrance to the North Walk's Carriage Drive. In 1962, the rent for the Brick Kiln Cottage was 30 shillings per month.

Below is an amazing and beautiful, unique photograph of all of the remarkable Angell family together, taken in front of Brick Kiln Cottage, which was then known as *Angell Cottage*. This must have been a very special occasion, for everyone is dressed in their best clothes.

BACK ROW LEFT TO RIGHT: Ron, George, Walt, Bert, Doug and Frank.
FRONT ROW LEFT TO RIGHT: John (christened Llewellyn Sidney but always known as John) with Dolly (Christened Doreen Frances but known as Dolly), Eli, holding Mary (the baby of the family, born in 1928), Alice, Norah, Jake (holding Mickey the dog), Vera and Gordon.

The two-bedroomed Brick Kiln Cottage was a *tied property*, occupied by Eli Angell (a farm labourer), his wife Alice, their 13 children and their dog, Micky. Several of the Angell children were born there; Frank (the 7th of Eli and Alice's offspring) was the first to arrive in September 1915, followed by Ron (1917), Vera (1920), Gordon (1922), John (1924), Norah (1925) and finally Mary (in January 1928).

It is difficult these days to comprehend how fifteen people and one dog could have lived in that small 2-bedroomed cottage, especially as they had no kitchen, no bathroom, no sanitation that we would recognise today, no gas or electricity and all water had to be drawn from a garden well. Eight boys and the four girls slept in one of the bedrooms, with a partition wall having been put in place to provide a modicum of privacy for the girls! The boys slept *'topped and tailed'* in two double beds and the girls did likewise in another double bed. This still left one boy without a bed place, so for several years George (4th eldest boy) slept at the Mizen's house along the road at No. 8 Chequers.

The family photo was taken in 1933 shortly before two of the boys, Doug and Frank set sail for the Far East with the Wiltshire Regiment, for what was meant to be a seven-year deployment. They served in Singapore from the beginning of January 1934 until the end of January 1936, before moving on to India. Frank was stationed in India until the end of April 1940, while Doug remained there for another three years, until April 1943.

In June 1944 Frank, Doug and their youngest brother John fought in Normandy as part of the invasion force. On 22 July 1944, John was badly wounded by a high explosive shell while his section was advancing on a German position, known as Hill 112 at Caen. John was initially presumed dead and it was only due to his good fortune that he was thankfully rescued after one of his friends heard him groaning. John suffered severe damage to his legs and buttocks, including a fractured left femur and serious injuries to his left foot, left knee and right thigh.

Their mother, Alice was badly shaken by the news of John's injury and the shock, together with the worry of another four of her son's, (Doug, Frank, Ron and Gordon) fighting in the war, is thought to have been a significant contributory factor when she suffered a heart attack and died just a few days later, on 11 August 1944. R.I.P.

In March 1945 John was discharged from the Army on medical grounds as a result of the injuries he had suffered. Doug, Frank and Ron continued to serve in the Army throughout WW2, while their brother Gordon served in the RAF.

Frank was awarded the Military Medal (MM) for a conspicuous act of bravery on 26 November 1944. Part of the citation recommending the award of his MM reads, *'On two occasions, without referring to anyone and when the shelling was at its worse, Cpl Angell went out on his own to repair the vital line from BnHQ to the Coys of Tripsnorth. Such devotion to duty in the face of the greatest danger was an inspiration to all the Signals Platoon, and showed a sense of fearless initiative far greater than could normally be expected'*. Such fearlessness and bravery was a recurring feature of Frank's Army service. When he was finally discharged from the Army, Frank's Commanding Officer recorded that he was, *'Very capable and quite fearless under all operational conditions'.*

The Angell family were not able to gather again as a complete unit until the final members were discharged from military service in 1946, by which time mother Alice had died. The photograph that had been taken in 1933 is thus the only image of the full family.

The Angell family were well known at the time, as shown in the Wiltshire Times and Trowbridge Advertiser article below of Saturday 25 June 1932:

FAMILY OF 13 BROUGHT UP BY FARM WORKER. *'Large families are not common in these days; thus it is somewhat of an achievement to bring up a family of 13 children on the wages of a farm labourer. That is what Mr. and Mrs. Eli Angell of Brick Kiln Cottages have done. Of their family of 13, nine were boys the youngest is 5 years and the oldest 29 years of age. Today, 12 of them are living at home and five of them are going to school. One girl is at Northampton, and all the boys are engaged in farm work and live with their parents who were married 30 years ago.'*

Norah and Mary revisit their old home. In September 2000 Karen Lloyd, paid a call to the cottage. Karen told the tenant that her mother, (Norah Pritchard – formerly Angell) and several of her siblings had been born there. Karen asked the tenant whether he would allow her mother and aunt (Mary Hemmings – formerly Angell) to have a look at the garden of what had been their home, as a special treat to mark Norah's 75th birthday. Not only did the tenant allow Karen, Norah and Mary to visit, but he also invited them in for a cup of tea and he allowed them to see the inside of the cottage. Needless to say Norah and Mary were absolutely delighted and extremely grateful.

The Lime/Pottery/Brick Kiln. In the 1800s a crushed stone track used to run immediately in front of the cottage (at right angles to the main road). The track led to the Lime/Brick/Pottery Kiln Quarry which lies 200 yards or so east further into the fields behind the cottage (as you look towards

Chippenham). All you can see from a distance is a large wooded area, long since overgrown with trees and brambles. Deep inside, are several large green ponds, covering the remains of the quarry that was once a hive of industry. Nowadays, the only signs of life are a few old discarded beer bottles, a badger set, and a strange and eerie atmospheric ecosystem of wild plants and wildlife.

Apart from the production of bricks and pottery, Lime/Brick kilns were also one of the most effective methods of charcoal production. They have been used for decades, low in capital cost, moderate in labour requirements and capable of giving surprisingly good yields of quality charcoal suitable for industrial and domestic uses. The brick kilns would also have been used to burn crushed limestone at very high temperature, to produce 'quicklime', 'burnt lime' or 'unslaked lime', all which can be put to many uses.

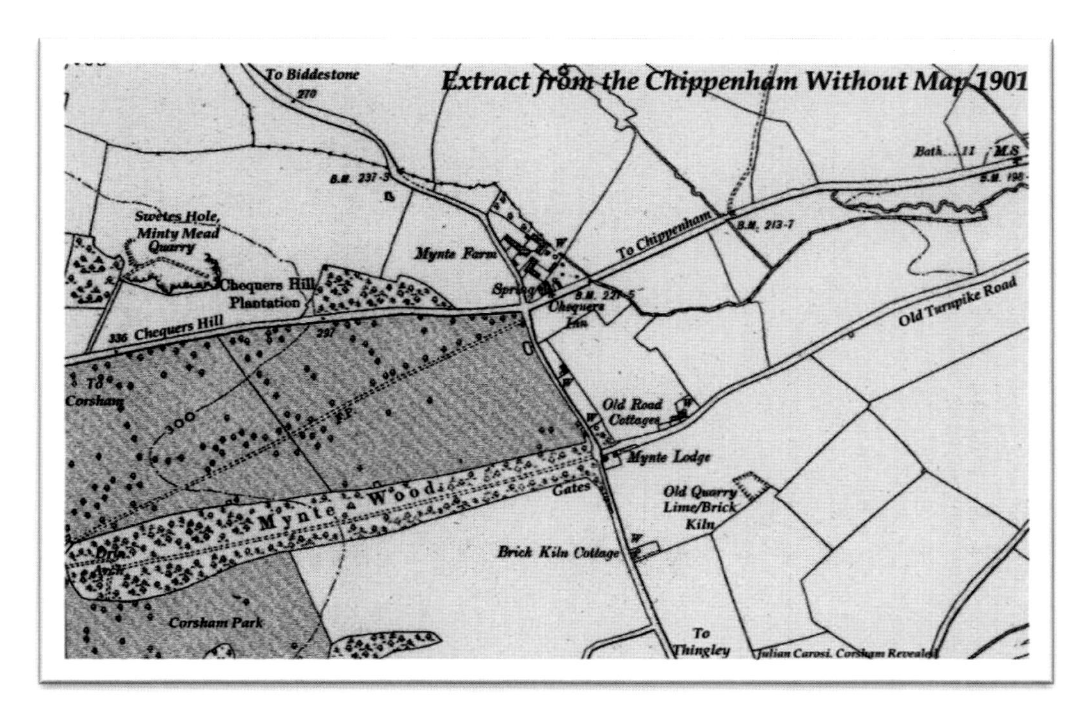

This old Corsham/Chippenham Brick Kiln quarry - hidden deep in the town's history, would have been a thriving little brick-baking, lime-slaking and charcoal making business in its time. The bricks would have been made nearby, with kneaded clay-bearing soil, sand and lime dug out from the quarry; then fire-hardened using wood-burning fuel to make them durable, or air-dried, and then sold off for use in masonry construction. And for the construction of Box Tunnel *(see Chapter 4).*

In 1805 a Pottery, Brick Kiln was auctioned for sale on Wednesday 3 April at the Angel Hotel in Chippenham. It was described as a most desirable FREEHOLD POTTERY and BRICK KILN in acres of rich meadow land, possessing a deep saturation of clay of peculiar excellence for bricks of pottery with all suitable erections thereon. The kiln at one time burnt off 30,000 bricks, included covered shade for stacking, two long drying houses for tiles and pottery, 15 feet by 50 each, a pottery house 75 by 18 feet with other conveniences. Also a neat COTTAGE adjoining, not much more than half a mile from Chippenham.

In 1840 James Martin (a carter working for John May of the Hare and Hounds) and another man named Pritchard, were racing their horse and cart too fast down Chequers Hill at 5 o'clock in the morning, on the way to collect bricks from Mr. Hunt's Brick Kiln near Chippenham, for use at one of the Box Tunnel shafts being built at the time. One of the cart's wheels went over a pile of dirt at the side of the road and violently shook James Martin from the cart. Both wheels of the wagon passed over James Martin, severely injuring him, he died three hours later. A young boy who was sat at the front of the wagon very narrowly escaped the same fate.

Special thanks go to the present occupier of the *Brick Kiln Cottage* and to Geoffrey Forshaw (whose grandfather was Eli Angell), for the information concerning the Angell family in this chapter *(the photo shows Geoffrey in 2015 outside of the Brick Kiln Cottage).*

NOTE OF WARNING: The following is a gruesome and mysterious (as yet unresolved) story concerning the details of a dismembered newborn child's body found nearby in a separate Lime Kiln near Starwell at Stowell close to Biddestone in 1933.

In June 1933 an inquest opened on 24 May on the discovery of a dismembered body of an infant child found in a field in the lime kiln near Stowell Farm. When Mr. Thomas Clarke of Sheldon Road was out walking with his wife and two children on 21 May of 1933, they decided to walk over one of the Mynte Farm fields to look at an old lime Kiln near Starwell.

At the edge of the lime kiln Mr. Clarke held up one of his sons so that he could see down into the kiln, when Mrs. Clarke with a shocked exclamation, pointed to something on the ground. Lying side by side were the two completely severed legs of a very small child. Telling his children that they were pigs' feet, Mr. Clarke quickly hurried them all away.

After a search on Monday May 22 at 7:45p.m., Police Sgt. C.W. Perry subsequently found the trunk of the new born child wrapped in bloodstained brown paper. A further search the following day revealed the two missing arms at the bottom of the kiln.

The remains were taken to Corsham mortuary and an inquest was opened the following Wednesday by Mr. A.L. Forrester (County Coroner). The first witness at the 24 May inquest was Doris Clarke, a young girl aged thirteen of 29 Palmer Street, Chippenham, who said; *'That on 22 May, she had heard about this pair of legs that morning from a girl who said she had seen them when out with her mother the night before they were found. I and another girl went to have a look for the legs and if we found them we were going to report it. We went to Holywell along the lane, into the field and across to the lime kiln. By the side of the kiln were these two legs. They were very small and rather white; they were uncovered and there was a piece of newspaper and my friend got frightened. We came away and told my mother, who went for the police.'*

At this point, the coroner adjourned the inquest until 27 June pending further Police enquiries. At the second inquest held on 27 June, no further evidence was provided and the mystery still remains unsolved to this very day. Dr. H.E. Cresswell of Corsham told the Coroner that he had concluded a post-mortem examination of the remains the same evening that they were found. He concluded by saying that the body was a female child and in his opinion it had been dead for more than three days. When asked how the legs and arms became severed, he said; *'I think they have been torn off with the aid of a very blunt instrument. It was very badly done'.*

He continued by saying that he believed that the child had been born alive but had died shortly after birth. Asked whether he though the amputations were done during the life of after death, Dr. Cresswell replied; *'I do not think it possible that such mutilation could have been done during life.'* The child had been subjected to violence before death, for there was also bruising of the scalp and a fracture of the scull.

Nobody ever came forward to own the child but this was hardly expected. **R.I.P.** The Coroner recorded an open verdict of 'found dead' adding that the cause of death was inattention at birth. Dr. C.E. Perry said that:

'The child had been born alive, but perhaps through inattention had received violence at birth'.

Chapter 24. Lypiatt Hostel No.15 Camp.

The name Lypiatt comes from the Saxon word Lepegate, which is a low gate that can be jumped by deer, but not other animals. This probably dates back to when Melksham Forest spread close to the settlement of Corsham. The camp is situated to the south of Great Lypiatt Farm near Neston.

At the beginning of World War II, the field opposite *(and south of)* the 127 acre Great Lypiatt Farmhouse in Neston *(owned then by Geoff Knapp)*, was commandeered for the war effort and the twenty-five acre Lypiatt Camp for 1,000 men was constructed with 122,837 sq ft of buildings available to provide accommodation for those working in the underground Corsham depots.

In 1946 it became an army transit camp for military personnel leaving the UK; the hostel closed on 15 March 1950. Lypiatt was just one of a number of hostel camps near Corsham, associated with the wartime use of the underground quarries for ammunition storage, factories or military headquarters. The hostel sites were run by the National Service Hostels Corporation Ltd. *(an agency of the Ministry of Labour)* and planned by Alexander Gibb and Partners.

The accommodation blocks were originally simple single-sex, one-storey structures, with the married quarters (MQ) sited elsewhere in the larger prefab bungalow estates in and around Corsham. Some hostel sites also had dance halls such as the one in Lypiatt which survives today, with the dance floor remaining unchanged and the bar to the left of the entrance.

The following is a list of all the WWII local hostel (HS) and married quarters (MQ) sites in Corsham: HS1 Westwells, HS2 Gorse Farm, HS3 Thorney Pits, HS8 Potley, HS9 Westwood, HS10 Kingsmoor, HS15 Lypiatt, HS16 Leafield, HS14 Rudloe, MQ1 Corsham, MQ1A Corsham, MQ1B Corsham, MQ2 Boxfield, MQ2a Boxfield, MQ3 Westwood, MQ4 Quarry Hill, MQ5 Chippenham, MQ6 Chippenham. The Lypiatt Hostel site is the only functioning hostel site remaining in Corsham!

The No.23 Army Married Families Lypiatt Camp originally consisted of basic prefab bungalows with a galley kitchen and sleeping rooms. Between 1956 and 1960, these were used for housing military families returning from abroad. Some families were housed whilst waiting for their husbands to join them back in the UK. Military wives who were estranged from their husbands, were also temporarily housed there with their children who would attend the small primary school on site. It was an ideal place for families needing to adjust to life outside of the Ministry of Defence (MOD). The site also had a cinema, NAFFI and a cookhouse where meals were served at set times.

In the 1950s the *Lypiatt Camp Country Dancing Club* was created there. Also in 1950 the Local County Council tried to obtain the land to build houses on. But the Principal Regional Officer, Ministry of Works stated that they had been informed that the Lypiatt Hostel, vacated by H.M.S. Royal Arthur, was required by the War Department and it was regretted that it would not be possible to put it at the disposal of the local authority for housing. In 1953 the Lypiatt Married Families Camp Commandant invited the residents of Neston in, to see the Queens Coronation on the camp's television in the morning. Dancing, fireworks and a bonfire were provided in the evening. All the children were provided with refreshments by members of the committee and the ladies from the various Neston Village organisations.

The Lypiatt site is now used to house members of all three armed services and is known as the Services Cotswold Centre. The Services Cotswold Centre (SCC) (post code SN13 9TU) is a tri-service facility managed by Headquarters Army Welfare Service (AWS) and funded by Headquarters Support Commands (HQ Sp Comd) on behalf of the MOD. It provides short term transit accommodation for service personnel, their spouses, civil partners and families. The accommodation comprises of sixty self contained chalet style homes. The gardens have previously won Corsham in Bloom a number of times and been nationally recognised for how gardens can play a part in helping soldiers transition back into civilian life. In September 2015 horticulturalist Alan Yandell and the gardening team were crowned as joint Inspiration Street winners in David Domoney's ITV series *Love your Garden* competition which aimed to promote the stories of community spirit and success.

Also within the base is Lypiatt Primary School (ages 4-11) and Early Years Centre which occupies the larger buildings at the northern end of the site. It is the only primary school in the country serving the families of our armed forces who need temporary accommodation following separation, bereavement, or discharge from the services or for other welfare reasons. The two newly built accommodation blocks were more recently used for severely wounded soldiers and their families following injury during the Afghanistan conflict. In the 80's the camp was referred locally as 'Tenko' *(after the BBC 1 series about a female POW Camp in Japan)*, as in those days it was full of military wives who were *between* marriages!

Wiltshire Times and Trowbridge Advertiser 25 December 1880: On 19 December 1880 at 4 o'clock, sixteen year-old Paul Shrewing who was looking for mistletoe, found the body of child inside a hollow tree in Lypiatt Lane, Corsham. At the inquest he said. *"There is an oak tree standing by the roadside which is quite hollow. I went up to the tree looking for mistletoe. After getting up onto a low dry stone wall, I noticed marks of blood. About 8 feet from the ground is a hole in the trunk which is about 8ft to the ground and full of leaves. Lying at the bottom was what I thought was the naked body of a child".* William Hancock the town Constable, accompanied by Inspector Bullock, went to the tree to investigate. The body was removed to the Station Hotel where a post mortem was carried out by Dr. Garlike from Sutton Benger. The child had been neglected at birth, as the umbilical chord had been severed but not tied off, resulting in the child bleeding to death. The tree is about a thousand years old and it is particularly mentioned in the Doomsday Book. It was 4 feet in diameter and capable of holding three or for persons in a standing position. The verdict was, *'Found dead in a hollow tree'*!

Chapter 25. Machine Breakers - and Captain Swing.

AN ORIGINAL PORTRAIT OF CAPTAIN SWING

In 1813 Thomas Davis, steward to the Marquis of Bath produced a report on agriculture in Wiltshire, that stated that labourers in many parts of this county may truly be said to be in a wretched condition. There was a surplus supply of labour in an era when mechanisation was beginning to have an impact on agricultural working practices for the first time.

Whereas farmers had previously provided their labourers with a full time job with a 'tied' cottage, they were cutting back on their costs and employing casual workers *by the job* or *by the season*.

Farm workers now found themselves in the position of casual labourers, moving from farm to farm as required instead of having the regular jobs which they had enjoyed before. By 1830 there had been years of war and high taxes, three years of poor harvests (which meant less income) and their living conditions were meagre (very often little more than hovels).

Fuel and food was scarce, and the lack of spinning work for women and children meant that the village poor were unable to live by their industry. In 1830 the labourers in Wiltshire, along with those of the other southern counties, rose up in protest over their poor living conditions, low wages and the introduction of the new thrashing machines (first invented by Scottish mechanical engineer, Andrew Meiklefor and used in agriculture in 1786).

Cases of arson started to occur, and a thrashing machine was destroyed in Kent. The machines were seen as taking away the work of the farm labourers. So called *'Captains'* were chosen from the community, to lead riots demanding higher wages and reductions in the tithes.

The discontented labourers in gangs began destroying thrashing machines and burning hay stacks and barns and stealing sheep and money as they went from village to village. Letters were sent to houses in Chippenham threatening to burn homes. Some of the farmers themselves were also in a predicament, as landlords would not lower their rent, which meant that the farmers did not have enough income to increase the wages of their labourers.

The protesters used the name *'Captain Swing'* when signing off the letters that were delivered to land and farm owners.

The letters were a means of protesting against the starvation and poverty that these new grain threshing machines had created. They also demanded that farm labourers' wages increased or at least stayed the same.

The following is an example of a short Captain Swing letter: *'Sir, Your name is down amongst the Black hearts in the Black Book and this is to advise you and the like of you, who are Parson Justasses, to make your wills. Ye have been the Blackguard Enemies of the People on all occasions, Ye have not yet done as ye ought. Swing'.* Or more succinctly: *'Sir, This is to acquaint you that if your thrashing machines are not destroyed by you directly we shall commence our labours. Signed on behalf of the whole, Swing'.*

Few of the letter-writers were ever brought to trial. In addition, it is not known how many letters were real, and which were fake or which were created by an *agent provocateur*.

Captain Swing was a *made-up name* designed to spread fear among landowners and to protect the real protest leaders from being discovered. Troops were dispatched along with special constables (including Mr Stratton from Shaw) to quell the riots. The rural magistrates dealt out severe punishments to those arsonists who were captured. By December 1830, almost 2,000 men and women had been rounded up awaiting trial. Hampshire, Berkshire, Buckinghamshire, Dorset and Wiltshire were the worse effected counties. There were 18 cases of arson in Wiltshire and 97 threshing machines were destroyed, by far the greatest total compared to other counties.

A **Proclamation** dated Thursday 23 November 1830 by King William IV, was printed in the local papers, commanding all Justices of the Peace, Sheriffs, under-Sheriffs and all other Civil Officers to use their utmost endeavours to discover, apprehend and bring to justice the persons concerned in the riotous proceedings. A bounty of £50 would be given to those who apprehended any perpetrator found guilty of riots, and £500 for those found to be guilty of setting property on fire and destroying corn, hay buildings and such like.

Those who were *rioters* would be convicted but would also receive the Kings most gracious pardon with a view to quelling the riots. But those found guilty of setting fires and destroying property would be liable to be prosecuted for the same.

In 29 November 1830 in a move to help quell the rioters, the Magistrates acting for the Division of Devizes sent out a newspaper message that if order is restored in the area, whilst they would not accede to any demands, they would apply themselves to remedy the grievances and adopt the best means in their power to secure a just and proper amount of Wages to Labourers. They also recommended to all landowners and occupiers of land in the area to ADVANCE forthwith the AMOUNT of WAGES to their LABOURERS so as that every able body Labourer shall receive his full labour wages at the rate of 10 shillings per week. They also requested that proprietors and tithe owners should openly and candidly declare what rent REDUCTION they intended to MAKE to their tenant farmers.

The whole population of Steeple Aston and West Ashton came out voluntarily to offer their services as special constables to help quell the riots and prevent fires. Farmers in the neighbourhood of Bishops Cannings agreed to increase the wages of their workers thereby ensuring that no damage was recorded against their property.

Two hundred Machine Breakers at Heytesbury fled in all directions at the sight of Warminster troops, several of the rioters fell into the River Wylye, five or six feet deep. Twenty of the rioters were captured and conducted to Old Bridewell in Devizes.

In Christian Malford, a mob of two-hundred had assembled and were met by Paul Methuen (Corsham Magistrate), Thomas Clutterbuck and Walter Coleman (three magistrates presiding in the Chippenham Courts). Asked what they wanted, the rioters replied, *an increase in wages to enable them to provide for their families without having to applying for parish relief, for the local clergyman to lower his tithes, for landlords to lower rents and for the farmers to pay them ten shillings a week in the winter and twelve shillings in the summer.*

The magistrates promised the mob what they wanted and that they should have the wages that they desired. On hearing this, the mob gave three cheers and disappeared without the slightest bit of trouble. The local clergyman promised to reduce his tithes in proportion to reduced rents by the landlords.

In Corsham, sixty horsemen enrolled to protect the peace and stand together in the strongest defensive array against the rioters, most of the Corsham men being young and active. On Tuesday 25 November 1830 thirty-eight of the Corsham contingent were on the road along with the local yeomanry within an hour of their assistance being requested. Fortunately there was no occasion for action this time. Each evening in Corsham, between 6 and 7 o'clock, ten of the Corsham horsemen would patrol the town, starting at one point and going out in indifferent directions to prevent the rioters from attacking the farms in the Corsham area. They would return at 11 o'clock when the Corsham foot patrol would take over responsibilities until 4 or 5 o'clock each morning.

Many of the rioters were captured. Capital offences were judged in Salisbury and minor offences before the Magistrates in Devizes. Two hundred and eighty prisoners also rioted in the Devizes House of Correction, 100 of who were subsequently charged with rioting. Forty-six prisoners were committed to Fisherton Gaol in Salisbury for unlawfully destroying threshing machines and for extorting money by threats and violence.

The various sentences were as follows: Sentenced to Death 252: Commuted to life transportation 233: Executed 19: Transported 505: Imprisoned 644: Fined 7: Whipped 1: Acquitted/bound over 800. The riots continued into 1831. Agricultural labourers continued to be the worst paid, worst fed and worst housed of all the working communities at that time.

Below, are a few recorded local incidents that occurred during the riots, along with some of the severe punishments given out to a few of the Wiltshire rioters.

- Peter Withers wrote several times to his wife in Wiltshire to join him in Tasmania, but heard nothing from her until 1844, by which time he had married again. He wrote back saying, *'I sent a great many letters before I took a wife, so not 'earing from you, and I being a young man, I thought it a proper thing to look for a partner which would be a comfort to me in my Bondage, so we must not think about coming together again'.*
- On Sunday 4th December 1831 it was reported that a cart house, with a wagon inside, and some hay, were discovered to be on fire in the evening, the whole of which were consumed. There was no doubt that the fire was the work of an incendiary. The property belonged to Mrs Barton, a widow who lived near Monks, in the parish of Corsham.
- At Mr. Dark's farm in Broughton Gifford, two hay ricks, (containing 40 tons of hay), a wheat stubble rick, six cow cribs, and a large cow shed were destroyed. The fire spread so rapidly, that there is scarcely any part of the farm unconsumed. The damage was about £200 (£1,600 in today's money).
- Thomas Day, was convicted of breaking open the house of Robert Lawence, of Corsham, and stealing nine yards of Irish Cloth, and other articles. He received a sentence of 'Death'.
- The same sentence was passed on John Whale, who was convicted of stealing a wether sheep, from the same property belonging to Robert Lawrence.
- Stephen Withers was convicted of stealing a pan of butter at Melksham, and was sentenced to seven years transportation.
- John Salmon was sentenced to death for stealing a sheep from William Edgell at Trowbridge.
- George Whale was found guilty of stealing four sheep, the property of John Henly at Calne, and a judgement of death was recorded against him.
- Thomas Whale was found guilty of receiving the sheep skins knowing them to be stolen, and was sentenced to 14 years transportation. ***They were certainly very harsh punishments in those days!***

On 8 March 1833 at the Lent Assizes in Wiltshire, two years after the Swing Riots had ceased, Henry Harren a coal dealer from Corsham (his father James Harren was a Carrier of the High Street) was found guilty and transported to Sydney, Australia for life, for sending a letter, threatening to murder James Davis Horne of Corsham. The handwriting was clearly proved to be that of the prisoner. The letter signed SWING, said, *'I am determined to do what I am going to tell you: me, and 93 of my party are determined to have Reform, quietly if can. You had better not buy coals of strangers. If we can't have Reform quietly, we shall have it by loss of a few lives. There is no harm in poisoning or shooting you and Tailor. Unless you leave off buying coals of strangers, your cattle will die, your house will be on fire, and your lives will be lost.'*

In 1835 two hundred and sixty four of the transported 'Machine Breakers' were pardoned and many more in the years that followed. Most stayed on in Australia making new lives for themselves.

Chapter 26. Miscellany Corsham Newspaper.

The Corsham Miscellany,
AND GENERAL ADVERTISER.
No. XVII. MAY 1st, 1855. Price, One Penny.

TO ADVERTISERS.
Every Three additional Lines,—Sixpence.

HIGH STREET, CORSHAM.
ROBERT SCOTT,
Printer, Bookseller, Publisher
BINDER, STATIONER, &c.
An extensive assortment of
Bibles, Prayers, and Church Services,
with a NEW and GREATLY ENLARGED STOCK of
Standard and Modern Works.
IN PLAIN AND ELEGANT BINDINGS.
TYPE-PRESS & COPPER-PLATE PRINTING,
ENGRAVING, &c.

GOUT AND GRAVEL SPEEDILY CURED!
Ask for C. GEE TAYLOR'S
ORIGINAL DROPS.
OF SPEENHALAND, NEWBURY, BERKS
(Prepared from the Prescription of a Medical Gentleman.)
In Bottles price 2s. 9d. and 1s. 1½d. each; a bottle at 2s. 9d. contains as much as three bottles at 1s. 1½d., which is a great saving. With full directions for use.
Tic-Doloreux cured at Frome.
HANNAH TOMKINS,
Rheumatic Gout cured in Devizes.
HENRY BUCKLEY,
VEGETABLE ANTIBILIOUS PILLS,

THOUSANDS HAVE BEEN CURED
DURING A PERIOD OF 50 YEARS, BY
BROOKE'S
MELLIFLUOUS COUGH BALSAM!
WHICH IS ACKNOWLEDGED TO BE THE
BEST MEDICINE EVER KNOWN!
The following extracts from testimonials will show its efficacy.
Corsham at SCOTT'S Patent Medicine Warehouse.

In 1855, over 150 years ago, Corsham had its own newspaper called *'The Corsham Miscellany And General Advertising',* costing one penny.

The local news was very scant in content, with most of the paper taken up with national news items, and local advertising, particularly *R. Scott's of the Corsham Post Office*.

He seemed to sell every cure in tablet form known to man; like the beautifully named medicine called *'Mellifluous Cough Balsam'*, which purports to be the **'BEST MEDICINE EVER KNOWN'**.

Goodness knows what damage these untested so-called medical cures will have done to our poor Corsham predecessors! It makes your eyes water to think what the advertised *'Page Woodcock's Wind Pills'* would have done to your insides, despite its claim to *"remedy WIND in the STOMACH, and BOWELS, SPASMS, Costiveness, Giddiness, and sick headache, Heartburn, Indigestion, Disturbed sleep, Palpitations of the heart, Colic, Jaundice, Gout, Dropsy, Asthma, Sore Throat, Ague, Biliousness, Erysipelas, Female Complaints, Lumbago, Piles,, Tic Doloureux, Scurvy, Eruptions on the skin etc."*

The paper shows that Amos Jackson, son of James Jackson of the Nagg's Head Lincoln, *found relief in the first dose and was quite cured on taking the third dose of Woodcock's Anti-Cholera Drops!*

The advertisements were guaranteed to make you chuckle with their unbelievable claims! One so-called *cured* gentleman was purported to be so ill, *"as to be near gone as possible"* prior to taking *Woodcock's Anti-Cholera Drops!* And no doubt the ladies of Corsham were not slow in trying out some of, *'Nurse Lilley's Royal Female Pills' - for Green Sickness and Flutterings of the Stomach!*

Another advert offer's **CART GREASE - good quality at 3p per lb at A. AYLIFFE'S Sadler and Harness Maker Corsham.** And rented housing was also available: **Desirable Villa Residence. To Be Let. With Immediate Possession. Within five minutes walk of the town and railway station, containing two sittings and four Bed Rooms, Water Closet, suitable Offices, excellent Garden and plentiful supply of water!**

Mr Garrard at the Corsham G.W.R. Railway Station's Bath Coal Company could also supply you with all your *'very superior quality'* coal needs at reduced prices. Orders will be promptly attended to, and coals may be weighed on the Town Engine, for the satisfaction of customers, free of charge.

And how about Brooke's Improved Chemical Marking Ink which purports that the oftener it is washed the *Blacker* it will appear? *Yeahhhhh - pull the other one! [Ed].*

Chapter 27. Monks Chapel.

Monks Chapel United Reformed Church (URC), Gastard, Corsham. On the edge of Corsham, sits the old quaint Monks Chapel, with its *'horse-box'* pews and quainter rows of nails and hat pegs, where regular Christian Sunday worship has continuously taken place since it was built in 1662. It is believed to be the only *'Five Mile Chapel'* in which worship has remained unbroken since the 1600s. The chapel itself was built using stone taken from an open quarry in the adjoining field to the south some 300 yards away.

The Grade I listed building has altered very little over the years. The interior is intact with a gallery on three sides, including the original box pews, and pulpit. When you enter the chapel, it's like going back in time nearly 400 years! The Chapel is called 'Monks' because the ground (including the graveyard) was given to the church by a Mr. Monk who lived in the nearby farmhouse.

Where is Monks Chapel? The chapel is situated off the B3353 as you travel between Corsham and Gastard. Immediately after going past the narrow Lindleys cottages on the B3353 Corsham to Melksham road, turn right up Monks Lane at the crossroads. Monks Lane was previously known as Cock Street in 1570. The little Monks Chapel can be found on the right, a quarter of a mile from the crossroads. You can park in the large Leafield car park on the left when visiting. The Chapel is a little further up the hill on the right hand side, behind a high dry stone wall.

The address is Monks Chapel, Monks Lane, Corsham, Wiltshire, SN13 9PH.

Current services still take place there each Sunday between 2:45 pm to 3:45 pm and the chapel is licensed and approved to carry out Wedding Ceremonies. The current URC Minister (2018) is the Rev. Heather Wilson from Canada; the Rev. Heather also has pastoral responsibility for: Melksham, Whitely, Monks Chapel and Shared Pastoral Responsibility for Bradford-on-Avon.

The interior of the Chapel is whitewashed and depicted on the ceiling is a boy's face, still in its original state, probably painted there to interest bored children. The gallery, which is reached by either of two wooden enclosed staircases, has enclosed choir seats opposite the pulpit with wooden shelving for a stand. The gallery also housed the first organ of the church. On the outer edge of the wooden panelling of the gallery, it is still possible to see the wooden pegs on which men hung their hats; there are more hat hooks on the walls.

External shutters (which were fastened on the inside) were fitted to protect the windows against attack from those seeking to disrupt services. The highest window is in the gallery and still has a pulley wheel by which the outside shutters could be pulled together from the inside. This window when seen from the outside forms the distinctive *eyebrow* shape over the main door that makes the Chapel so recognisable.

Monks Chapel has a very tall pulpit, where the Preacher had a good view of the countryside and could spot any troublemakers making their way to the Chapel. Chapels like this were frequently raided. There is a door under the Pulpit that is reputed to lead to a possible secret underground tunnel exit through which the Minister could make his way to safety if the chapel was raided by the authorities, enabling him to surface some 500 metres away in the security of nearby Monks House. If true, that would have been a very long crawl through a tiny claustrophobic tunnel! The high boundary dry-stone wall surrounding the chapel may have been created as another form of defence.

The tunnel may have simply been an earth trench covered by large flat stones (obtained from the nearby quarry opposite) and topped with soil as a roof. But no tunnel starting point in the chapel has ever been found. In the 1950s when locals Mr. Bert Smart and Mr. Bill Painter were investigating subsidence near the top of Monks Lane just above the chapel, a hole was revealed under 'tilted' flagstones. When asked if it could have been the cellar of an old house, they replied, *'No! It was definitely a tunnel and we didn't fancy going along it'*. The area was subsequently cemented over. Following an investigation by the well-known dowser Mr Donald Reeves of Corsley (with no local knowledge whatsoever), Reeves stated that he was of the opinion that a deep tunnel ran east underground from outside the building at the rear of the pulpit, and then south to the top of Monks Lane.

Unfortunately no early documents exist regarding the religious work carried on at Monks as they were kept by Mr. Spackman. On 18 January 1849 Mr. Spackman's shop in the High Street, Corsham, was discovered to be on fire, and within a short time the whole of the premises, with its contents, was engulfed (see Chapter 13).

Following the downfall of the Cromwellian regime and after the monarchy was restored to Charles I's son, Charles II in 1660, there was an accepted freedom for a range of Protestant groups and faiths to practise their beliefs undisturbed and without unsettling others. Quakerism began as a sect whose members believed that there was a piece of God within every person and that everyone could communicate with God directly. This was a radical view at the time. In general, the English government and the Church of England (at that time), misunderstood the Quakers and their actions. Quakers, along with other religious groups that were not part of the mainstream establishment (Nonconformists) suffered from religious persecution. The English establishment often harshly persecuted the Quakers with long imprisonments, starvation, beatings, whippings, and other forms of punishment. This form of religious domination was common in England at that time, and the government used this tactic of oppression to try to silence not just the Quakers, but other Nonconformists as well who opposed the traditional religious and civil authority.

Monks Chapel was built in response to the 1662 *Five Mile Act* passed by Parliament, when King Charles II and his Parliament took it upon themselves to revise the English Prayer Book which required Ministers to use *'fixed forms of service'* and to give their agreement/oath and consent to the New Book of Common Prayer. In short, it required all religious Ministers to accept the revised English Prayer book. Up to 2,000 Ministers across the Country (60 from Wiltshire) left the established Church (some becoming local schoolmasters for a living) after being ordered not interfere or try to change the *Government* of the Church. Many were evicted from their posts for rejecting the new rulings because of their belief to worship as they chose.

Ministers who did not conform, where known as *'dissenters'* and prohibited by Law to preach within five miles of a borough town (then Chippenham). Corsham was not large enough at that time to be considered to be a borough in the regulations. This lead to the Quakers secretly building Monks Chapel in 1662 so that they could worship as their conscience dictated. The chapel was built just outside the five mile radius of the Borough Town, Chippenham, thus conforming to the Act.

Those worshipers with an independent mind quickly joined the new movement and would walk (or ride on horseback up to 15 miles to get to Monks Chapel. A small walled-in field to the west of the Chapel was used as an enclosure for the worshipper's horses. This field, and access from the road, is shown on a local farm map as 'Meeting House Ground', whilst the one adjoining the north side of the Chapel is named 'Meeting House Mead'. Worshipers would bring food and drink with them, using the Chapel's (now closed in) fireplace to cook their food. The time of their return home would be governed by the phase of the moon, guided back home by its light across the fields or along the tracks to their dwellings. When there was no moon, services finished early, as worshipers only had the feeble light of their lanterns and nature to guide them home across the dark landscape.

The Act of Toleration was later passed in 1689 and in 1690 the Independents (the Congregational church) came to own Monks Chapel and in that year the gallery was built. The Toleration Act 1689 (also referred to as the Act of Toleration) an Act of Parliament, meant that Dissenters were required to register their meeting locations and were forbidden from meeting in private homes. Any preachers who dissented had to be licensed. The Toleration Act gave all non-conformists, except Roman Catholics, freedom of worship, thus rewarding Protestant dissenters for their refusal to side with James II. They had to promise to be loyal to the British ruler and their heirs.

In 1662 the Vicar of Corsham was ejected from his living because of his non-conformity. However, he later returned to the Established Church, being persuaded to that course of action by the Bishop of Bath and Wells. *'The Quaker Act of 1662'* made it illegal for Quakers to worship together. The Quaker Act also made it illegal for people to refuse to swear the Oath of Allegiance to the Church of England. Two years after the Quaker Act was passed, the English Parliament passed the Conventicle Act in 1664 which restated that no other religious meetings could take place except those carried out by the Official Church of England. About that time, Benjamin Flowers, a Minister of Cardiff in South Wales refused to accept the revised English Prayer Book, and headed home where his father was the Vicar of nearby Castle Combe. In 1674 the Vicar of Chippenham wrote of Flowers and *'that nest of vipers at Corsham'*, saying that they were a *'squadron of irregulars'*. As well as opening a Presbyterian church in Chippenham itself, Benjamin Flowers also established non-conformist worship in Corsham with meetings in houses, barns and in Monks Chapel, thereby making Corsham a centre for Independent Worship and Preaching.

To minimise the chances of the militia from finding the chapel being used as a place of prayer meeting or any other services forbidden by law, Monks Chapel was purposefully built in the form of a cottage by the Quakers in 1662 complete with a chimney and a fireplace. The Quakers were strong in the area, and were supported by several local dignitaries such as, Thomas Beavan of Melksham, Adam Goldney in Chippenham, and the wealthy Captain Francis Dickenson and later his merchant son Caleb Dickenson of Monks House.

The words, *'It is a good thing to give thanks unto the Lord and to sing praises unto thy name O most high'*. [Psalm 92:1] are printed inside, above the eyebrow window. On the outside are carved the words, *'KEEP THY FOOT WHEN THY GOEST TO THE HOUSE OF GOD'*. [Ecclesiastes 5:1]

In 1972 Monks Chapel was badly in need of a face-lift. Under the chairmanship of Ivor Tilley, restoration contributions were gathered from many organisations as well as from hundreds of ordinary folk who wished to ensure that the Gospel would continue to be preached in the 'Old Chapel'. Monks Chapel now has a sound, waterproof roof, a box-pew interior free from woodworm, improved heating and lighting, secure plaster walls - and none of the old world charm has been lost.

A renovation *Thanksgiving Service* was held on Saturday 28 June 1980, when the Moderator, the Rev Michael Hubbard was the preacher. In May 1986 Monks Chapel was officially accepted as a United Reformed Church in Corsham; this was confirmed at an URC General Assembly in Blackpool.

Abutting the outer wall north of Monks Chapel is what is probably a merestone which marks a boundary. In this case, it may separate the Chapel (which is officially in Neston) from the nearby cottages which are in Gastard. A roadside stone opposite Great Lypiatt Farm is also likely to mark a boundary. The polling wards of Neston & Gastard are separated by a path between the Chapel and the cottages. This line then takes the centre of the road up Monks Lane, turns right and then turns left down Pond Close lane to the Wansdyke.

Thomas Gay, a local quarryman living at 3 Monks Lane, was from a family of dissenters who worshipped at Monks Chapel. Thomas was crushed by a falling slab of stone aged 66. His son George Gay (1771-1833) went on to become a self-taught composer, poet and an organ builder. In 1827 he published a volume of sacred music. It took three years for George to build the organ at Monks Park chapel where he was the organist. George went on to compose fifty Psalms and Hymn tunes of the late 18th / early 19th century, including seven Set Pieces, and a Cannon (in one volume) and several anthems on loose sheets. Some of his hymns were called, 'Monks', 'Neston', 'Corsham', 'Williton', 'Westrop', 'Patterdown', and a hymn tune in short metre (3-4 time) in G major which he called Chapelnap (see photo); all local names originating from this part of the old parish of Corsham.

The hymes were published in 1833 as, 'A Collection of Tunes', (known locally as *Hawkes Tune Book*) for use by Wesleyan and Methodist Societies, arranged by Thomas Hawkes, a land agent and surveyor of Wilton, Somerset. A copy is held at Taunton Castle Museum. The preface contains reference to the 'double G clef', devised by George Gay, it is said to *stop women squawking!* On 26th July 1833 George Gay committed suicide and was buried at Monks Chapel with his second wife, Jane. His music continued to be played after his death. The curved grave stone top in the burial yard, on which the name 'Gay' is inscribed in large letters, is apparently the same stone on which George Gay (also a land surveyor) took his own life 'under sad circumstances'. The stone was subsequently shaped by his quarry stonemason workmates and placed on top of his grave. **R.I.P.**

274th Anniversary of Monks Chapel 23 June 1936.

Chapter 28. Murder in Swete's Hole, Mynte Mead 4 August 1606.

The Corsham Parish Registers, once held in St. Bartholomew's Church, are now held by the Wiltshire and Swindon History Centre, Cocklebury Road in Chippenham; the contents of which can now be viewed on microfiche. Evidence of a mysterious killing in Corsham, has been found in the form of the following scrawled note *(see photo below)* at the very front of the oldest Corsham Register of 1563. It concerns an argument that took place over four-hundred years ago in the Chequers Inn between two Corsham men named Swete and Bricker. The argument concerned a woman. The two men left the Inn and walked halfway up Checkers Hill into a quarry where a duel ensued with swords which resulted in one of them being killed. The memorandum in the Parish Register is as follows.

'1. Memorandum of Swete's Hole, in Minty Mead, August 4th 1606. Here William Swete and - Bricker fought with swords concerning a Woman and in Fray [an affray] the former was slain and the latter acquitted. This Hole is open'd every year to perpetrate the memory thereof.'

In the 1606 burials section of the register, it is further noted that:
'Willm Swete slayne 4 Aug & buried the 6 Aug'.

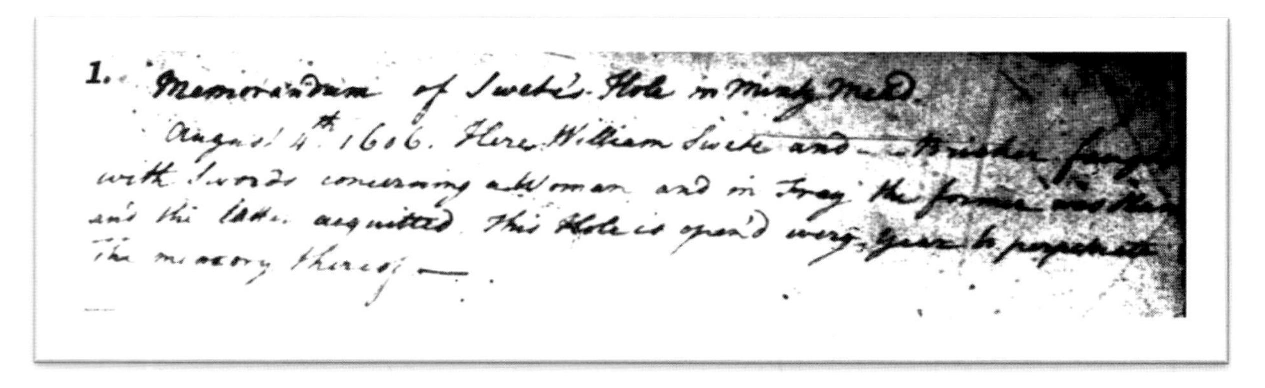

1. Memorandum of Swete's Hole in Minty Mead.
August 4th 1606. Here William Swete and — Bricker fought
with Swords concerning a Woman and in Fray the former was slain
and the latter acquitted. This Hole is open'd every Year to perpetrate
The memory thereof —

In those days, the quarry would have been an isolated place away from prying eyes; perfect for a dual of such heated passion! The nearest house was Mynte Farm about half a mile away at the bottom of Chequers Hill at the crossroads between Corsham and Chippenham on the A4.

For nearly 200 years, in memory of Swete's death on the 4 August 1606, Swete was commemorated every year by a gathering at the quarry until the late 19th centenary, by *'opening the hole'* in memory of him and to lay flowers. Thereafter, the quarry was called *'Swete's Hole'*.

The surnames Swete and Bricker were both popular family names in Corsham around that time. The Cross Keys area was once known as 'Brickers Barn'. The 'Bricker's Barn Trust' were responsible for building and maintaining the turnpike road in 1761, that ran <u>*behind*</u> the Cross Keys Inn, then across the fields to Hartham Church, accross the end of Middlewick lane, alongside Pickwick Lodge Farm and then coming out at the top of Box Hill alongside the old Rudloe Manor RAF site (see Chapter 53).

The Corsham Marriages Register show that in 1613 on 15th Nov, John Bricker married Webb Alice. In 1603 on 3rd Oct, Nathaniel Russell married Joyce Bricker and in 1608 on the 2nd Oct, Christopher Horte married Jane Bricker. In 1611 on the 17th June, William Jones married Suzan Sweete.

The exact location of Swete's Hole (or Swete's Hollow as it was sometimes called) was discovered in a 1765 hand drawn map showing 'Swete's Hole' as an arable pasture of land, along with a corresponding listing (identifying the location as being in Field No. 9 worth £2. 2s. 14p); both documents were discovered recently in the Swindon and Chippenham History Centre and can be seen in the photos. [Ed].

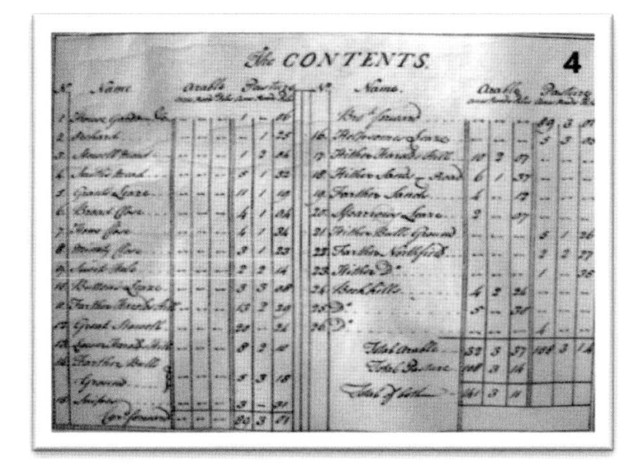
The CONTENTS

4

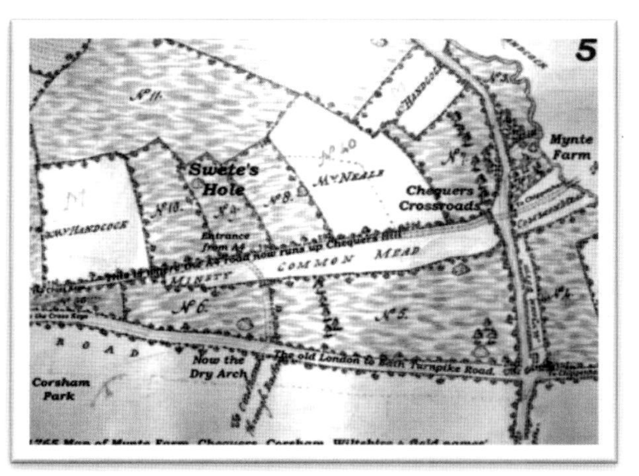

The map also shows the position of the old London to Bath turnpike main road, which in those days, ran a quarter of a mile to the south of where the A4 runs up Chequers Hill today and along where the Dry Arch is in Mynte Wood! Another note of interest shown in the map is the original location of the Chequers Inn, which in those days was sited alongside the old turnpike road and opposite the large gates that lead into the Corsham Court's North/East carriage drive of years gone by. It was several years later that the Chequers Inn moved into the large building a quarter of a mile north at the A4 crossroads in front of Mynte Farm at the bottom of Chequers hill.

The location of Swete's Hole today is just inside the northern boundary of the Corsham Estate's (Chequers Hill) plantation of trees that line the north (left) side of Chequers hill as you drive down towards Chippenham. Halfway down the hill is an entrance to the woods, barred across with a metal farm gate. Swete's Hole was about 50 metres inside the wood, directly northwards from the metal gate towards the far boundary.

There is no Public Right of Way through the woods, so please keep out.

There is not much left of Swetes Hole, as the open quarry has now been filled in and levelled out.

It was used as a rubbish tip in the 1950/1960s and was levelled out later when the extensive tree plantations took place there some years ago. The small quarry was probably used originally to provide the stone used for local building and for the surfacing of the nearby old London to Bath turnpike road. In the late 1950s early 1960s, you could see the old quarry rubbish tip from the top deck of the double-decker bus that ran to and fro between Corsham and Chippenham.

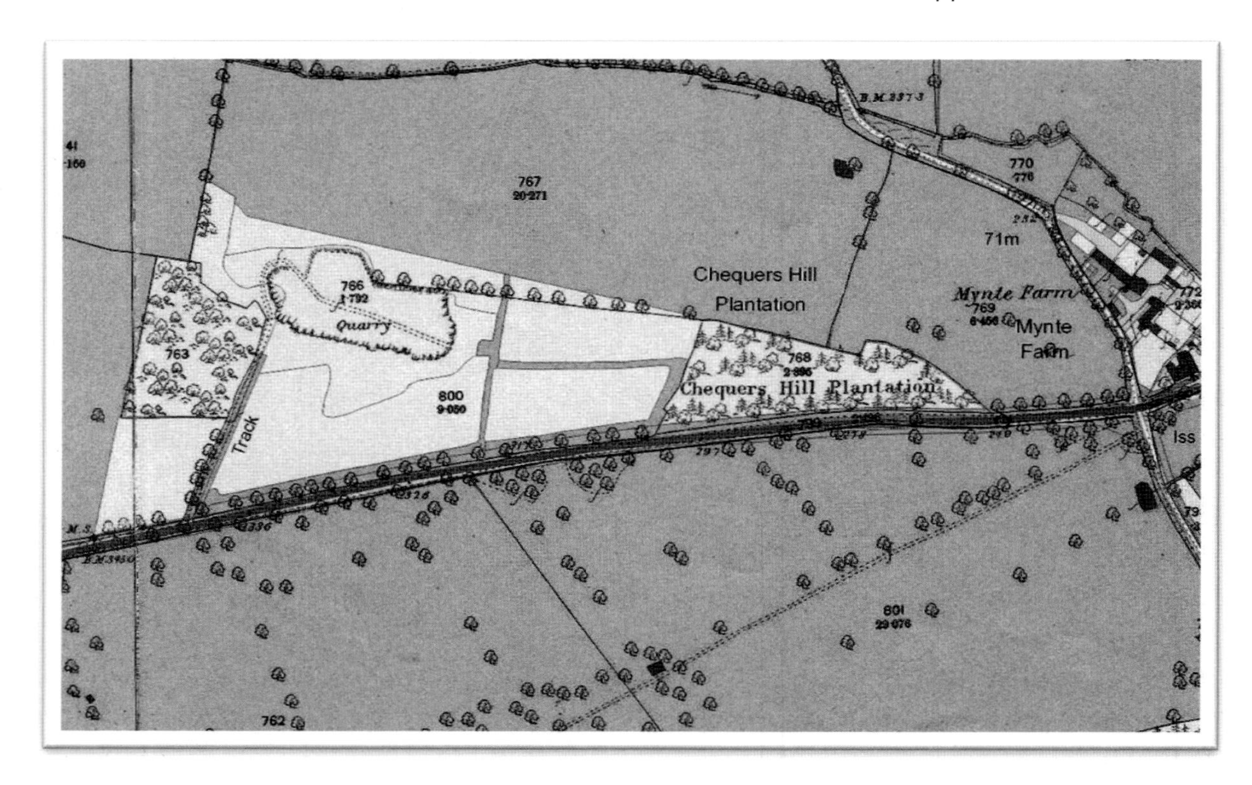

The following is a 1953 newspaper report:

In November twenty year-old Robert A. Collins of no fixed address, previously from Trowbridge, who had been sleeping for some time in a hut at the rubbish tip in the Swete's Hole on Chequers Hill, stole a fowl on 3 November at 12:20p.m., valued at 15s from Mr. Arthur Foster's farm in Chippenham.

At the trial, Collins said, *'I have tried to find lodgings for my girl [a married woman] and her baby son and myself but without success. I saw some fowls in a fowl house and as I knew my girlfriend and her baby were desperately hungry, I decided to steal one of the fowls and kill it. As I was leaving the farm I realised I had done wrong and threw the fowl behind a cart in a cart shed. I can only say that I am sorry I have done this. I realise that it was a stupid thing to do.'*

Collins, who had spent most of his young life in care, was placed on probation for two years.

There is an old ghost story about this particular stretch of road from Chequers Hill to the Cross Keys that maybe - just maybe, could be the ghost of William Swete returning to seek his revenge! *See Chapter 16 Ghost Story No. '2', Horror on the A4, for more detail.*

Chapter 29. Murder of Harry Long 1594.

(Henry Danvers, Earl of Danby)

One of Corsham's great events was perhaps this murder done here on the night of Friday 4 October 1594.

Sir Walter Long, his brother Mr. Harry Long *(youngest son of Sir Robert Long of Wraxall)*, Mr. Thomas Snell of Kington St. Michael, Mr. Anthony Mildmay, Henry Smyth esq *(then owner of Corsham Court)* and a group of magistrates, were sitting at meat together as friends in the middle of the day between the hours of 11 and 12 o'clock. Harry was sat next to his brother Walter.

By Canon Jason: One of the company saw a small boy peep in at them and then disappeared. It was supposed that this was done to discover the position of Harry Long. Immediately after, the door burst open and seventeen or eighteen men presented themselves, lead by Sir Henry Danvers and his brother Sir Charles. Sir Henry fired a small pistol at Harry Long, the charge from his pistol entered the heart of Harry and he was instantly a corpse. The villains then rushed out of the room. The Danvers brothers along with their retainers fled on horseback and arrived at Southampton the next morning (Saturday). They crossed over Southampton Water to Calshot Castle inhabited by Henry Wriothesley, third earl of Southampton.

Lady Danvers wrote a petition in which she described the insolent and violent behaviour of the Longs as provoking the affray at Corsham when, in order to save his brother Charles's life, Henry Danvers shot Henry Long.

A coroner's inquisition was held, and the Danvers brothers were outlawed, but no immediate indictment seems to have been preferred against them either by the family or the government, but some of the followers, from both sides, were subsequently hanged for being involved in the escape and causing an affray. John Aubrey (1626-1697) the famous English antiquary later wrote. *'My great-grandfather, R. Danvers was in trouble about it; his horses and men being in that action. His servants were hanged.'* Aubrey also noted that '*R. Wisdome was then lecturer and preacht that day and Henry Long expired in his arms'*.

An order was issued later from the Lords of Council to apprehend Charles and Henry Danvers, *'Whoe beinge accompanied to the number of twentie and fower persons armed with pistolls and other weapons did enter a house with force and did murther Captaine Henrie Longe also one Barnard a servant watinge at table. It is said a foot-boye was expressly sent to see in what order they were sett at table and to bring word to the said Charles Danvers wee praie you to cause the same boy to be also apprehended'*.

Quote by Harold Brakspear of Corsham: *'Before William Snelling, coroner of our lady the Queen within the liberty of her town of Cossam, on view of the body of Henry Long Esq., there lying dead and on the oath of twelve men, presented that a certain Henry Danvers, late of Cirencester, Kt., and others, not having the fear of god before their eyes, did on the 4th October, between the hours of 11 and 12 of the same day, at Cossam, with force of arms, viz., swords, &c, did assault the aforesaid Henry Long, and the aforesaid, Danvers, voluntarily, feloniously, and of malice prepense, did discharge in and upon the said Long a certain engine called a dagge, worth 6/8, charged with powder and bullet of lead, which Danvers had in his right hand, and inflict a mortal wound upon the upper part of the body of Long, under the left breast, of which he instantly died, and that immediately after the felony they all fled.'*

The Earl of Southampton already knew something of the incident as he instructed his servants to hide the murderers in his lodge where they stayed until Tuesday. In the meantime, there was a hue and cry that murder had been committed at Corsham and a warrant was eventually issued for the arrest of Sir Henry Danvers and Sir Charles Danvers who were thought to have escaped to Southampton. The Earl quickly secreted the perpetrators onto a boat belonging to a man called *Read*, who anchored them off-shore near the Southampton coast.

For the next few days, they were supplied with victuals by a man named *Drudge* using Mossill's boat! A man with a warrant managed to get onto the boat but was told in no uncertain terms, that they *(the murderers)* would teach him to mind his own business and threatened to throw him off the boat if he did not depart immediately with his warrant. A few days later, they were secreted in Whitley Lodge, near Tichfield House and afterwards to Calshot Castle opposite Cowes and from there escaped to France and later back to London where they managed to evade the Law by continuously changing their residences.

Sir Charles Danvers who was very friendly with the Earl of Essex, later joined him in a plot (the Essex Rebellion) against Queen Elizabeth. For that, they both lost their heads on Tower Hill 6 Feb. 1601. Beheading was already a rare event and Essex was the last person to be dealt with at the Tower.

In her 1960 book *'Wiltshire Forefathers'*, June Badeni described the murderer Henry Danvers as, *'Succeeding to the baronetcy at his brother' death and was a perfect master of the French, a historian, tall and spare, temperate, sedate and solid'.* He was a distinguished soldier, fighting in the Low Countries, In France and in Ireland.

The assassin Sir Henry Danvers wandered about until the death of Queen Elizabeth in 1603 (nine years after the murder). When James I came to the throne, Sir Henry Danvers eventually managed to get into the King's favour and his crime was reversed. Twelve years after he had committed the murder, the law cleared Sir Henry Danvers of all the consequences of his act. In court, Sir Henry Danvers did not deny that he had given Sir Henry Long a death wound in the breast. Sir Henry further pleaded that although he had indeed discharged his *"engine called a dagge worth 6s. 8d. charged with powder and lead"* in and upon poor Harry Long, inflicting a mortal wound, yet the words *percussit cum* (he struck him) had been omitted from the charge, although commonly used in indictments. Here the court wavered; it thought *percussit cum* should have been set down by the coroner, and Sir Henry Danvers (Lord Danvers) walked out discharged, an outlaw whose outlawry was reversed.

James I made him a Baron, Lord President of Munster and Guernsey. Charles I made him Earl of Danby and a Knight of the Garter. He died in Cornbury Park, Oxfordshire, on 20 January 1643 (fifty years after committing the murder) and was buried at Dauntsey.

There is some confusion over the actual site of the murder. Some say it occurred at *'one John Chamberlaine's house'* (a common baker around that time), or in one of the Church Street houses. It is more likely to have been in the *'Golden Ball'* public house which appears to have been situated in Church Square, as the initial gathering included Henry Smyth of nearby Corsham House (Corsham Court) and a number of magistrates. The dying man could have been taken to the house of Mr. John Chamberlyn? The late John Poulsom (author of 'The Ways of Corsham' believed that 'Ridge Farm' at Neston (then owned by the Longs) could have been the site of the crime.

The quarrel dated back to the Wars of the Roses. The ongoing feud between the Danvers and the Long families is explained by the following information from Mr.W. Chitty of Pewsey. The Wiltshire village of Dauntsey formally belonged to a family of the same name. Joan Dauntsey who died in 1455 brought the village as her dowry to Sir John Stradling when she married him.

They had a very large family. Some men came into their house one night when they were all asleep and murdered the whole family. Luckily, Anne Stradling, one of the daughters was staying in London at the time and subsequently she inherited all of the family property and money.

Anne later married Sir John Danvers of Culworth. Sir John Danvers had a grandson who was also named John, who later becomes Sir John Danvers himself. He had ten children, seven daughters and three sons, the two eldest being Sir Charles and Sir Henry Danvers who murdered Harry Long in Corsham.

At this time, family feuds were very common amongst the aristocracy, often resulting in violence being committed. Parliament allowed the gentry to employ *retainers* for the purpose of keeping up family quarrels. The *retainers* never did any work as such; rather they followed their masters and fought their battles. Unpunished murders like the one in Corsham were often committed.

There had been a bitter hatred between then Longs and the Danvers for a number of years. It had been whispered amongst the Wiltshire gentry that the first Danvers (Sir John Danvers of Culworth) who obtained Dauntsey by marrying Anne Stradling knew something about the murder of her sleeping family.

Whether Anne Danvers (nee Stradling) knew anything about it, will never be known, but it is possible that she did not. Whispering increased to loud talking, and after a while, Sir John Danvers was openly charged with the family murders, but this could never be proved.

The Longs cherished the idea that Sir John Danvers murdered the family and that the deed was done by his command to his retainers. This created a bitter enmity between the Longs and the Danvers which only increased with rancour as time went on.

But the foul murder of the Stradling family was continuously being talked about and the feud waxed hotter and hotter as the tongues wagged, culminating in the 1594 murder of Harry Long in Corsham.

Chapter 30. Osborne House.

The Battle of Osborne House 1968.

Osborne House protrudes out like a sore red nose at the road junction near the bottom of Pickwick Road, opposite the Methuen Arms. It does seem a strange place to have built such a grand house, squashed in with one side bordering immediately alongside the main road and the other acting as a *sort of* lean-to for three tiny cottages. You either love Osborne House *(now a Grade II Listed Building)* or you hate it! With the advent of the motor car, most buildings such as these (that obscure visibility at road junctions) have long since been knocked down; but not so Osborne House - despite an *all out attack* to destroy it in the 1960s. It can't be denied, that this peculiar looking building remains *'a part of the very fabric of Corsham'*. If you are one of the lucky ones to have been inside, on one of the building's *open days*, you will have seen a very tasteful and thorough renovation that retains many of the building's original features.

1720: Osborne House (1 Station Road) originates from early to mid C18 and was built on virgin land, against the rear of the Horsefair Cottages *(3, 5 and 7 Station Road - Grade II Listed Buildings C17 reconstructed in C19)* which predate Osborne House by about 100 years. It is thought that Osborne House may have originally been called Horsefair House.

The Corsham Cricket field (previously The Corsham Common including the 'Pound') was once the site of an ancient Fair which was granted to Corsham by Royal Charter in 1285. The Pound was a small enclosure abutting the boundary of the Cricket Field. It was created to confine animals which had strayed into the open fields. The entrance was in Station Road where the position of the gateway can still be seen as part of the boundary wall by the Bowls Club.

The granting of a Fair by the King showed Corsham to be a town which was the natural centre for trade in its area. At the Fair, horses were sold on the site of the cricket pavilion i.e. in front of the 'Horsefair' cottages. The Fair ended on 2 March 1899 having, it is said, been sited in the adjoining field to the south during its latter years. Just before that time, the Fair had started to peter out and the holding of it was no longer viable.

Horse Fairs, were local events traditionally attended by gypsies and travellers; a place where they could buy and sell horses, meet with friends and relations and to celebrate their music, history and folklore.

On the afternoon of Monday 4 September 1852 a less than successful Horse Fair was held in the cricket field in Corsham. *'The supply of sheep was good, wethers (ram or billy goat castrated at a young age) and lambs sold well at good prices. Pigs had realised their full value. But a number of hacks and cart horses remained unsold. The pleasure fair was less than usual. There was a total absence of shows, music and the usual common excitements of the occasion, which naturally diminished the attendance of sightseers'.*

Another Horse Fair also took place each year on 7 March, inside iron railings where the Town Hall now stands. There was an interesting auction advertised in the *Devizes and Wiltshire Gazette on Thursday 25 December 1823*, concerning the sale of, *'two dwelling houses, orchard, garden and timber-yard adjoining, containing two acres (more or less) at the bottom of the Horse Fair, in the several occupations of Mr. William Butler, Mr. James Langford and Mr. Bromley'.* These *may* have been situated somewhere near to where the cricket field is now, as the Cricket Club appears to have been formed later in 1848.

The Osborne Family later took up residence in the Osborne House. They became one of the most important families of builders and stonemasons in the area.

Osborne & Sons - masons taken in the yard at the rear of Methuen Arms in 1933.
Photo courtesy of Gordon Williams.

TOP ROW: Arthur Newbury, Bill Frankham, Billy Hatter, Bob Oatley, Fred Gale, Bob Wright, George Chamberlain.
MIDDLE ROW: Verdon Cole, Charlie Hampton, Cecil Selman, Walter Gingell, Ted Wooten, Ken Taylor, Arthur Gingell, Frank Taylor, Sam Gale, Arthur Coleman, George Cole, Joe Dew.
FRONT ROW: Stanley Osborne, Carl Buckle, Ted Say, Bill Taylor, Ernie Cole, Billy Brown, Jack Lumpkins, Frank Fletcher, Bob Lambridge, Alf Reed, Billy Fry, Bill Young, Henry Williams, Lawrence Waite, Walter Baker, Jim Mines, Jack Simmons, Bert Osborne.

The workers were nicknamed *'The Silver Assed Carpenters'* because of the white aprons they wore.

The Osborne & Sons firm was established in 1775. Later, William Osborne's son Bert was in charge until his death in the early 1960s. Bert was also an undertaker as well as a stone mason and also a keen member of the Corsham Amateur Dramatic Society. On 14 June 1940 Mr. Clare Spackman's funeral (provided by Bert) cost the Spackman family a total of £27. 1s. 6d (just over £1,000 in today's money). Bert was also an accomplished cellist and his two daughters Madeleine Marie and Muriel also became musicians. Bert was also a local actor taking part in several *'dramatics'* at the Town Hall. Madeleine had gained honours at the London College of Music and at the local eisteddfod; she married Sgt. Harry Lambert on 3 August 1940.

1924: The high quality craftsmanship of Osborne & Sons (now headed by Bert Osborne) was awarded a Bronze Medal at the British Empire Exhibition, Wembley. The Mayo Fountain in Corsham, is one fine enduring example of Osborne & Sons' work; built around 1890 at a total cost of £115 10s. The War Memorial situated at the Junction of Lacock Road was also built by Osborne & Sons and designed by local architect Harold Brakspear, who also oversaw its construction in 1896. The Regal Cinema was also built by the Osbornes.

Mid 1950s: About this time, Messrs Smith and Lacy Ltd. left their builders' yard (where Williams Grove is today) and took over the old stonemasons' yard at the rear of Osborne House and used it as their new builders' yard, shop and associated building for a number of years. Towards the end of their residence there, the yard becomes an eyesore to those passing along the narrow stretch of road alongside the Methuen Arms. The use of Osborne House as a *hairdressing salon below, with living accommodation upstairs* was later proposed by the builders Smith and Lacy and Lacy. Ltd (on the ground floor); but this was refused.

1965: In the period between 1 Sept 1965 to 18 Oct 1968 a total of 11 accidents occurred at, or very near to the dangerous Osborne House road junction (1 fatal, 2 serious, 6 slight and 3 no injury).

[Ed] Whoever recorded this, could not count!

1967: County Planning Officer J.P. Thomson agreed that the present junction alongside Osborne House was unsatisfactory. One of the options proposed to improve the road junction was to completely demolish the house.

John Methuen described the house as, *'Almost a slum inside, an eyesore on the two sides and in almost condemnable condition.'* He had a point, as at that time it held the unflattering title of, **'the dirtiest house in Corsham'**. The north facing side of the building is directly joined to a busy narrow road with a junction at the front elevation. The sheltered north side of the house is a haven for the development of black carbon, grime and algae growth, all combining over the years, to produce the building's 'dirty' look. Thankfully, the lower Bath stone block work bordering on the main road was repaired in early 2018, after 400 years of gradual damage due to the incessant traffic splashing rainwater and muck onto its surfaces.

Frederick William Beresford-Smith, a Chartered Accountant from Bath and advisor to Bath Abbey, proposed another *'audacious'* plan to improve the road junction, by building a *NEW ROAD* diagonally through several buildings (see following plan), which he said at the time were, *'not important and their loss would not be a catastrophe'*. This would have obliterated several historic buildings (including the old Methuen School) as can be seen on the sketch of the proposal.

Another proposal was to build a new road across the cricket field! Mr Holman said, *'That a suggestion of a new road through the sports field, leaving an island with four houses on it, was unthinkable.'* Mr C.J. Poulsom also objected to, *'houses being pulled down willy-nilly'.*

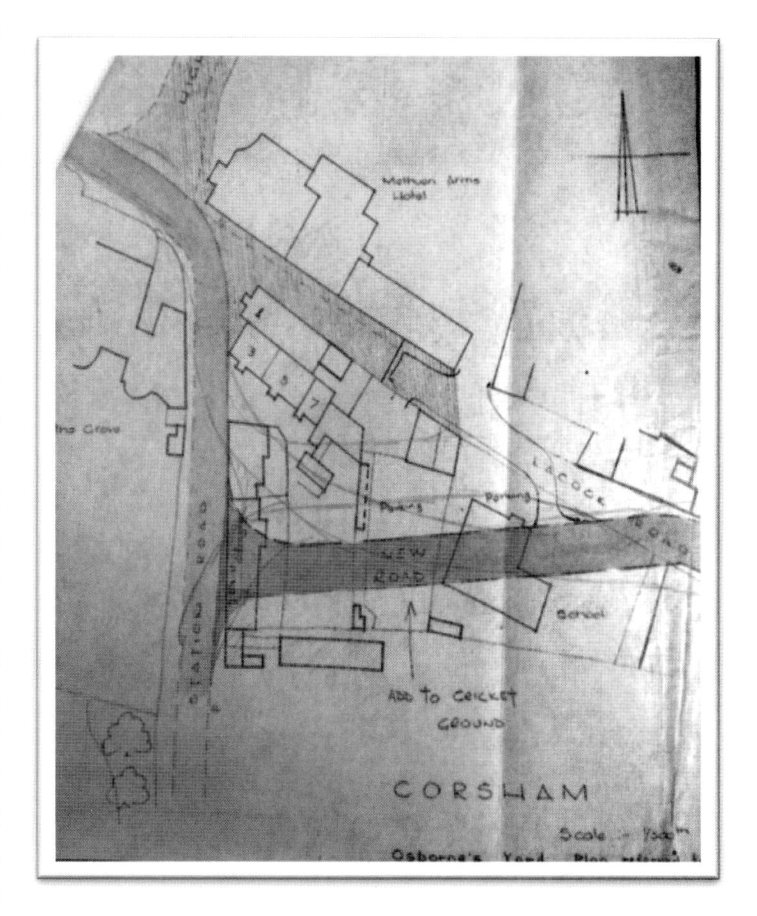

1968: A vote was taken by the Corsham Civic Society members to save Osborne House from being demolished. Thankfully, of its 80 members at that time, 50 were in favour of seeking a *'building preservation order'* to save Osborne House and 20 against. A campaign was subsequently launched by the Corsham Civic Society to preserve Osborne House. The Society believed that although the building at that time was greatly dilapidated, it was structurally sound and had a value of considerable importance in the street scene of Corsham.

The Society adopted as its battle slogan, the words of Professor Colin Buchanan:

'Do not allow your historic buildings to be sacrificed for the sake of through traffic.'

Mr John Betjemen described the idea of demolition as, *'A footling piece of destruction'*. Letters of support were received from far away, such as from Jennifer. W. Nash who wrote from New York.

'I wish they could see the towns here in America, how ugly they are. I'm terrified, that when I next visit Corsham, which I love very dearly, it will be turned into a series of blocks of flats and offices and little boxes.'

The small Corsham Civic Society was up against nearly all of the 'big guns'. The battle was on! The following were in favour of demolishing Osborne House; Wiltshire County Council, Corsham Parish Council (agreed to demolition by 10 votes to 5), Corsham Chamber of Commerce, nine local clergymen and John Methuen. The nine local clergymen from all of the Corsham Churches (who were later accused of meddling with affairs that were of no concern to them) banded together to produce a letter, also signed by Bishop Denis Hall (former Bishop of the Niger, West Africa) supporting the proposal.

Canon E. Marshall Hall, the vicar of Corsham said at the time: *'The preservation of life was more important than the preservation of the building. We do not want our parishioners to be sent prematurely into the next world'.*

Supporting the Corsham Civic Society's campaign to *'preserve'* the building, were the Minister of Housing, the Royal Fine Arts Commission, and the Calne and Chippenham Rural District Council, via its vociferous Chairman William Light who lived in Corsham and said;

'That it would be a mistake to destroy something which can never be replaced for the want of a little thought'.

A public inquiry lasting several days was held in Corsham Town Hall beginning on 6th November 1968, to seek a *'Building Preservation Order'* to save Osborne House. Thankfully, Corsham Civic Society was successful, and a *'Building Preservation Order'* was placed on Osborne House.

A 'NO RIGHT TURN' was proposed as a possible solution to the nearby dangerous road junction. The installation of traffic lights was also considered. In the end, it only took *'a little thought'* to provide the solution of what to do about the dangerous junction. A simple scribbled plan on a note passed to the Inspector at the Public Enquiry on 7 November 1968 from Robert Eden was the catalyst for providing a sensible solution at minimal cost. Eden suggested that, *'By the simple expedient of painting a white line at this position, very many difficulties can be overcome.'*

The stop line position suggestion by Eden on his plan was originally on the main road, forcing motorists driving up from the Lacock direction to stop on the edge of the junction just outside of the front door of Osborne House, thereby giving the Station Road traffic priority to enter Pickwick Road. It did not take too long to adopt Robert Eden's idea and improve it by placing the stop line at the end of Station Road instead, giving priority to the greater volume of traffic coming along Pickwick Road. Along with a 'Halt' sign and a 'No Right Turn' sign, this simple low cost, low maintenance solution has proved to be a success (without having to demolish a part of Corsham's history).

The safety of this junction was greatly improved five years later, after the completion of the new *'Valley Road'* relief route, the precinct shopping centre and the pedestrianisation of the south entrance to the High Street in 1973 (making it essentially a 'T' junction instead of a crossroads), thereby greatly decreasing the volume of traffic at the Osborne House road junction. In years gone by, this junction gave access to a main transport artery along Station Road, leading to a busy Corsham Railway Station and onward routes to the Potley and Neston districts and beyond.

The building was later used successfully as a Veterinary Surgery for a number of years.

1996: The new owner restored the architectural features. The original floor plan was sensitively restored and enhanced to reflect its early eighteenth century elegance. A walled garden and parking was provided.

2006: Robert Fleming Masonry and Stone Conservation Ltd near Bath cleaned-up and conserved the stone facades.

2007: A Civic Society Building/Restoration Award was presented to the owner, celebrating the successful culmination of the restoration project.

2015: A final sale of house contents took place on Saturday 20th June. The five-bedroomed Osborne House Osborne House now has new owners and the crime and damaged stonework alongside the main road has been cleaned and beautifully restored.

Chapter 31. Parish Chest v Mrs. General Lightfoot!

When you next visit St. Bartholomew's church in Corsham, take a quick look at the old Parish Chest situated front left of the Chancel, alongside *'Our Lady's Chapel'* on the north side. The chest dates from the second half of the seventeenth century and is in remarkable condition considering the use it must have had over these past four hundred years or so! There were two chests; these were stored in Corsham Court whilst the church underwent restoration in 1874. The chest above was returned but the much larger one below remains in Corsham Court.

There were originally three locks on the above chest, one for the priest, and one for each of the two church wardens. The left-hand lock has been cut out, presumably due to a lost key in years gone past. The chest is made of six solid planks of wood and measures approximately 136cm in length, 59cm wide and 74cms to the under side of the lid.

The sides of the chest are 6.5cm thick, the lid, 5cm, and the sides a chunky 10cms of solid wood! The ends are enclosed with two 6cm wide iron straps, with two further straps across the bottom and partly up the right front and back. The lid is hinged with two further strong iron straps. The chest would have housed the church's important documents, such as the Chained books, Vestry Books and the church Registers, which date back to 1563; now held by the Chippenham and Swindon History Centre in Chippenham (Ref: 1157/1).

At the very front of the oldest Corsham Church Register of 1563 *(which would have been originally stored in the chest, but is now held by the Chippenham and Swindon History Centre)*, is scribbled the following curious entry:

"Memorandum of Swetes Hole, in Minty Mead, August 4th, 1606. Here William Swete and - Bricker fought with swords concerning a Woman, and in the fray the former was slain and the latter acquitted."

If you are interested in this story, see Chapter 28 entitled *'Murder In Swete's Hole.'*

The Case of Mrs General Lightfoot v The Vicar of Corsham December 1860 *(reports from the newspapers of the time):* Mrs. Cornelia Lightfoot, widow of the late General Lightfoot, recently came to Corsham to reside with her two daughters. Whilst her house (previously occupied by Dr. Pennefather) was undergoing alterations, the (1858-66) Vicar of Corsham Parish the Rev. Mr. James (Josh) Abbott (who did not reside at the Vicarage) consented to allow Mrs Lightfoot to reside in the Vicarage for a couple of months at a mere nominal rent, until her house alterations had been completed. This would save her the inconvenience of living at a local Inn whilst the work was completed.

The conditions were: (a) that the Vicar's servant who had charge of the furniture, should be allowed to remain, and (b) free access should be given to the Vicar to a certain locked room in which the Parish Chest and other parochial property were deposited, and (b) none of the furniture in that room was to be used or moved.

Mrs. General Lightfoot agreed to this, but within a week of her moving in, not only had she *turfed out* the Vicar's servant but positively refused to allow access to the locked room; she also moved some of its furniture. More than that, she refused to let the Vicar into his own Vicarage! It was only after Rev. Abbott threatened legal action against her via his solicitor, that he was able to obtain possession of the Parish Register, which in those days was a very important document. It was then agreed with her, that she would allow all of the items in the locked room to be removed. But when the Rev. Abbott sent around a cabinet maker to remove them, Mrs. Lightfoot changed her mind. She was importuned by the Rev. Abbott three or four times to consent to the removal of the items without effect. The Rev. Abbott then went to the house himself with the cabinet maker and insisted that the things should be either removed or locked up. An altercation ensued, the result being that some of the items were removed and the remainder locked up in the room. It was hoped that all unpleasantness had now ceased.

Five days later, Mrs. Lightfoot went before a magistrate and accused the Vicar of Corsham of threatening her with violence! A case was brought before the Bench for a hearing.

Mrs Lightfoot read out a long statement before the Bench about the altercation but it afforded no evidence of her accusation of threatened violence by the Vicar.

The Vicar was quite prepared to have gone fully into the case and to have shown that Mrs. Lightfoot had put an entire misconstruction upon anything which he had said or done.

The Vicar's solicitor avoided any cross-examination of Mrs. Lightfoot which might have been hurtful to her feelings. The case was dismissed. And the vicar later rues his decision not to cross-examine.

At the close of proceedings, Mrs. Lightfoot said that she was ready to receive an apology from the Rev. Gentlemen. The Rev. Abbott replied, *"That after the course that she had taken against him, he could offer no apology, as he had done no injury and especially as she had attempted to distort matters with the view of making a public case to his prejudice."*

One would have hoped that peace had returned to Corsham........but no.......read on!

Mrs Lightfoot took exception with the 13 December 1960 newspaper report of the case. A month later in January 1861 Mrs Lightfoot asked the editor of the *Devizes and Wiltshire Gazette* newspaper to print a statement from her in their Thursday 10 January 1861 edition. This included the following statement that she had read out at the proceedings in December:

'On Monday evening November 12th. 1860, I met Mr. Abbott in the Post Office: he accused me of a falsehood and treated me with great rudeness in consequence of my denying I had dragged his furniture that was in a room upstairs all over the house. He said he would put a lock on the door: I refused to permit it. He then followed me across the street and persisted in his rudeness. I, and also my daughter, told him that he was quite at liberty to remove his effects any day after my invalid daughter had left her room, which would be at 4 p.m.'

The next day (Tuesday November 13th) Mr. Abbott himself handed over a letter from his solicitor Mr. E. Turner Payne to Mrs Lightfoot, stating that, *'At 6 o'clock this evening (13th Nov. 1860) Mr. Abbott and a competent person would arrive to remove his furniture and possessions'.* The letter went on to say that if she refused, Mr. Abbott would consider that as being tantamount to Mrs Lightfoot converting the furniture for her own use, which in Law would render her liable for lawful proceedings to the recovery of the detained items.

The letter was not what you would call written in a friendly way as it finishes off with the Solicitor's statement: *'As my instructions are peremptory to take immediate legal proceedings in the event of your non-compliance with this demand, I would respectfully urge upon you the desirability of your no longer detaining Mr. Abbott's property. I am, Madame, your obedient servant.'*

Mrs Lightfoot replied to the solicitor saying that she had rented the Vicarage at £7 for two months on the clear understanding that she was at liberty to use any furniture except that in the locked room. Because of the *tenor* of the solicitor's note to her, she wrote back and said that she was at a loss to understand why she now, *'Had to give up **all furniture and effects** belonging to Mr. Abbott, in the House or on the premises. What were I to do with an invalid daughter in an empty house? I wish you to send me an explanation of your note as early as possible, with a list of what Mr. Abbott claims. I have nothing of his in my custody, or ever had, except the furniture in daily use, therefore am unaccountable for any other'.*

The solicitor replied that it was only the goods in her custody - and not the furniture in daily use that was at question. He also accuses her in his letter of; *'Being evasive and that she should get herself a solicitor to act on her behalf, so that he may not have to resort to serving a writ on her personally.'*

Mrs. Lightfoot said that when Mr. Abbott came for his papers he had entered the house and said; *'Am I to have the parish papers as they are required for a Parish meeting?'* Mrs. Lightfoot told him, *'That he could have anything he wanted downstairs, but that he would have to wait for her invalid daughter to wake before going upstairs.'* He replied that, *'He should not be dictated to by her'*. He then said, *'I will swear [to the magistrate that] you will not let me have the parish papers'.* Mrs. Lightfoot replied, *'But you know I have not refused them'*. He said, *'He did not care, he would swear she had refused'.* He said, *'Madam, I will go upstairs'*, she said, *'You shall not'*. He stamped his foot, clapped his hands and said, *'The meeting is waiting and that the household will be filled with policemen unless the papers were given to him'*. She said, *'That his noise and violence would put her daughter in convulsions'.* He said, *'He did not care'*. She said, *'I will never enter your church again'.* He said, *'You may please yourself, I shall never be sixpence the richer for you'*. She said, *'There is a power above that will protect me'.* He said, *'And there is one below and I will make you fear it'.* Mrs. Lightfoot, fearing for her daughter's health, told him to go upstairs and fetch the papers. He came down two minutes later with nothing in his hands. The Rev. Abbott asked his man to come up with him and they did so. They came down a few minutes later with still nothing in their hands. The man said, *'There are no papers'*. The Rev. Abbott told his man, *'To go upstairs and put a staple on the door to put on a padlock'*. She said, *'You may not, my daughter is now almost in convolutions'.* The man, seeing that Rev. Abbott was getting angry again, said to Mrs. Lightfoot, *'A screw will do for now, may I come back when the young lady is better in the evening?'* She replied, *'You might'*. The Rev. Abbott said', *'The Vicarage was his and he would come in whenever he thought proper'.* She then implied that he had entered her house on false pretence as there was no Parish Meeting.

A final postscript by the newspaper's editor said. *'That the Rev. Mr. Abbott let the premises to Mrs. Lightfoot purely out of kindness, there can be no doubt, and we fear Mrs. Lightfoot has occasioned the Rev. Gentleman much annoyance.'*

Other reports from the newspapers of the time: Before she came to Corsham, Mrs. Lightfoot in 1856 had appeared before the Cheltenham Crown Court in a dispute with one of her servants Jane Jones who wanted to recover her wages. The Judge did not believe Mrs. Lightfoot's story and the judgement went with the plaintiff Jane Jones, with a fine of 15s for Mrs. Lightfoot. It is interesting to note that in 1866, five years after the Corsham incident, Mrs. Cornelia Lightfoot was summoned by Sergeant Matthews for removing two cows without a licence. Mr. Balch, butcher appeared as agent for Mrs. Lightfoot and pleaded guilty. It appeared that she had a licence for removing one cow, but she allowed the other cow to accompany it. The magistrate convicted Mrs. Lightfoot and issued her with a penalty of £1 (about £80 in today's money) including costs. In 1868, Mrs. Cornelia Lightfoot was involved in a Windsor Court case of the wrongful dismissal of her servant Ellen Robinson. In Maindenhead in May, Emma Hunter, one of her servants, is sentenced to 14 days hard labour for stealing one sheet, five clothes and a petticoat on the 18th May. On another occasion at the end of December 1877, Mrs. Lightfoot appears in the Hemel Hempstead court accusing her servant Hannah Goddard of stealing a piece of pork and various other articles. Hannah Goddard was acquitted. It seems that Mr and Mrs Lightfoot had appeared in many court cases in the past! Most of them referring to their servants and with most of the servants being acquitted! Including the assault case (Thomas White v Gen Lightfoot) held in the Cheltenham County Court Friday 18 April 1857, all to do with the plaintiff's wife being roughly pushed around for not being able to serve a dinner on time. Judgement was given to the plaintiff, with damages of £1 1s to be paid. **AMEN to all that!**

Chapter 32. Pickwick District School.

The Grade II Listed St Patrick's Church building which stands alongside the A4 road on the west side of Corsham, has not always been a church – it was originally built as a mid-Victorian 'Pickwick District School' for up to 165 children in 1858 on land gifted in 1846 by Lord Methuen and his tenants, Sir Gabriel Goldney and Arthur Knapp.

The 'Deed of Covenant' defined Lord Methuen's gift as *'all that piece of land now marked out, containing one acre, part and parcel of a certain close called Curtis, lying at Pickwick in the County of Wilts.'* The purpose was *'for the education of children and adults of the poorer classes of the labouring and manufacturing people in the district of Pickwick.'* It was to be conducted in accordance with the principles and practice of the Established Church in England.

The local architect Henry Edmund Goodridge of Bath was asked to produce a design which would provide schooling facilities for 48 boys, 48 girls, 50 infants and for 200 adults to use the school on Sundays and Good Friday. The design was exhibited at the Royal Academy in 1857. The building was designed in the Victorian Gothic style with gables and a bell tower and had therefore an ecclesiastical aspect from the outset. The two entrance porches open respectively onto the (A4) London and Park Lane roads. The school was opened in 1858 and placed under Government Inspection in June 1860.

Teaching was conducted in a large room partitioned by a curtain. The infants were taught in a gallery also surrounded by a curtain. Windows were placed well above the pupils' heads to avoid distractions. Heating was originally via a Tortoise stove with the lighting firstly provided by oil lamps and then later by gas. The original managers of the school were Mr & Mrs Goldney of Beechfield House, Pickwick. The first teachers were Thomas Vincent and his wife Elizabeth. They left the school at the end of December 1865. Apparently they hated the school, disliked the children and were disillusioned with teaching in general. They used corporal punishment at the slightest excuse! Yikes!!!!

The exterior of the building survives virtually unaltered. The 'Boys' and 'Girls' each had a separate entrance at the rear of the school. The 'Girls' entrance is now the rear entrance to the church (the name 'GIRLS SCHOOL' is carved into the stone above the door). The 'BOYS SCHOOL' entrance was to the right; this can be seen in the old photo at the beginning of this chapter. But nowadays, the BOYS entrance can only be seen from inside the building, as it is enclosed inside an extension to the original building.

Most entries in the school logbooks of 1863 and 1887 refer to the progress of pupils but some entries are more illuminating:

'Commenced the week by giving William Fido a sound flogging for his impudence. The school visited by a lady-friend of Mr Goldney's who was most gratified.'

'Sorry to write that Stephen Hancock again grossly mis-conducted himself, the necessary fruit of over-indulgence at home.'

'Work going on very well in all the classes. All the teachers present.'

'Ink spilled, through Fanny Bezer's disobedience for which she was severely cautioned.'

'The afternoon of every Friday during the winter finds the school very thin, so many children being sent by their parents to Hartham Park for soup.'

In September 1878 fourteen year old Thomas North was charged with indecently assaulting the five year old daughter of Edward Hatherell the school master on 10 September. He was found guilty and sentenced to two months imprisonment.

In 1892 the Pickwick School master Edward Hatherell *(sometimes spelt Hatherill)*, a teacher for 35 years) was summoned to meet his creditors in May, after getting into a large cumulative debt of £99.2s due to losing his first wife in 1888, a large family and paying off interest on previous loans.

Edward Hatherell failed to appear when first summoned to attend at the Bath Bankruptcy Court because he had to teach on that day! He was made bankrupt the following month. He appeared in May 1892 and because he was now bankrupt he had received notice to leave his post which he had held for 25 years as a teacher. Three years ago, because he could not pay his creditors, he borrowed some money from a Mr. Edwards to whom he paid £30 for £20 received. He had two loans at this rate and paid them off. There was another loan on which something was owed. He had paid Edwards more than he had received and now Edwards claimed £30 and had threatened him. He sold his furniture and had a fair prospect of paying off his debts and getting straight again, had it not been for the pressure and tremendous interest charged by Edwards. *[Ed] I'm not sure what happened to Edward Hatherell, but one hopes that he pulled though, in what must have been a difficult time for him.*

In January of 1895 the Rev. Canon Awdry referred to a case of *'gross insubordination'* at Pickwick School when a London boy was punished for a small offence. Following his punishment, the boy produced a stone from his pocket which he intended to throw at his master's head. Other boys also had stones in their pockets with which to back up their comrade if needed; this would probably have caused a riot if the attempt of the London boy had succeeded. The Reverend said that the boy was to be pitied as he had never heard of the fifth commandment. Financial problems led to deterioration in the building which was criticised by His Majesty's Inspectors for poor ventilation, bad lighting and damp.

A fall in the local population after the Great War prompted the closure of the school in 1922 and the sale of the building in 1928 for £900 by Mr. Woods.

The little Roundhouse near the school used to be a sweet shop kept by a little old lady. Her customers were the children from the school, who called it the *'Pepper Pot'* sweet shop. In 1840 when this round building was used for a short while as a Toll House, the Keeper was brought before the Magistrates at Corsham, for demanding 4½p, for a metallic spring cart when the legal toll was 3p only.

The old schoolhouse was used for as while as a glove factory during the 1930s, and later became a gas mask factory for a short while during WWII.

Due to the need of hundreds of Catholic Irish workers suddenly arriving in Corsham (from 1938 onwards) to build the military underground facilities in WWII, the building was purchased in 1944 by Bishop Lee from the Diocese of Clifton, who blessed and opened it as the Corsham Catholic Church on 17 April 1945. It was dedicated to Saint Patrick as a tribute to the Irish workers and Father Ryan conducted the first Mass. In the late 1950s the interior of the church building was opened up and several of the separate spaces were combined to form a larger area for worship.

On 2nd September 1957 Father John Supple was appointed as the first resident Parish Priest of Corsham since the Reformation in the 16th century. At first, he stayed at Mrs Eden's house in Pickwick and later at Miss Sheppard's in Meriton Avenue.

A presbytery was built in 1959. A parish hall was later constructed in the gardens at the rear which initially served as a Sunday School for the local Catholic children. The original wooden hall has been replaced by a new modern building. The church was enlarged to take in the whole ground floor of the old school and a *'fine new Rectory costing £5,000'* was completed in 1959. The fittings these days are mostly modern but include the Stations of the Cross carved in wood by a nun of Henbury and a statue of Our Lady carved in 1980 by Michael Penny of Atworth.

A beautiful oil colour painting (shown in black and white below) by *A. Perrone* of the Nativity was presented to the Catholic Church in Corsham, by Italian prisoners in 1945 from the Ladyfield Hostel in POW Camp 89, which was the Easton Grey POW Camp near Malmesbury.

[Ed] - My father was interned in Eastern Grey as a WWI Italian P.O.W. in 1945!

Chapter 33. Pickwick Motors.

Pickwick Motors & Engineering Works Corsham.

Sperring's Pickwick Motors Garage, c 1920.

Mr. W. Sperring is on the right of the photo. His assistant Mr. Hemmings of Broadstone (whose brother Gerald was also a motor mechanic) is sitting and Mr. Sperring's brother-in-law, Harry Batley, is in the centre. Note the 1920s style pump in the background *and the nonchalant smoking of cigarettes near to the petrol pumps!* The dog seems to be the only one not smoking! Mr. Sperring Senior came from Salisbury to Pickwick during 1922 and both he and his son Hugh saw many changes in fashions and the style of motoring during their seventy-five years as motor engineers in Pickwick.

Mr. W. Sperring's son Hughie, single-handedly kept the *Pickwick Motor and Engine Works* garage going for many years after his father had died. Hughie always seemed to have time to have a chat with you whenever you *'filled up'* with petrol at his garage, even when your visit interrupted his mechanical repair work inside the garage.

For many years, there was a beautiful 1935 MG SA Tourer Charlesworth car on display in the garage window. Everyone who saw it - wanted it! But how did it get there? This splendid MG SA was built at the Abingdon Motor Works and left it as a Charlesworth sports tourer. It is thought to be one of very few original Charlesworth tourers in existence. It was delivered new, in English Cream over red leather, to its first owner Mr. Alfred Nencini, on 29 May, 1937.

In November 1939 Mr. Alfred Nencini was involved in an accident, after which his beloved MG was taken to W. Sperring's garage in Pickwick, where it was repaired and subsequently painted black. When the work on the car had finished, Pickwick Motors and Engineering Works attempted to contact Mr. Nencini to settle the invoice. Their letters were returned unopened. Mr. Nencini's insurance company finally explained to Mr. Sperring, the proprietor of Pickwick Motor Company, that Mr. Nencini had tragically taken his own life ***(more on this later!!!).*** In lieu of payment for the repairs and in agreement with the insurance company, Mr. W. Sperring chose to inherit this fantastic sports tourer. The car was infrequently used and remained gathering dust in the garage's display window to the envy of all those *(including me [Ed])* who set eyes on her over the years whenever they visited the garage.

Tech Details: Chassis no. 1771, 75 bhp, 2,288 cc OHV six-cylinder engine, four-speed manual gearbox, solid front and live rear axles with semi-elliptic rear springs, and four-wheel Lockheed hydraulic drum brakes. Wheelbase: 3,124 mm.

In 2002 the car was purchased from Pickwick Motors by a new owner. That same year, the MG was sent to the world-renowned TT Workshops for a total restoration where it was returned to its original cream colour with red leather seating.

When it was taken to Le Mans in 2004, the car won an award for the best MG. It was described as a very usable tourer and the owner had taken it on several long runs through Europe, including journeys to France and to the Le Mans Classic.

The photo above was taken on Wednesday, 26 October, when the MG SA Tourer Charlesworth went to Auction in 2011 and sold for £70,000. It had a limited mileage since its total restoration in 2002. It is one of just five Charlesworth-bodied SA Tourers known to exist.

This fantastic MG SA is certainly among the most desirable MGs with its six-cylinder power plant and lovely low open sport coachwork by Charlesworth. Well-known journalist Laurence Pomeroy wrote of the SA in *The Motor* (7 June, 1938) magazine, *'I can quite honestly state...that for the sheer pleasure in driving, I have come across nothing which pleases me more than the car now reviewed.'*

Murder of Kathleen Emily Nencini and suicide by Alfred Hector John Nencini at The Rise, Hillingdon, Middlesex on 14 December, 1940.

Alfred Hector John Nencini (the man who never came back to Pickwick for his 1935 MG SA Tourer Charlesworth) later murdered his legal wife after committing bigamy and then shooting himself in a double-killing on 14 December, 1940. Nencini from Buxton, once passed an Intermediate Exam as an Accountant in 1937. He was also a keen tennis athlete; playing doubles matches with his partner A.E. Irons in the All-England Championship in Derbyshire 1931. Alfred Nencini was born in Uxbridge, Middlesex in 1908.

The car's first owner Alfred Hector John Nencini (aged 32) and his wife of three years Mrs. Kathleen Emily Nencini (aged 26 and born 1915 in Uxbridge Middlesex) were married at Gretna Green.

They were both found dead in 1940, by a maid in their house at The Rise, Hillingdon in London. Mrs. Nencini was found sitting in a chair.

Pathologist Dr Skene Keith sated that, *'Both the man and the woman had bullet wounds to the head. But while that of the woman could not have been self inflicted, the man's could'*. The bullet that had killed Kathleen, passed through her head and lodged itself inside a china cabinet after smashing through the glass panel.

Mr. Alfred Nencini subsequently killed himself with a bullet shot through the head.

Six weeks previously, his *first* wife, Mrs. Kathleen Nencini went into the country, taking her three-month-old baby with her. Mr. Alfred Nencini told the maid that he was going away on business. Instead, he drove to see his other wife in his second marital home!

His second wife, gave her name at the inquest as Ellan Margaret Nencini (born 8 June 1908 Birth Registration District Swindon Wiltshire). She had met Mr. Nencini on 30 November. They were married at St. Mary's Roman Catholic Church in Chippenham and spent their six-day honeymoon in Devon. They went to live at Swakeleys Road in Uxbridge. Mr. Nancini had told Ellan (his second wife) that he had a revolver which a friend had given to him as a souvenir from Dunkirk.

On the day of the tragedy, as they had arranged to go away for the weekend, Mr. Nencini told Ellan that he would be home early at 12 o'clock. But after he had arrived home at 12.30p.m., he told Ellan that he had just remembered that he had an appointment to see about some furniture being moved. He drove away in his car and she did not see him alive again. Instead, Mr. Nencini drove to The Rise in Hillingdon to meet his *first* wife Kathleen.

Mrs. Kathleen Nencini (his *first* wife) had returned from the country a day before the tragedy and had gone back into their home in *The Rise*, to remove a box which contained letters, papers and a revolver. She took the letters and left the papers and revolver in the box.

She did not stay in the home, but met Mr. Nencini there the following day as arranged. It was there, where they were found by the maid, both shot by bullets fired from the revolver inside the box.

Mrs Ellan Nancini (his *second* wife) went on to live a ripe old age and sadly passed away in 1998 in her 90th year. **R.I.P.**

Chapter 34. Police Station - Pickwick Road.

The postcard shows the old 'County Police Station' at 62 Pickwick Road, Corsham.

The first professional policemen in England, known as 'Peelers' or 'Bobbies', were set up in London in 1829 by Robert Peel, the then Home Secretary, after *'The Metropolitan Police Act'* of 1829. The 1856 County Borough Police Act created a system for government inspection, audit and regulation for the first time, which forced the whole of the country to set up police forces. It would probably have been around this time that the first Corsham Police Station was set up. Prior to this, most counties retained their own Parish Constables.

The first Corsham Police Station was in a building on the left-hand side of Post Office Lane. It is said, that the policeman on duty downstairs could, if he needed assistance, poke a stick through a hole in the ceiling to alert the officer above! The building later became the home of the Hancock family of coal merchants and has since been demolished.

The second Police Station, known as the *County Police Station*, was located in the building at 62 Pickwick Road. This building was later converted into flats for a while in the 1960-1970s. The house is now a smart private residence; with 'County Police Station' still carved boldly into the wall above the front door (see photo below). In the near-right foreground of the early 1900's postcard view above, you can see the iron railings that once fronted the County Police Station when it was located there. These were cut down in support of the WWII war effort and have since been replaced by the current owner. When the building was in its prime, it also had a tall white flagpole in the front garden, just ahead of the front door.

Two Corsham policemen who worked there, were PC. Perry and PC Beard and in the 1930's Inspector Reakes was the governor! In 1915, it was manned by Sergeant Henry A Nicholas, and one constable. In the sketch here, you can see the original hand-drawn plan for a new prison cell, which was built at the back of the building at 62 Pickwick Road, for locking up the Corsham miscreants!

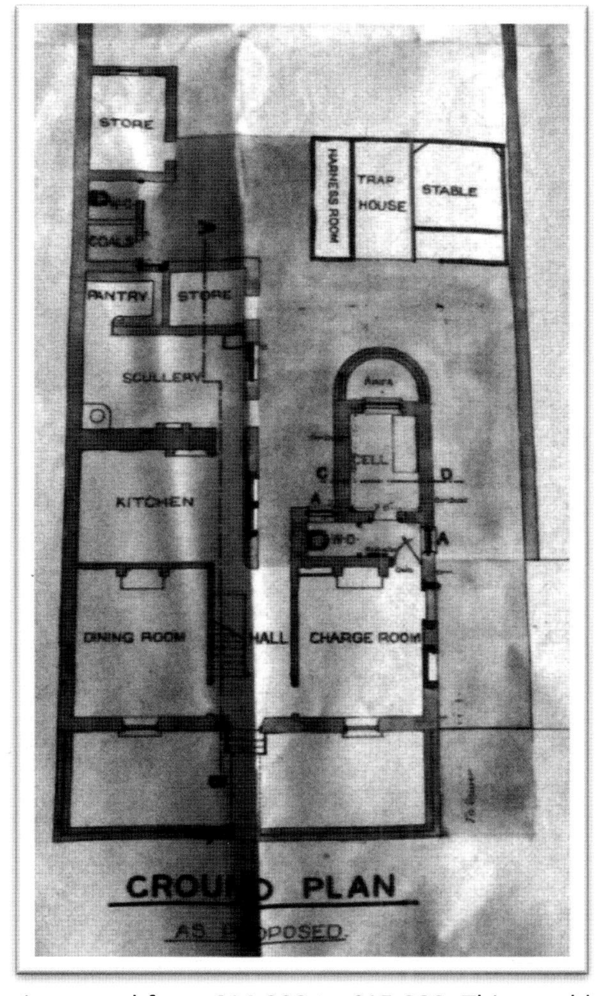

The plans are held by the Wiltshire and Swindon History Centre in Chippenham (reference F10/100/83/6HC Corsham Police Station Architects Plans).

The next location for the Police Station was at the top of Priory Street.

In 1947 there was a tetchy battle between the Wiltshire Housing Committee, who wanted the new Police Station to be built on the Corsham Estate owned land at Ivy Fields, but the Chief Constable was adamant that he wanted it built on the edge of land earmarked for new housing at the top of Priory Street.

In 1949 the estimate for the new Police Station was increased from £14,000 to £15,000. This would include three police houses and three garages. In 1950, the Wiltshire County Council received a Ministry of Health sanction to borrow £15,709 (repayable within 30 years) for the erection of a new Police Sub-Divisional Headquarters in Kings Avenue at the top of Priory Street in Corsham. The Chief Constable eventually *got this own way*, and the building was erected at the top of Priory Street in due course. This meant a reduction of eight houses being built on the new Regis Council House estate.

The red-bricked Police Station at the top of Prior Street was knocked down between the 1st - 3rd July 2015 with the Corsham Police team moving into the new Corsham Campus in Beechfield Road during June 2014. It is ironic, that on the old Priory Street/Kings Avenue site, ten new houses were built in 2017. The result being an increase on that corner site of two more houses than were originally planned for!

One of Corsham's early crimes was reported in 1892, when John Buckland an innkeeper of Atworth, was summoned by Inspector Cruse of Corsham, for being drunk in Corsham when in charge of a horse and trap on 20 January. He was also further charged with maliciously breaking a window at the Corsham Police Station the same night. Buckland admitted his wrongdoing and said. *'It was his first offence and more of an accident than anything wicked'.* He was fined 10s for being drunk and 1s for breaking the window, plus costs of 8s 6p - a total of about £90 in today's money.

In the photo below, are two original Corsham Police Truncheons from the 1800s, courtesy of Kieran Aust. The 'WR' initials on the top truncheon commemorate King William, 'The Sailor King' who (at 64) began his reign from 1830 until 1837.

I wonder how many Corsham heads have been 'tapped' with these over the years!

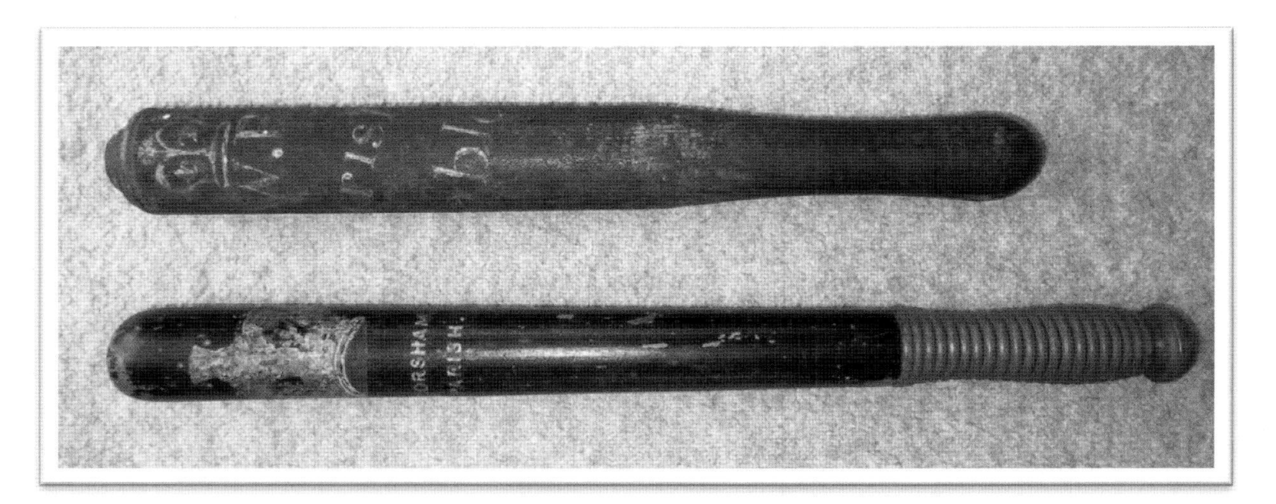

In 1897 Inspector Gale retired from the Corsham Police Station, and was replaced by Inspector Elkins from the Swindon Division. Two years later in 1899, Inspector Elkins was reduced to the rank of Constable for an offence that he committed. It concerned a Corsham family tradition. For many years past, Lord Methuen and his father before him, had given an annual gratuity of £3 to the Police Inspector stationed at Corsham for services rendered in protecting Corsham Court. But according to Police Rules, officers cannot accept gratuities without sanction of the Chief Constable. The money was given to the Inspector's wife.

For three or four years past, Lord Methuen had been absent from Corsham Court, and his Agent (it seems without the knowledge of Lord Methuen) made a new departure and divided the money by giving £1 to the Inspector's wife, and £1 each to the wives of the Constables stationed at Corsham and Biddestone.

Elkins *had not* been found guilty of dishonesty (otherwise he would have been thrown out of the constabulary), rather he had been deemed to be disobedient to a Standing Order which directed that gratuities should never be received without the sanction of the Chief Constable. The Methuen tradition had been applied for many years, even before Elkins had taken over as the Corsham Inspector. It was felt at the time that it was very unfair to penalise one Inspector, when others before him had done the same (i.e. received £3 annually from Lord Methuen) *and got away with it!*

The Corsham Parish Council at the time, very much regretted Inspector Elkins removal and reduction in rank to Constable. They felt that he had been very harshly dealt with, as during his tenure, there had been a marked improvement in Corsham. In 1901, Elkins tried to appeal his case to no avail. It seems like Elkins continued as a Constable elsewhere for some time, making many arrests in his duty. Even though Elkins, who had been in the service for 15 years should have known the regulations inside out, looking back, it seems a rather harsh punishment for a man who was obviously very dedicated! One can only imagine the *stick he must have received* on the beat with other constables. [Ed].

Above is part of a plan to build a new prison cell in the Pickwick Road County Police Station

In May 1904 a 17 year old tramp was charged with assaulting Viola Kennedy, daughter of Mr. Kennedy of the Chequers Inn, Corsham. On the previous evening, the girl was returning home from Chippenham Secondary School when the prisoner molested her and used improper expressions. She ran home and told her father who was a retired police inspector. He went in quest of the prisoner whom he found and took to the Corsham Police Station. On the way, the prisoner begged the ex-inspector to *give him a good hiding and let him go!* He was committed for 14 days.

Below is a photo of the Priory Street/Kings Avenue Police Station in its very final stage of being built in the early 1950s.

Chapter 35. Poorhouse/Workhouse.

Drawing by Oswald Brakspear.

The Corsham Poorhouse was situated immediately to the right of the Royal Oak in the High Street and alongside a small alleyway known as *Paradise Lane*.

In 1974 a fire destroyed the Poorhouse's gable end and part of the buildings behind. The shop-front (No.70 High Street) appended to the front, now completely hides the old Poorhouse buildings from the street view.

The shop-front has accommodated many businesses over the years, including for periods, the butchers *'Coates and Sons'* and later the *'N.W. London Meat Company'*, and now *'ES Electrical Contracting'.* The old High Street pump once stood on the opposite side of the High Street.

The Corsham Poorhouse was situated in an area (also once known under several other names, Catherine's Court, White's Court and Scavenger's Court), slightly tucked away from the High Street next to the Royal Oak. The old photo below, showing the top story and gable end of the Poorhouse, was found with the enthusiastic help of a great team of volunteers, misfiled deep in the dusty archives of the Devizes Museum.

It is not known exactly when the paupers were first housed in the Corsham Poorhouse, but the Parliamentary Papers Vol. 21 Part 2, page 1258, does mention that in 1772, four 17th century cottages [that stood at right angles to the High Street], were *lately* converted into the Workhouse. The Rectory court book-notes also show that the *new* Poorhouse was there in 1728. The cost to the Vestry *(the pre-Parish Council committee)* was £400.

Following the introduction of the Chippenham Poor Law Union, an ornamental gable (the top of which can be seen in the old photograph here and later destroyed by fire) was added to the street end of the cottages when they were converted. On its completion, the Poorhouse then consisted of five dwellings and cost £240 in 1836 (about £2,000 in today's money).

In September **of 1781** an advert was placed in the Bath Chronicle seeking '*a man that understands clothing business to take care of poor at Poor House in Corsham'.* Any person of good character may apply to Churchwardens & Overseers of Poor of Parish.

The care of the poor was originally managed by a private contractor, but this abuse was done away with in 1798. In 1799 it was resolved that those poor souls from Corsham who became its occupants should be employed in spinning and weaving. In 1800, a Master and Mistress were therefore appointed to manage the Poorhouse on a salary of £12 a year, plus 2d. out of every shilling of the earnings generated by the inmates. The Poorhouse children who were *old enough*, were *'put out'* to work in the local trades. The Policy of a Poor House was to make conditions worse inside than those prevailing outside; so that the able-bodied would do all they could to stay away and work. Married couples under 60 were separated and parents were not allowed to see their children. Smoking was prohibited, meals taken in silence and inmates confined indoors except to attend church!

Anyone born in the Parish of Corsham who became destitute, no matter where they lived, were *sent down* and housed and fed in the Corsham Poorhouse by the Parish Council. For example - in 1808, to negate an extra ongoing charge on their own poor rate when there was already great hardship amongst their poor, East Molesey Parish Council spent £40 in forcibly sending a woman back home to Corsham in Wiltshire, because they objected to paying for her keep! Thankfully, there was always room for the Corsham destitute in our Poorhouse.

Photo of Catherine Court and the rear of the Poorhouse buildings under repair after the 1974 fire, taken from the Old Malt House, looking south across the car park at the rear of the Royal Oak.

In 1818 one of the early masters of the Poorhouse, Mr. Sam Horne passes away.

In 1832 a sum of £200 was ordered to be borrowed for helping Corsham paupers to emigrate. Sixteen 16 men, 10 women, and 27 children were selected. They were conveyed to Bristol in two covered wagons, where someone was appointed to meet them and to help them purchase any small things that they required, prior to seeing them safely onboard their ship.

In 1833 the year before the passing of the Poor Law Amendment Act, the Colonial Land and Emigration Commissioners (CLEC) organisation was set up to manage the programme of emigration to Britain's colonies (Canada, Australia, New Zealand etc.).

Under the new regime, some emigrants could qualify for a free passage if they were under forty, capable of labour, of good character and having been vaccinated against smallpox. Or if they had come from occupations such as agricultural labourers, shepherds, or were female domestics or farm servants. Young married couples, preferably without children were viewed as the ideal candidates. Assisted passage was also available with less stringent restrictions to healthy able-bodied labourers whose moral character could be vouched for.

In the year from **June 1835 to July 1836** the County of Wiltshire emigrated 347 people at a cost of £2,042. From 1835 to 1899, the overall number of Poorhouse emigrants that had been sent out from England and Wales reached 36,000.

In 1834 the *'Poor Law Amendment Act'* replaced the parish *'Overseers of the Poor'* act, established under the old Poor Law. The Chippenham Poor Law Union's board of guardians, (which was officially declared on 17 November 1835) took on the administration of the workhouses within the local parishes (including Corsham), either by order of the 'Poor Law Commission' or by the common consent of the parishes.

Each civil parish in the union was represented by at least one guardian on the board, with those with larger populations or special circumstances having two or more. The Chippenham Union initially used the former parish workhouses in the Butts at Chippenham and at Lacock, the latter of which was specifically used for accommodating children.

A new purpose-built Chippenham Union Workhouse was erected in 1858-9 on a site at Rowden Hill to the south of Chippenham (where the Chippenham Hospital is now); some of the original buildings still exist. The building cost £13,100 and was capable of holding 401 inmates.

There were five Workhouses within the Chippenham Union; Chippenham, Corsham, Lacock, Box and Colerne. The Chippenham Union is divided into four districts, with Corsham being District No. 4, covering Corsham, Box, Ditteridge, Colerne, Biddestone Saint Nicholas, Biddestone Saint Peter and Slaughterford. Population of 6085 and a Poorhouse master's salary of £110.

In 1835 the Corsham Poorhouse housed 35 people. The maximum that could be held there were 90, but the greatest ever held in Corsham at one time was 45. The Governor/Master at that time was M. Arnold. The buildings were rented at £30 per annum.

To give you a flavour of what it must have been like for Corsham paupers in the 1800's, the following is a harrowing tale that appeared in the *Devizes and Wiltshire Gazette on Thursday 07 December*

1843. 'A woman of the name of Elizabeth Manley, 69 years of age and a native of this town [Chippenham], but belonging to Corsham parish, for many years obtained her living by carrying water from the river; but having caught a chill in her leg, she became an inmate of the Corsham workhouse. On the formation of the Chippenham Union, she appeared before the Board, and was ordered into the workhouse; but on stating to the Guardians that her only relative lived in Bradford-on-Avon, they allowed her 1s. 6p. per week. By some oversight, this poor creature, though so lame as to be obliged to walk with a stick for support, was forced to go to Corsham, a distance of eight miles, once a month for her 6s. She had repeatedly requested the relieving officer to pay the money to some person in Bradford-on-Avon, to save her this unnecessary trouble, but he had always postponed doing so. On the Saturday preceding her death, she left home at 7 o'clock in the morning, to go to Corsham as usual. She reached that place at mid-day taking 5 hours to go 8 miles. Being very much fatigued and unable to return the same day, she requested an old acquaintance to allow her to sleep in her house that night, which she was permitted to do on top of some clothes which the woman *shook out* on the floor for her. The next morning, Sunday, at 10 o'clock, she started back for Bradford-on-Avon, where she arrived at 4 p.m., so worn out with fatigue that she was obliged to take to her bed. The medical gentleman, Mr. Baines, who attends the district in which she resided, was called in and promptly attended to her case, but she died after an illness of five days.'

Another story that had a much better ending, started when one night, an infant was brought to the Corsham Workhouse after being found abandoned in a basket in Pickwick. He was named 'Moses Pickwick'; his Christian name given to him as a foundling and his surname from the village where he was found. Moses was brought up in the Workhouse until he was old enough to labour in the stables at the Hare and Hounds (very near to where he was found) where the London to Bath mail and stage coaches stopped. By his good conduct and intelligence, Moses later became head ostler there, and eventually a coach proprietor in Bath. His coaches, with the name 'Moses Pickwick' emblazoned on their side, regularly stopped at the Hare and Hounds.

In 1874 Mr Thomas White (later of Keary, Stokes and White) purchased the Poorhouse property for £441.9s and further rebuilding was carried out by Osbornes the local builders and stonemasons who employed a huge team of men, working the stone in their yard at the rear of the Methuen Arms.

The Chippenham Union, later established a children's cottage home at Velley Hill, Gastard, near Corsham. In 1924, the home could accommodate 12 children, with E. Swain as its Superintendent.

In August of 1974 the part of the Poorhouse building fronting the High Street was seriously damaged by fire whist it was being used as a storeroom for the butchers shop situated at the front. The first floor and the roof space were completely destroyed. The following year, the Corsham Civic Society (with the backing of Robin Eden) battled in vain to stop Wiltshire District Council from demolishing the upper two stories and rebuilding with a flat roof over the ground floor.

The move to save the Poorhouse was also supported by the Corsham architect Mr. Oswald Brakspear, who stated;

'It is not difficult to see what a delightful group the Poorhouse would make here with its neighbours. When we see what admirable work the council is doing in paving the other end of the High Street, it would be doubly tragic if this charming and architecturally valuable building were allowed to go'.

Two thousand pounds was raised by the Corsham Civic Society to make the building safe, pending an eventual (estimated £38,000) rebuild of this Grade II building - but it was never to be, as the Ministry of Environment issued a court order to compel the owner to make the building safe or to demolish in within 21 days. Demolition started on 27 January 1976. The result is that we have a very odd looking, flat roofed frontage, which is certainly not in keeping with the rest of the beautiful Corsham High Street.

Mike Slater, a local resident living in the High Street, watched the fire being fought in 1974 from his upstairs window opposite. When he wandered through the remains of the fire afterwards with Chris Shergold, they found this old wooden whistle, about an inch long, underneath where the floorboards had collapsed; possibly lost down a gap by a former inmate or maybe one of the wardens!

In the old photograph below *(kindly supplied by John Cuthbertson)* you can see *'Coates & Sons'* the High Street butchers, with the original Poorhouse facade looming up over the top of their small fronted shop. It's a fabulous image of Corsham's High Street of days gone by.

Spare a thought for the poor Corsham inmates when you next pass by!

Chapter 36. Porch Entrance of St Bartholomew's.

St Bartholomew's church in Corsham has a fascinating history which would fill many books. This is just a small example of the beauty of our Corsham Church for you to enjoy.

When you next visit St Bartholomew's church in Corsham, take a moment to have a much closer look at the main porch entrance which is in the second bay of the south aisle. This substantial late fifteenth century porch took the place of an earlier one. It is roughly 9 feet square with a little store room called a *Parvise* above.

Front face of the Porch: The parapet on the front is adorned with the usual Hungerford shield of nine quarterings and the crest, a garb (sheaf of corn) between two sickles. Beneath is the motto 'ET DIEV MON APPVY' and the date ANO. DOM. 1631 *('God is my Support 1631').*

The porch facade has three 15th century niches in its walls; each holding a statue of an important Saint. The original statues were destroyed during the 16th-century Reformation when Popery *(the doctrines, practices, and ceremonies associated with the Pope or the papal system; Roman Catholicism)* was violently overthrown.

On the outside left of the porch is a stone tablet carved with the following words:

'IN MEMORY OF CHARLES AND MARY MAYO, AND THE REV ROBERT MAYO. THE THREE FIGURES WERE PLACED ON THIS PORCH ST. BARTHOLOMEW'S DAY IN 1919.'

St BARTHOLOMEW: On the left wall of the porch facing west and looking along Church Street, is a *gruesome* depiction of St Bartholomew the patron saint of the church. Christian tradition says that St Bartholomew was skinned alive before his death; the skin of his body cut into strips, and then pulled off, leaving his body open and bleeding for a long time. He was then crucified, head downward. In the statue's right hand, the Saint holds a 'fleshers' knife. In his left hand he holds his flayed skin as depicted in Michelangelo's *Last Judgment*. St Bartholomew's body was washed up in the waters of the small island Lipari, near Sicily and a large part of his skin and bones were deposited there. In 809, these remains were moved from Lipari to Benevento in 983.

St PETER: If you look up from the outside, on the left corner of the porch front, you will see St Peter, one of the Twelve Apostles of Jesus Christ and the first Bishop of Rome. In his right hand St Peter holds two huge keys of heaven! In the Gospel of Matthew 16:19, Jesus gives the care of the whole Church and its government to him by saying, *'I will give you the keys of the kingdom of heaven, and whatever you bind on Earth shall be bound in heaven, and whatever you loose on Earth shall be loosed in heaven.'* Since the 16th century, every time that a Pope dies, a symbolical pair of keys are created and buried with them.

St PAUL: On the right corner of the porch is St Paul. In his right hand, he holds a two-edged sword which is a reminder of the means of his martyrdom. He was beheaded in Rome in 67 AD.

(Heb 4:12) 'Indeed, the word of God is living and effective, sharper than any two-edged sword, penetrating even between soul and spirit, joints and marrow, and able to discern reflections and thoughts of the heart.'

Other portrayals of St Paul show him as a martyr, with his severed head under his arm and accompanied by the sword that killed him. In his left hand, St Paul holds a bible which represents his gospel in the New Testament part of the Bible. St Paul wrote some of the most beautiful and important passages in the whole of the Bible.

St Peter and St Paul are often depicted together (as they are in Corsham) as *'pillars of the Church.'* The three figures - St Bartholomew, St Peter and St Paul - were provided by subscription in memory of Mrs. C.T. Mayo and the Rev R. Mayo who were constant friends to the church during their lives.

East face of the Porch: If you look up at the hidden east facing wall of the porch, you can see on the middle merlon *(solid upright section of a battlement)* of the parapet, that it bears the arms and crest of Halliday (a name of Anglo-Saxon origin), with the strange *Halliday* family motto, *'QVARTA SALVTIS'* beneath.

The *Coat of Arms* granted to the 'Halliday' family was a black shield, with three silver helmets (two over one), garnished gold, and a silver border engrailed, the Crest being a demi-lion rampant, holding a blue anchor. The Motto, *'QVARTA SALVTIS'* translates as, *'The fourth to heal' or 'A fourth to salvation'*. The first recorded spelling of the *'Halliday'* family name is shown to be that of Suein Halidai, which was dated 1188, in the *'Pipe Rolls of Nottinghamshire'*, during the reign of King Henry II, known as *'The Builder of Churches'.*

The name 'Halliday' *(descended from Walter Halliuay, styled the Minstrel, Master of the Revels to Edward IV)* cames to Corsham in 1620 via Margaret Halliday who married Sir Edward Hungerford. The two similar merlons either side depict the quartered arms of both the Hungerford and Halliday families. The letters E.M.H. beneath presumably stand for Edward, and Margaret Hungerford.

Photo shows the porch before the statues were added.

Porch interior: Inner Staircase: Just inside the main entrance on the porch's east wall, is a door that used to lead to small staircase annex made for Lady Margaret Hungerford to gain access to a private gallery which she had built in 1631 in the south aisle for herself and household and which continued to belong to Corsham Court until the gallery's destruction in

1874. The gallery was lit by two dormer windows in the roof each side of the porch *(see photo);* these were removed when the new tower was completed in 1878. The stairs are now gone and the annex now houses the boiler for the church's central heating system.

In 1810 the upper part of the church spire had to be removed as it was dangerous.

In 1815, the rest of the spire was removed leaving the tower square, as the piers beneath could not support the weight. It was not until 1878 that a new tower and spire were built in its present position to the left of the original squared off tower as shown in the photo.

Porch Ceiling: In the centre of the vaulted porch ceiling, is a boss *(protrusion of stone*) bearing a King's head. The stone ceiling itself rests on a stone corbel *(structural piece of supporting stone)* in each of the four corners, supported on the carved heads of a Bishop *(north-east),* a Queen *(south-east)*, an Angel *(south-west)* and a King *(north-west).*

Inside the porch above the apex of the church's main entrance door is another moulded stone corbel which looks as though it was meant to hold another statue, but instead, above it is a plaque stating:

'IN THIS CHURCH PORCH LYETH Y BODY OF WILLIAM TASKER GENT WHO CHOOS RATHER TO BE A DOOR KEEPER TO THE HOUSE OF HIS GOD THAN TO DWELL IN THE TENTS OF WICKEDNES. HE DEPARTED THIS LIFE IAN THE 20TH AN 1684 AGED 69 YEARS'.

William Tasker chose to be buried in the porch, rather than in the churchyard or inside the church itself, because he despised the hypocrisy of the wealthy and their ostentatious monuments inside and out! [Ed] AMEN to that!

The coat of arms hanging high up on the wall above the porch door, just inside the church is that of King William and Mary, who were unusual as they both reigned together from 1688-1702; hence the letters on the coat of arms *WM RR* meaning *William and Mary, Rex Regina.*

On either side of the porch interior are stone seats. The floor is paved in stone. The little square-headed window above the entrance door was walled up before 1874. The porch is crowned with a battlement parapet with two large stone water shoots on the west side to drain off the water. In the centre of the battlement wall, are the faded remains of a large sundial.

Chapter 37. Post Office.

1800s: THE 1st POST OFFICE:

The Post Office in Corsham has been located in several places around town. In the early 1800s, the very first Corsham Post Office was established in the Methuen Arms and called the new *'Commercial Inn and Posting House'*. One of the early Postmasters was John Sweatman, the landlord of the Methuen Arms in 1830. He was responsible for managing the letters that arrived from the Chippenham sorting office every morning at 9 o-clock and ensuring that all outgoing mail was despatched by 4 o'clock in the afternoon. Mail coaches and passenger coaches also stopped daily at the Methuen Arms. For example, in 1839 a coach called *'The Accommodation'* stopped at the Methuen Arms at 9am on its way from Chippenham to Bath and stopped there again on its return journey later at 6.30pm.

Today, the Methuen Arms looks very much like it did around 100 years ago. The hotel is rich in history. John Aubrey the historian claimed that this was once the site of a nunnery. There was once a building on this site called Winters Court with the Nott family owning the site from the 15th century. Family member Christopher Nott attempted to open an ale house here, as far back as 1608. The building became the Red Lion and was a coaching house. In 1779, the building was passed to the Methuen family and subsequently renamed the Methuen Arms in 1805.

1804: As early as 1804 advertisements were appearing in newspapers showing the Corsham Post Office as a point of contact for job replies. For example, on Monday 2 April 1804, an advert appeared in the Salisbury and Winchester Journal seeking a middle aged person with perfect knowledge of the *'Superfine Broadcloth and Cassimere Manufactory and Wool-Dying Business' to act as a factory Superintendent. Replies to be sent to John Jones at the Post Office Corsham.* In January 1808, another advert appeared seeking; 'A*n apprentice to a Surgeon and Apothecary in a respectable neighbourhood, with replies to be sent to A.A. Post Office Corsham'.*

If you look very carefully, at the lintel over the top of the window to the left of the (chequered) side-door of the Methuen Arms (on the main road side), you can still see evidence of the first Corsham Posting house. In large faded capital letters across the lintel are the words *'Post Office'*. In the section of the old postcard photo above right, from the very early 1900s, are the words *'Order Office'* above the window and *'Posting House'* on the large notice on the hotel's wall.

1825: The Post Mark for Corsham was the *'fleuron'*.

1844: The first Corsham Postmaster and landlord of the Methuen Arms, John Sweatman aged about 60, comes to a gruesome and mysterious end as he dies from poison! Having quit the Methuen Arms in adverse circumstances, Sweatman and his wife had been living in Bath but in 1832, Sweatman's wife Mary sadly dies aged 52. In June 1844 John Sweatman left Corsham on his way to Chippenham, for the purpose of receiving some money which he said was *due to him* from the estate of the late Mr. Joy at Hartham. He had told a person in Corsham before he had left, that if he did not get the money, he did not know what the consequences would be. This money he did not receive. On his way back home, he called in at the Chequers Inn for two to three hours to see the landlady who he was well acquainted with. He only drank one glass of beer and smoked two pipes of tobacco. The landlord, seeing that Sweatman was downcast, tried to get him to remain the night, offering him anything that the house could afford him to restore his spirits. But Sweatman left the Inn at 8 o'clock with a depression of spirits and did not return home as expected.

On his way home, Sweatman had been seen by some people walking by. They watched him lie down under some trees not far from the footpath leading from Chippenham to Corsham through Lord Methuen's park. Supposing him to be intoxicated with liquor, they did not approach or disturb him. On the following morning about 10 o'clock he was found at the same spot, dead and cold! Nearby was a corked bottle which contained a small portion of oxalic acid. Mr Little, surgeon of Corsham who made the post-mortem stated that he had found the stomach in a state which clearly indicated that poison had been swallowed in a quantity that had caused Sweatman's death. The jury at inquest held in the Pack Horse, returned a verdict that Sweatman had, *'Died from poison, but how or by whom administered, there was no evidence to show'.*

1855: A postal number was allocated to the town. Mr. R. Scott of the Corsham Post Office advertised his goods in the *'The Corsham Miscellany And General Advertising'* local paper, promising every cure known to man in liquid and tablet form, like the beautifully named medicine of 'Mellifluous Cough Balsam', which purported to be the 'BEST MEDICINE EVER KNOWN'. (See Chapter 26).

1859: THE 2nd POST OFFICE: The post office moves into the ironmonger's shop owned by builder James Bromley. The shop was somewhere near to the corner where Post Office Lane joins the High Street. The small road, then a cul-de-sac leading to the Golden Path towards Alexander Terrace, was named *Post Office Lane*. The road still retains that name, even though the Post Office is no longer there! Later in the century, the ironmonger's shop (with its integral Post Office) was managed by Mrs Sarah Bromley. Foot messengers were regularly despatched from Chippenham to Corsham at 6am each day. The Mail box was closed at 10p.m. After closure, a fee of 1 penny was charged for each letter until the despatch was made up.

1885: THE 3rd POST OFFICE: The Post Office moved out of Post Office Lane and into the large building at No. 15 High Street, opposite where the *Green Ginger* shop is today. Mr Fred J. Bryant *(the Bank Agent of the Capital & Counties Bank)* became the Postmaster there until he retired in 1940. Harry Simmonds later became the postmaster there. In those days, letters were delivered at 7am, 1pm and 6.30pm and were despatched by rail from Corsham station at 9.15am, 11.30am, 2.50pm, 6.50pm and 9.15pm. It was not unusual to post a letter to London in the morning and to receive a reply during the evening of the same day.

The building at No.15 was once used as an Employment Exchange and then the Halifax Building Society. Much earlier in 1830, it was occupied by Mr. Peglar, a butcher and seller of beer. He called

his house 'The Lamb'. If you look carefully, to either side of the window to the left of the main door at No. 15 High Street, you can still see where the letter box was once embedded into the wall. Also above the door you can see a round symbol with a face of the Sun in its centre; this is a copy of a rare Sun Fire Insurance Plaque. The first to use the mark was the Sun Fire Office established in 1710.

Fire insurance marks were metal/lead plaques marked with the emblem of the insurance company which were affixed to the front of insured buildings as a guide for the insurance company's fire brigades that were used in the eighteenth and nineteenth century, in the days before municipal fire services were formed. Another 'Sun Insurance' plaque was located at No. 5 Pickwick. The original plaque had a piece missing, but the owner Mr Lewis had a replica made by Andrea Garrihy and Galena Leadworks, which is now visible at the front of the house in Pickwick. The original plaque is retained under lock and key. The Telegraph Office based at the railway station had the letters 'R.S.O.' added (Railway Sub-Office) to their postmark.

The mail train collected and despatched the mail bags at a location just east of Corsham Railway station. This was done when the train was in motion; a *'snatcher'* mechanism was used to collect the mail bags which were hung from a bar horizontal alongside the track. Incoming mail bags were off-loaded from the train at the same time, down a chute.

1888: The Post Mark for NESTON is a single ring.

1903: The Secretary to the Postmaster General stated that an evening delivery of letters to Gastard would be made in future.

1932: In October 1932 the Parish Council failed in their attempt to get a *Stamp Machine* placed outside the Post Office, due to the early closing each day of the office. By the end of November, the Council were informed that a new Stamp machine would be provided; a hearty vote of thanks was sent from the Parish Council to Capt. V.A. Cazalet M.P. for the assistance he had rendered in this matter. But five years later, things were not running smoothly with the Stamp Machine, as it was beginning to give trouble. The problem was caused by light, bent or damaged coins being used, which meant that no stamp would be obtained, and the person coming next with a full-weighted coin would get both a stamp AND the previous person's *bent* penny back!

1934: Houses in Corsham had not yet been numbered, causing difficulty for postman to identify people, especially those having the same surname. In the High Street alone, there were some dozen persons with the name of Smith! Nobody knew who was responsible for providing house numbers.

1938: THE 4th POST OFFICE: The Post Office moves to its present location at No. 84 High Street under the new postmistress Mrs Adams. This building had previously been occupied by Joseph Essery Eastmans, a firm of builders, hardware, plumbers and decorators. The Post Office and post box were now opposite the Town Hall but it took a lot of negotiation to get another post box placed at the other end of the High Street. The shop in Station Road was deemed too close to become a sub-post-office. Street name plates were put up for the first time in the urban parts of Corsham, making it easier for postman to find the correct house. Most Corsham houses now had numbers.

1940: The office at Corsham was still classified as a sub-post office. The Parish Clerk sent a strong appeal to the Postmaster at Chippenham asking for Corsham to be raised to that of a 'salaried' post office. Owing to the large increase in Corsham's population and the amount of business done, the town deserved a fully constituted Post Office. Mrs. Clifford had to resign her appointment as sub-post-mistress, due to her (sub-post-master) husband having been called up for military service (he would be expected to return to his post at the end of the war). A tribute was paid to Mrs. Clifford, recognising that she had been overworked and under-staffed during her appointment.

1944: The sorting office moves out to Westwells Road but Corsham residents are not happy with the *'Hawthorn'* post mark now being used on their letters instead of *'Corsham'*. The Postmaster said that he had no control over the Hawthorn *'non de guerre'* [i.e. an assumed name under which a person engages in combat] as it was invented to confuse the enemy about all of the defence establishments dotted in and around Corsham. **In 1951:** The Parish Council suggested to the Post Office authorities, the possibility of using the old Maternity Home in the High Street for a new Post Office, but this never materialised. When plans for the Shopping Precinct were being drawn up in the 1970s, there was considerable pressure for the Post Office to be incorporated into the scheme, but sadly this did not materialise and the Post Office remains where it is today.

2015: The letter 'P' disappeared for the best part of 2015 and the building became known for a while as the ***'Corsham Ost Office'.*** Much to everyone's relief, the 'P' is now back on the wall.

Chapter 38. Quarry - Tin Pan Alley - Cross Keys.

Just behind the Cross Keys, in what was known as the Hartham Hythe field *(the Cross Keys area was also known in the 1700s as Bricker's Barn)* there are the remains of two old surface dug stone quarries. These quarries do not feature in any of the local history books and have long been forgotten about!

The first and largest of the hidden quarries is in the circular wood immediately behind the Cross Keys Inn *(and known locally by children in the 1960's as 'Tin Pan Alley')*. It is a large hole, surrounded by fencing and hidden under the shade of a large number of trees. At the very bottom in the thick undergrowth is a Badger set and a haven for other wild life.

This quarry would very likely have been used to provide the crushed stone for lining the surface of the local Bricker's Barn Trust turnpike road which ran alongside the large quarry and *behind* the Cross Keys. The stone from these surface dug quarries was also used in the building of local dry stone walls and rubble-built cottages like the ones that you can see at the nearby crossroads.

The second, much smaller quarry is now just a 'pimple' in the landscape and has almost disappeared under years of infill with rubbish and soil. You can see the location of the quarries in the 1919 map.

In the 1700s the Bricker's Barn Trust turnpike road ran across the fields behind the Cross Keys Inn. Then past Hartham Church and across the top of Middlewick Lane through to the ex-Rudloe Manor site at the very top of Box Hill. This was once part of the main London to Bath road, before the A4 through Pickwick became the single main route, as we know it today.

In the days before tarmac was invented, the responsibility for maintaining turnpike roads lay with the parishes that they ran through. All parishioners were obliged to perform a regular stint of labour repairing the roads each year, or by providing horses and carts for transporting the crushed stone.

The local children from the nearby Corsham *prefab* bungalow estates of the 1950-1960s, used to slide down the steep quarry slopes on large discarded tin dinner trays that had been thrown to the bottom, holding on by their fingertips in fear of tumbling out (which they did almost every time).

The largest quarry was know as *'Tin Pan Alley'*, due to the large number of broken iron bedsteads, cookers, prams and sheets of discarded rusty corrugated iron that mysteriously found their way to the bottom of the quarry (there were no recycling centres in those days!) Some of the originally discarded tin sheeting is still visible today at the very bottom!

The quarry was also a prime source to enable the construction of wooden go-carts for children. The bases of metal prams were ideal as a sub-frame, along with their sturdy axils and wheels. All that was needed were a couple of planks of old wood, a hammer, some string, and a stout heart........ and BINGO, the Corsham children had a Formula 1 Racing Cart. Those children who were really astute, managed to get the front wheels to actually steer from side to side, by sawing off the front wheels and front pram axel and then hammering them onto a *'swivelling'* plank with 'U' shaped nails.

The steering wheel was any scrap of old rope, attached to each side of the front axel steering contraption or through two holes - and off they would go down the steepest hill they could find in Corsham; very often ending up in the hedge, due to some technical malfunction or other.

Braking was applied with the sole of a shoe directly onto the front tyres! The aftermath of any crash, was swiftly followed by regular quick Pit Stops for more spares from 'Tin Pan Alley'. And then, off again in their latest F1 model!

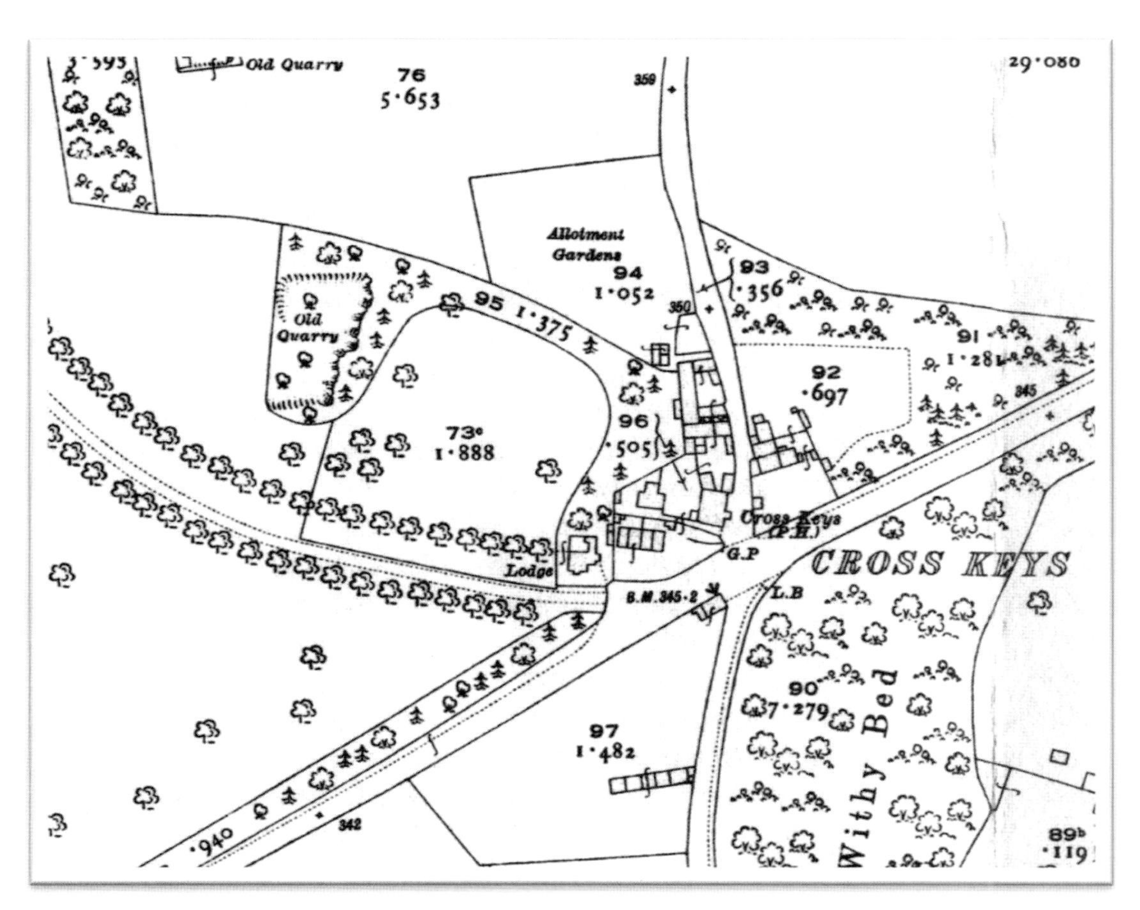

Chapter 39. Rising Sun Inn - a 'BLAST' from the past.

'I found civilians and fire officers in action, and these workers had to pass through a wall of flame coming out of the ground'.

That was the statement from PC Bosley when he arrived on the scene from Box in 1957.

The Rising Sun was a popular stopping place, halfway between Corsham and Box on the A4 main road and probably built around 1839 when the new Rudloe to Box road was built (now the A4). The building had two storeys at the front with cellarage below with three more rooms at the back. On the bottom floor was the outside lavatory, the bar, a lobby, a smoking room (or snug) and the skittle alley. This photo shows the Inn at around 1936. A feature of the Rising Sun for many years was the Christmas Party held each December for the local children.

Mrs. Joyce Griffin and Mrs. Barbara Rogers were daughters of the late Mr. Harry Smith who ran the pub from June 1933 - Oct 1936. Son-in-law Mr. William Graham Francis Cyril (Bill) Griffin and daughter Mrs. Joyce Griffin took over the licence. When Mrs. Barbara Rogers' husband died in 1954, she went to live with her sister Joyce to assist with the running if the Inn. Joyce could speak four languages and this was much appreciated by the Hungarian refugees who came to Thornypits in 1956 and frequented the Inn.

On the foggy and icy night of 4th of December 1957, the world resounded with a very loud bang in the middle of the night at 4:30 a.m. The explosion could be heard many miles away. This was the sound of a tragic accident. It looked like the flames of Hell were burning through the road reminiscent of a war time incident. The debris from the blast was strewn right across the road onto the opposite bank, completely blocking off the road.

The houses opposite had their windows blown out and parts of their roofs ripped off, other house windows for up to 100 yards away were shattered. Telephone poles and even the grass verges were set alight. At 10 o-clock another small explosion blew the back off a newly built bungalow near to the Inn. Mr. C. Baxter who owned a garage nearby thought that it was his garage that had exploded, but when he went outside all he could see was *a heap of rubble* where the Rising Sun Inn had been!

After the explosion, the first person to report the incident to the police was Lt. Cdr. A.E. Cheetham who lived immediately across the valley three miles away in Colerne. He said that he was awaken by the load explosion about 4:40 and thought at first that it was an aeroplane breaking the sound barrier! Two fire engines and three ambulances were sent to the scene.

The photo shows three of the rescuers who lived nearby: Left to right - Alec Thomas Dancey, Charlie Woodgate, and Howard Steele.

The Rising Sun Inn on the edge of the main A4 road, halfway down Box Hill, had been completely demolished by a massive explosion. The effect of the explosion was similar to receiving a direct hit by a wartime bomb. Only the left hand corner of the large building (part of the skittle alley) remained standing. The licensee (William Griffin) and members of his family were killed. Several other occupants of the pub at the time miraculously managed to escape death. Before the Gas Board managed to cut off the gas supply, further explosions occurred until about 12 noon; one beneath the house on the opposite side of the road!

An inquest was held on the three deaths - Landlord William Graham Francis Cyril Griffin 45, his wife Joyce Mary Victoria Griffin - nee Smith aged 42 and their four-year old son Andrew Phillip Griffin. Young Andrew had just celebrated his fourth birthday at the Guildhall in Bath the day before the explosion. Andrew was found wrapped in the arms of his father in the centre of the demolished house. William's skull was exposed on the left side front and injuries included multiple fractures of the skull. The cause of death was shock due to multiple injuries to the chest and skull. At the inquest, it was said that Andrew may have died up to 10 minutes after his father but was probably unconscious during that time. The deaths were all due to the shock, burns and from the huge force of the explosion, rather than by carbon monoxide poisoning. Mrs Griffin's wrist watch was still going when they found her on top of debris in the yard at the back of the building! She was dead. At the post-mortem, Dr. Bishton came to the conclusion that Mr. Griffin died first, Mrs. Griffin second and Andrew third. **R.I.P.**

The road was completely blocked by debris and a raging fire was burning. Several rescuers ran through the flames (many fires coming up though the ground) to try and save the occupants. Mrs Barbara Rogers (who was Mrs Griffin's sister) and her two children Susan (6) and Louise (3) were all buried in rubble on their beds. The landlord's dog Rex was saved after being heard crying under the rubble of the cellar. Mrs Barbara Rogers was found with her left arm and hand trapped by the rubble; her head was wedged in between large stones and her legs were pinned down. They all survived, and were taken to Chippenham Hospital. Mrs. Rogers said;

'I was awakened by the falling masonry I suppose, I did not hear a bang, but can remember first the stones falling, but I cannot remember them continuing to fall.'

The corner said that they were all very lucky to have survived the explosion. They had been sleeping in a part of the building furthest away from the explosion. Barbara was dug out of the rubble by Ron Barnett who lived opposite in 'Briardale'.

There were rumours that lucky survivor, the landlord's little two-year old (seriously injured) baby Jane Griffin, was 'blown into a tree', and if so, this would have contributed to her survival even though she was seriously ill. After treatment at Frenchay, Jane was later given into the care of her aunt Barbara Rogers who also survived the blast, and they all subsequently moved down the road, into Mrs Rogers' mother-in-law's home at 10 Hazlebury Hill. After the disaster Jane went on to live with her uncle and aunt in Beer in Devon; she later lived a happy life in Cambridgeshire, and had three children and was grandma to seven grandchildren. Sadly, Barbara Davies (formerly Rogers) died on 5th March 2016. Barbara was always reluctant to speak about this tragedy as it brought back such terrible memories. R.I.P Barbara.

The gas pipe fracture was caused by land movement. The hillside here is composed of huge Bath stone boulders and the gas pipe buried within the hillside had completely fractured. There was a large boulder weighing several hundredweight immediately over (and in direct contact with) the gas pipe's fracture position. But it was not the actual five-inch cast-iron main gas pipe that supplied the Inn, running up the hill under the pavement immediately in front of the Inn that had fractured, rather, it was the separate and unconnected much larger main twelve-inch gas pipe supply on the other side of the road close under the bank, which takes mains gas to Bath, Melksham, Chippenham, Calne and Devizes that had completely fractured. There was very thick fog with visibility 20 yards at the most that night and the road was icy, making driving very dangerous. Had the road not been frozen that fateful and foggy night, the gas would have probably escaped up into the air, instead of *seeping* underground along the crevasses under the road and then accumulating in the cellar underneath the Inn. It was not known how the accumulation of gas had ignited, but the Inn was heated by three fires each evening, which would have been allowed to burn down naturally. The Gas Board had previously been to the pub (to no avail) several times over the years, to try and locate and deal with reports of *'a smell of gas'*. Apparently, the smell was always there but no cause had ever been found. Seventeen gas leaks had been reported previously, over a distance of one and a quarter miles of pipe that ran down the hill alongside the pub!! There was often a smell of gas in the cellar.

The last complaint had been made a year before in February 1956. On a few occasions the pavement in front of the house was dug up and the gas pipe which fed the pub's meter was inspected.

Mrs Rogers said: ***'The smell of gas was still there after they [the Gas Board] had gone. We have got so tired of telling them. The smell of gas was always hanging around the house.'***

The inquest concluded that the explosion was due to a combination of three unfortunate circumstances - the presence of the boulder near the pipe, the washing away of the subsoil, and the surface of the ground being frost-bound, thereby preventing the gas escaping onto the atmosphere.

The Rising Sun site (alongside the bus shelter on the A4 Corsham to Box road) is now a grassed-over area overlooking the beautiful Box valley north towards Colerne. It's hard to believe that such a sad a tragedy happened there. There's little of the original structure remaining, but if you look closely, you can still see some of the footings and drains. It's certainly now a place of contemplation as the rest of the world hurtles by on the busy A4. The site should never be built on again.

At the end of July 2015 somebody leant on the old railings in front of the site, to take a 'seflie' photo, and the rotten posts collapsed, sending the person backwards down the slope hitting their head on the stones. Below is a 1927 plan of the Rising Sun.

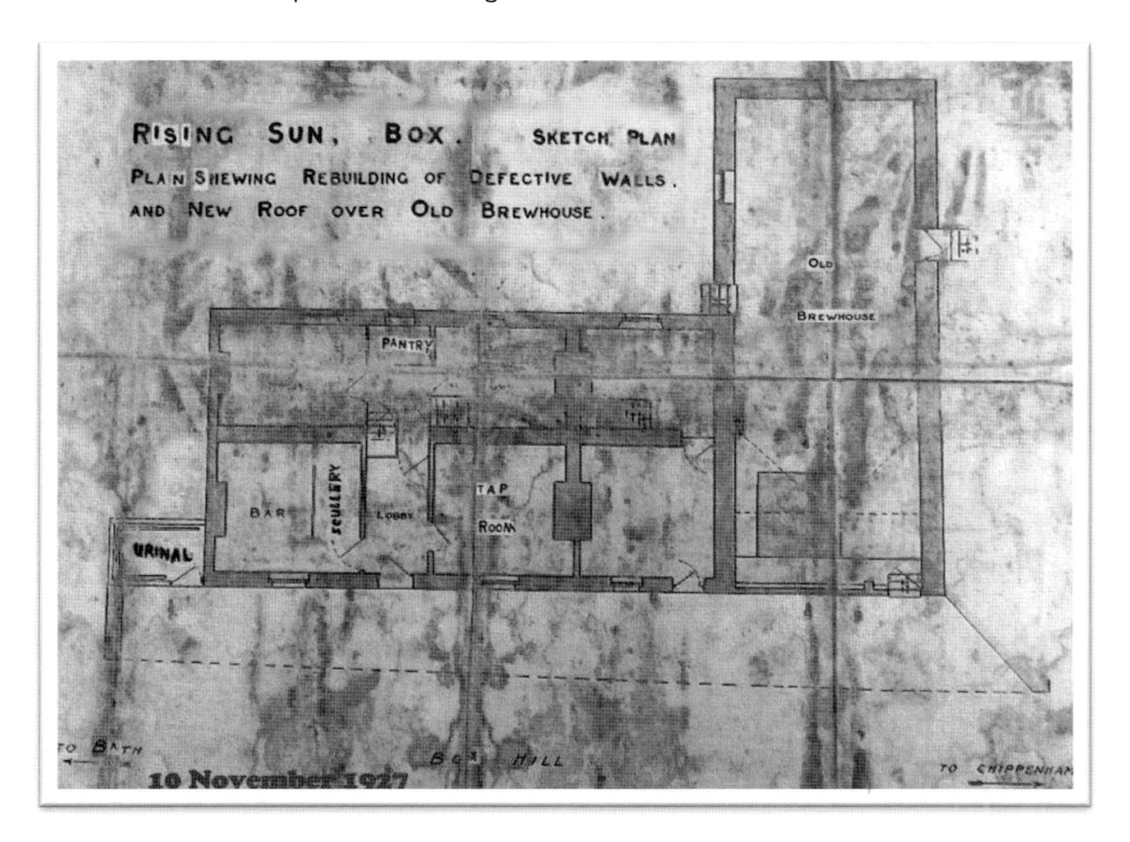

The site is owned by Wiltshire Council and was leased to Box Parish Council. The lease was recently handed back to Wiltshire when it came up for renewal and remains a memorial to the lives lost in 1957. The plot is small and subject to subsidence which would make it unsuitable to build on and there is presumably an issue of the cost of its maintenance including grass cutting.

An online petition called 'Friends of the Rising Sun View Point' to save the area was made in February 2018. ***When you pass by, give some thoughts to those who died there.***

Chapter 40. Road Signs - in WWII Wiltshire.

In preparation for a possible invasion in WWII many roads were blocked off at strategic points to prevent the enemy from using fast routes to their objectives.

Many of the road-blocks were semi-permanent, but some of these had to be later removed altogether, as they became more of an impediment to friends as to foes.

Removable blocks consisted of concrete cylinders of various sizes but typically about 3 feet (0.91 m) high and 2 feet (61 cm) in diameter; these could be manhandled into position as required.

In addition to blocking off the roads, in early June of 1940, nearly all of the country's entire road signs where removed and some were painted-out, on the premise that it would confuse the German army when they invaded England.

Railway station signs were also removed (like road signs); firstly for their metal content, and secondly to confuse the German invaders, if and when they ever did land, in getting around the cities and rural areas in England.

In London, some signs were changed so that they pointed in the wrong direction. The driving test was suspended for the duration of World War 2 and didn't resume until 1 November 1946. The examiners were redeployed to traffic duties and supervision of fuel rationing.

In 1942 some of the road signs were put back in their original location.

The Wiltshire road signs were all *stashed* in the Chippenham Council Depot during the war. Can you spot the ***CORSHAM/CHIPPENHAM*** signpost in the 1940 photo?

Chapter 41. Roman Coffin and Skeleton find at Hudswell Laboratories in 1942.

The discovery of a Roman coffin in Corsham in 1942 is the most significant major Roman *find* for our small town of Corsham.

Yet, the story of the young girl's skeleton and the location, has long disappeared from Corsham's history.........until now!

The young girl must have been an important person, as the coffin had been cut out from a solid piece of Bath limestone. Because she was found on the edge of where the Katherine Park housing estate is, I [Ed] have christened Corsham's Roman skeleton girl as *'Caterina'*.

The coffin was found on the site of the WWI Hudswell Laboratory. Tucked away, unbeknown to many of the residents of Corsham during World War II *(and for several years after)* there was a large security-fenced area consisting of several sizeable buildings dispersed around a hexagonal service road, whose purpose was the secretive examination and testing of large-scale ammunition. The Hudswell Laboratory site was located roughly where the Blackthorn Row, Privet Way, Elder Court, Black Acre and Bluebell Mead houses of Katherine Park now stand. Alongside the coffin's location these days, are also a number of beautiful lakes, footpaths and a large wood that borders onto Paddock Lane and Hudswell House to the west.

The Hudswell Laboratory:

The laboratory employed 300 men and women and was located at the back end of Hudswell in an area called *Black Acre*, a quarter of a mile North/East of Pockeredge Farm. The Hudswell Laboratory was an armaments ordinance testing factory, rather than a conventional laboratory. It was called a 'laboratory' to keep unwanted visitors away! The laboratory buildings were eventually demolished around the end of the 1960's. Only an old Marston shed and a few minor structures remained for a while. At one time, the old buildings could be seen if you looked south over the fence that ran alongside the old cinder running track that was known as the 'Peel Circus, Sheffield Ground'. The old running track now lies immediately beneath the large raised children's play-park on the Katherine Park estate.

The Hudswell Laboratories were part of the WWII fifty-acre Tunnel Quarry, underground Central Ammunition Depot (CAD), now completely empty of bombs, but still there in all its glory hidden 100 feet below the surface with all its conveyor belts and underground railways. The Hudswell Stone Quarry was originally opened in 1874 by Randell and Saunders and in 1875 was connected by a tramway running along Pockeredge Drive to the stone wharf alongside the main railway station in

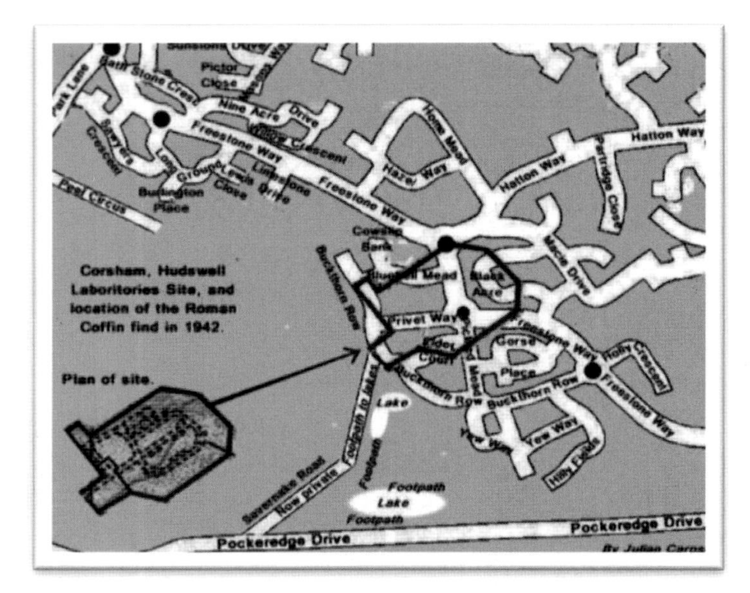

Corsham *(hence the local name Carriage Drive)*. The Hudswell Laboratory's main entrance was accessed via a narrow lane called Savernake Road *(now a small private track)* linking the laboratory to the end of Pockeredge Drive, near to Box Tunnel's eastern tunnel entrance *(on the Corsham side)*. On the right side of the Box Tunnel entrance near Potley, is a smaller opening which leads into an underground railway station platform where the ammunition trains where loaded/unloaded in WWII.

After the war, the Hudswell Laboratory was expanded to include new workshops where shells in dubious conditions were returned from distant battlefields to be examined, mechanically scraped, repainted, banded, stencilled and repackaged for long-term storage. Corsham residents often wondered at the time, where the loud bangs came from; it was from the two-cell proof yard, where ammunition was regularly test-fired. The laboratory site was so well hidden at that time that hardly a soul in Corsham knew that it was there at all.....or what its purpose was!

The Roman Coffin:

On the 3rd October 1942 a workman digging the foundations for a new building on the Hudswell Laboratory site, accidentally *'cracked'* off the corner of the coffin's huge lid with his pick-axe. Although the soil at the spot consisted of about 18 inches of virgin earth above brash, the coffin itself was only buried nine inches below in the surface. As the inquisitive workman gradually scraped away the soil, the Roman coffin started to emerge into the light for the first time in nearly 2,000 years. One can only imagine the workman's excitement at the time.

Col. A. H. Burn, a local resident and keen archaeologist, and Mr. A. Shaw Mellor of Box, a prominent member of the Wiltshire Archaeological Society, were summoned to inspected the site, unfortunately without discovering anything further of interest.

The coffin itself was carved out of one very fine piece of Bath stone, the exterior being well and carefully smoothed. It was quite plain with no recess for the head. Its exterior measurements were 5ft 6ins, long, 1ft. 11ins, broad and 1ft. 4ins, deep, with an interior length of 5ft. 2ins. The lid originally consisted of two pieces of stone each 2ft. 9ins. long.

When the huge stone lid was removed, inside appeared a skeleton considered to be that of a young Roman female of between 16-20 years of age. The skeleton was in good condition, the skull and teeth being especially well preserved. The body was lying extended on its back approximately in east to west alignment, with the left arm flexed at the elbow and with the left hand angled underneath the head as if she was sunbathing. No other objects were found in the coffin and it is somewhat surprising that no other remains have been found in the immediate vicinity. The coffin's probable date is somewhere between the second and fourth centuries A.D.

When Col. Burn and Mr. Shaw Mellor later carried out further investigations at Hudswell, they found pieces of Roman pottery in what appears to have been a Roman rubbish pit. These pieces were very fragmentary, although one piece was obviously of roof or floor tiling, approximately dating between the second and fourth centuries. The pottery was obviously of local manufacture; an Iron Age posthole was also found nearby. Previously, in July 1941, a bronze Roman coin identified later as belonging to Julian II (The Apostate, 355-363 A.D.) had been discovered from soil obtained near to the coffin site and then brought into the garden of a nearby house (probably in Paddock Lane).

Although the field where the coffin had been found had been trenched considerably for drainage purposes in the distant past, no trace of wall foundations were found. But the discovery of the coffin is regarded as inferring the presence not far away of a Roman habitation (as yet to be found!)

A two-page article concerning Caterina's find in 1942, written by the Royal Engineer's (RE) Colonel A. H. Burn, appeared in the Wiltshire Archaeological and Natural History Magazine (No. CLXXX June 1944 Vol. L). The exact location of Caterina, was detailed on a plan of the Hudswell Laboratory site at the time, but sadly the plan has long since disappeared. There was no mention of what happened to Caterina at the time, and the inference was that she may well have been covered back up.

Before the construction of the Katherine Park commenced during 2002-2010, an archaeological investigation by Bernard Phillips, *(at the request of Roy Canham, Wiltshire County Archaeologist)* took place, in an attempt to recover the Roman coffin.

The coffin was believed to be still in situ somewhere on the Katherine Park site, which at the time was being developed by Persimmon Homes (Wessex) Ltd. Large areas of topsoil were removed in two areas, totalling 300 square metres, but the investigation failed to find the burial site or the coffin. Nevertheless, three linear ditches *(earthwork believed to be a land boundary)* were encountered; one containing 2nd-3rd century pottery; and a fourth ditch was discovered of a more recent date. But no sign of the coffin or its incumbent was found on the old Hudswell Laboratory site...... and the bulldozers moved in.

After a long investigation by *Julian Carosi [Ed],* the Roman coffin has now been found! It lies in one of the dusty low cellars underneath the Octagon Room of Corsham Court, along with an old wooden placard explaining the coffin's history; confirming that the coffin was once exhibited for a short time at Corsham Court. In the 1940s, Corsham Court was probably the most suitable home for the large coffin. Further investigation via several museums and numerous different archived records has also revealed the whereabouts of Caterina's skeleton. Originally, the skeleton was sent to *'The Royal College of Surgeons'*, and from there to other scientific establishments. Today, Caterina's skeleton is held by the Natural History Museum in London where she now resides in two boxes!

The approximate date of Caterina's adolescent female skeleton is unknown, as it has not yet been radiocarbon dated. Access to Caterina at the Natural History Museum is possible for external researchers. Caterina's reference number at the Natural History Museum is NHMUK PA SK 3520.

Caterina is now part of the Natural History Museum's Romano-British comparative series, which has been studied by hundreds of researchers examining the human biology of the period that Caterina belonged to. The museum holds both the skull *(in its own box),* which matches that in the original find photo) and a partial set of postcrania i.e. part of the skeleton apart from the skull (more than is visible in the original photo) in its own box alongside the skull box.

We like to think that Caterina is 'one of us' in Corsham; and we'd love to have her back and lay her to rest in her home town of Corsham - but that seems very unlikely.

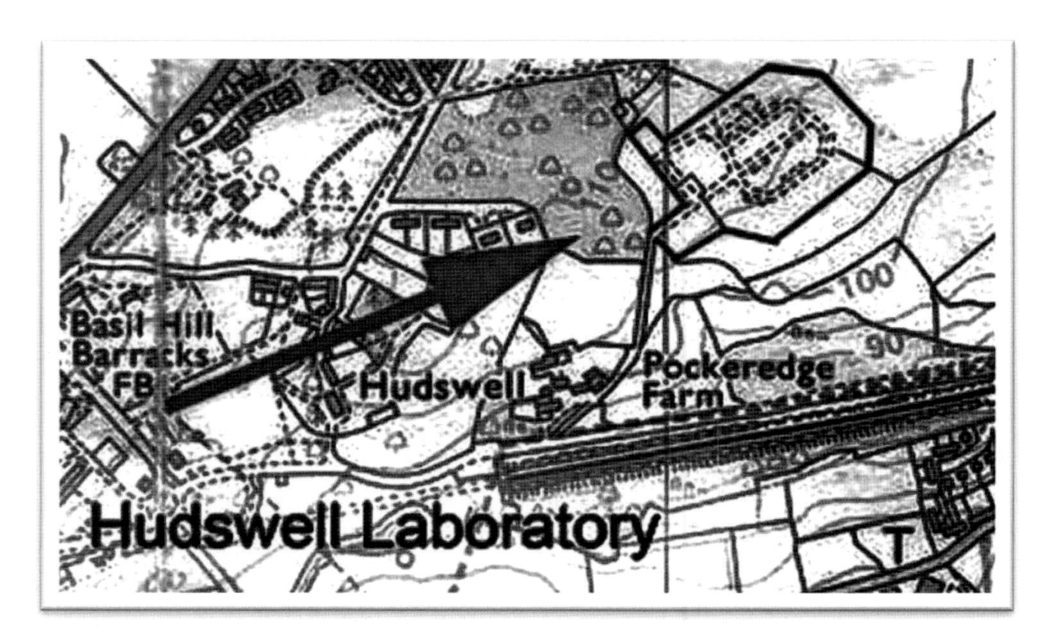

Many thanks go to the following people in helping investigate this article: ***Rob Kruszynski***: (Curator, anthropology collections, Department of Earth Sciences, Natural History Museum in London). ***Kate Tyte***: (Natural History Museum in London). ***Dr Marta Mirazon Lahr***: (Director of the Duckworth Laboratory, Leverhulme Centre for Human Evolutionary Studies, Department of Archaeology & Anthropology, University of Cambridge. ***Louise King***: (Archivist|Museums and Archives, the Royal College *of* Surgeons *of* England).
James Methuen-Campbell: (Corsham Court). ***Nick McCamley,*** Subterranean Britain. Second World. War Secret Bunkers. All the staff at the ***Devizes Museum.***

Chapter 42. Rossiter's Priory Stores Grocery Shop.

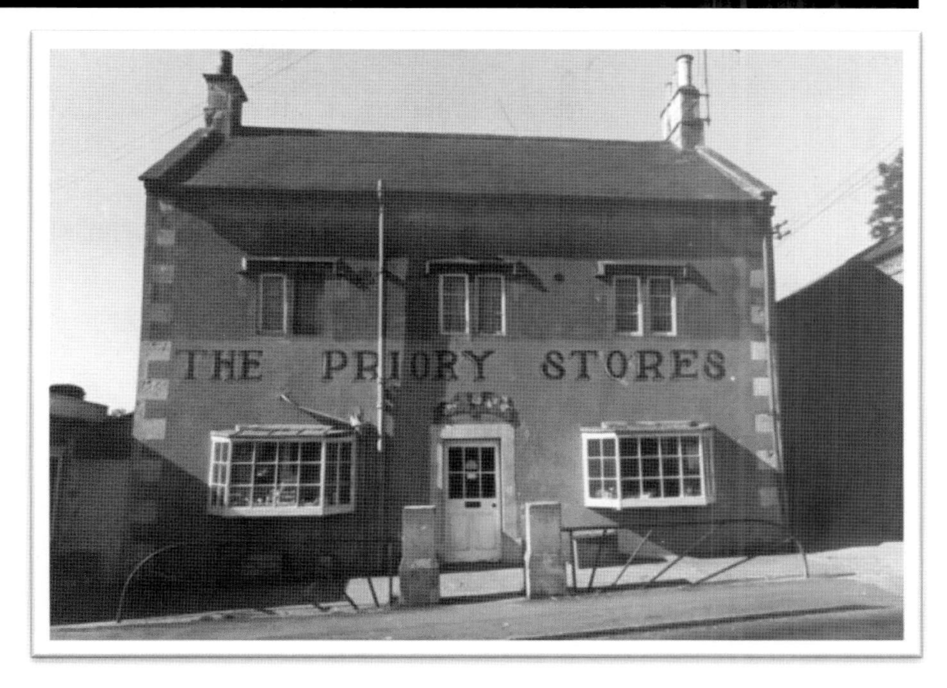

Can you remember Rossiter's general stores, halfway up on the left at 57 Priory Street, known as 'The Priory Stores'?

The previous owners of Priory Stores were Miss Bath and Miss Clifford.

The building was once a thriving source of sweets, groceries and many other household necessities.

It was the epitome of the *corner shop*, even though it was not on a corner! In the days before supermarkets in the 50s and 60s, Priory Stores was well used by Corsham residents.

The house is now a smart private residence and it's hard to believe that in years gone by, it was one of Corsham's most important shops. In one of the photographs below, you can see Joseph John, and Annie Rossiter standing by their back door which overlooked the rear of Arnolds Mead. Joseph was *previously a 'Decorator, Carpenter and General House Repairer'* and had a workshop in part of a disused cottage behind the Pack Horse Inn (now the Flemish Weaver) alongside the Town Hall.

The window of the little shop extension to the left front of the shop *(see photo on next page)* was always filled with weird and wonderful things! And the strange iron fence to the front of the building was an ideal place to lean your bike up against. Or for spinning yourself upside down on! I can still smell the *iron of it* on my hands to this day! The iron fence is still there today hidden in the hedge!

The houses in Priory Street have barely changed in the last 100 or so years.

In January 1950 the residents of Priory Street entertained the children of that street with a fancy dress party at the Regis School. This was followed by a pantomime 'Red Riding Hood' produced and presented by the junior helpers of the Priory Stores, under the supervision of Mr. Harry S. Rossiter. As the final curtain fell, Miss Geraldine Rossiter (ages 3) was presented with a bouquet of flowers by Bo-Peep (Margaret Pullen aged 3). Refreshments and films followed.

Can any of you remember Harry Rossiter's huge Octopus that stood in his front drive alongside the A4 opposite Pickwick Garage for many years?

Chapter 43. Skuse - Thomas. Thirty Years Afloat Abroad.

A True Experience of a Corsham Lad:

This is a small story about one of Corsham's forgotten souls who lived in the Victorian era. Thomas Skuse was born in Pickwick on the 4th April 1859, the son of a local shepherd who worked the fields around Corsham and Biddestone for 10s a week. Thomas had three brothers and one sister and his first job as a seven year-old was scaring the birds off the cornfields surrounding Middlewick Lane at 6p a week.

When he was eight years old, Thomas worked for one of his Uncles for 1s a week, and very often was rewarded by his uncle with *'boxed'* ears at work for some misdemeanour or another, and then 'strapped' once again for the same misdemeanour by his father's belt on returning home!

The photo here shows Tom as a lad of 15.

Thomas' mother died when he was only twelve-years old, and his father soon remarried. After an argument with one of his stepmother's visiting grandsons *(followed by a severe 'thrashing' by his father)* Thomas decided to leave home and live with his Uncle. Things were not much better there for Thomas, as his father later threatened to send him away to a *'Reformatory'*, which were evil places for treating children found guilty of minor crimes in the same way as adults. One can almost feel the pain of Thomas' situation, as rural family life in the Victorian era was obviously not quite as rosy as we'd like to believe it was.

Thomas went off to live with one of his Uncles in Wales, then into the coal pits in Newbridge, Pontyprid for 12s a week. He found the work too hard so he decided to run-away with one of his brothers. They walked all the way from Wales to Southampton and then on to Portsmouth - and later to London. It was a very long distance for those young legs! After his brother had enlisted, Thomas fell on hard times and had to spend some time in a Poorhouse, but managed to escape by enlisting *underage* into the Navy as an 'orphan'.

One of his early punishments in the Navy was to receive twelve *'stripes'* across his back on HMS Impregnable, dished out with a metal spoon tied to the corner of a dishcloth. One of Thomas' friends took eight of the stripes himself in his stead. It was probably the first time that Thomas had ever received an act of true friendship in his (so far) loveless young life.

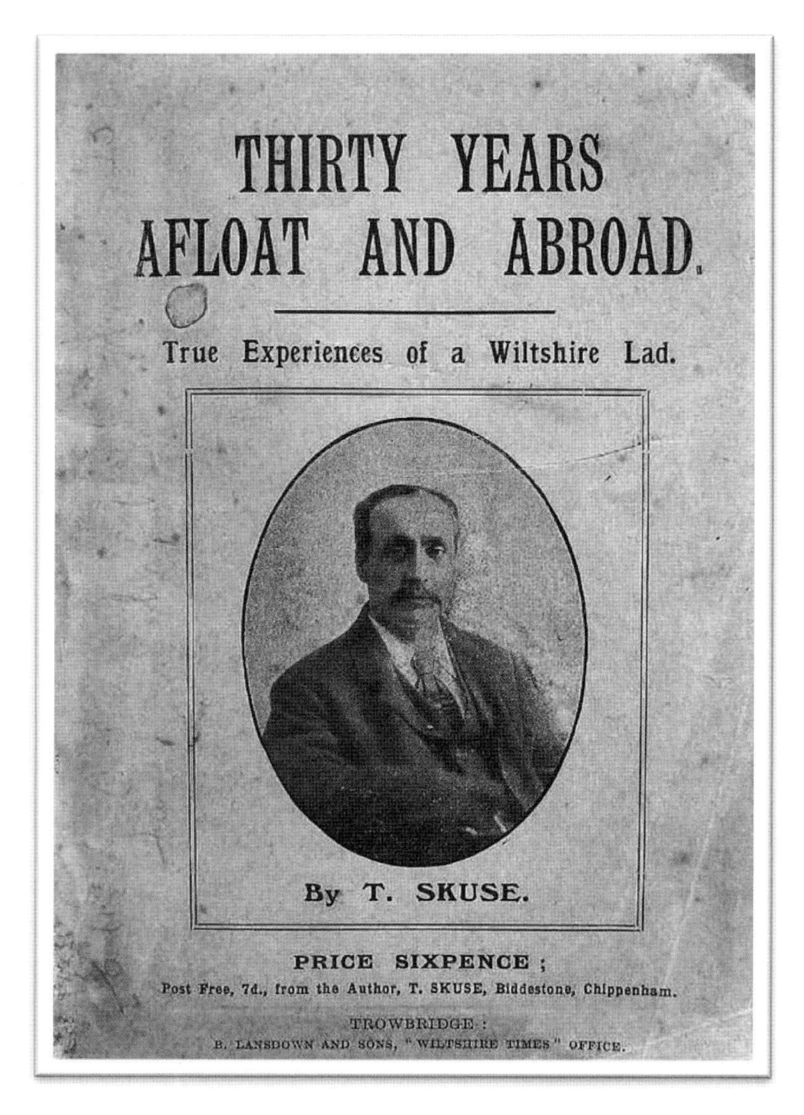

Thomas went on to travel the world. After three years service he arrived in Halifax, Nova Scotia on HMS Argus (a wooden paddle sloop). He then deserted the British Royal Navy and tried unsuccessfully to join the American Navy in Boston. Instead, he joined a working schooner bound for Lisbon and later the West Indies; and then back again to Boston where he was recognised by an old Naval chum Tom McQuire from the British man-o-war HMS Rover.

After 30 years afloat around the Americas and spending most of his money on drink, he arrived in Philadelphia and purchased a small plot of land during the *'Gold Rush'* there.

Thomas' luck changed, when he found a nugget of gold worth 50s *(about £200 in today's money)* in an Indian Reservation in California. He successfully carried on digging for more gold in the summer months and traded with the Indian tribes, all the way up to Oregon in the winter.

Thomas eventually married and settled down for a while, but his drinking demons never left him. On one occasion, he was so drunk that he fell down by the railway and stayed there until he was raised by a fireman's voice who saw him on the line, just in time to stop the engine from running over him. Then whilst walking home along the railway, he crossed a cattle guard and fell down into the four foot deep pit! He lay there oblivious to several trains which ran over the top of him as he slept off the effects of the alcohol!

He sold his Gold Mine, and invested £20 *(worth about £1,700 in today's money)* in oil stocks where he prospered for a short while. After his wife died, and was buried on Mt Vernon in Indiana, Thomas returned home to England via Southampton on 1st October 1902 after many years during which he lived 'life in the raw'.

Thomas moved to Biddestone, where he wrote a small booklet called *'Thirty Years Afloat Abroad'* outlining his life and dedicated to his deceased wife. Despite his troubles, Thomas was a religious man and throughout the book there are several biblical references; so his parents were obviously of Christian stock (even though the book calls them 'Primitives').

Thomas' story is a wonderful snapshot of life in those hard times, and you can't help but feel an affinity for him as a young child - you almost want to put your arms around him and take him back home with you.

The book was published in 1909 by *The Wiltshire Times, Trowbridge*. The small (120mm x 170mm) pamphlet contained 80 pages which included a plate of the author in naval dress at the age of fifteen *(see photo at the beginning of this Chapter).*

The following *Wiltshire Times* newspaper advertisement summarises Thomas's book: *'In his book "Thirty years afloat and abroad" (the true experiences of a Wiltshire lad), the author, Mr Tom Skuse who is a native of Pickwick, near Corsham, describes many wonderful adventures which befell him in different parts of the world.*

Early in life Mr. Skuse joined the Navy and became an able seaman, but whilst on a voyage, lured by the temptation of making money abroad, be escaped, and subsequently experienced much that was exciting and dangerous in South America, Portugal, West Africa, California, and other places.

He underwent many unpleasant experiences and hairbreadth escapes both on sea and land, his life, as he himself expresses it, ***being a tossed one, sometimes bidding fair, at other times overcome by evil.'*** *To those who have any idea of emigrating the book is recommended as a valuable guide, and certainly provides some entertaining reading. It has already gone through a first edition, and has now been issued in a cheaper form, the price being 6p.. post free 7p. It can be obtained from the author. Mr. T. Skuse, Biddestone, near Chippenham.'*

But times were much different in those days - and Thomas' story certainly brings this home. He suffered the addiction of the *'demon drink'* for great parts of his life, but you can understand how it would have offered him some solace in times of great distress and hunger and having a lack of fatherly love in his early years.

As he approached 60 Thomas (who had remarried) appears for a while in Chagford, a small market town and civil parish on the north-east edge of Dartmoor, in Devon. The following article appeared in the Western Times 29 April 1927:

CHAGFORD: The "Good News" caravan (??) is making a prolonged stay, in charge of Mr. and Mrs. Thomas Skuse. Mr. Skuse, who has served in the Navy and lost his right hand, has written two interesting books on his life experience, entitled, "Thirty Years Afloat and Abroad" and "Exciting Experiences in the Wild West".

We'd like to think that Thomas had some peace at the end of his life back home here in Wiltshire and later in Devon; and the following extract from the 1913 prefatory note written at the front of Thomas' little book by Pastor J. Smith, seems to indicate this.

'In the years that have passed, I have had further opportunities of seeing the life of the author, and my esteem of him has increased greatly. Without hesitation, I commend him to all, as a simple minded, sincere, persevering, and humble worker, and believer in our Lord's Kingdom.'

Amen to that - and you've not been forgotten by us in Corsham, Thomas Skuse.

Thomas Skuse. R.I.P

Chapter 44. Small Pox House and Small Pox in Corsham.

*Photo, courtesy of the Chippenham and Swindon History Centre of the old Small Pox House (*also known as the Pest House or Fever House*) alongside the crossroads opposite the Cross Keys Inn.*

The Small Pox house was originally a farm worker's cottage, part of farmer Burrow's Stowell Farm estate; the farm itself is about a mile or so away along the Allington road that turns left, off the A4 road just past the Cross Keys on the way to Chippenham.

The last occupants of the Small Pox house at 5 Cross Keys, Corsham (before it was demolished), were Mr. Pat Sythes, his wife Isabella and their young son Michael. Pat and Isabella met in Egypt where Isabella was an artist and Pat a serving Warrant Officer, Flight Engineer in the RAF; a career that lasted 36 years. Pat lost part of a leg below the knee due to shrapnel injuries received on one of his Lancaster Bomber missions in 1944 during the war.

In the late 1940s, Pat, Isabella and young Michael were living for a while with Isabella's sister (Mrs. Yvonne Marcella Leahy) in one of the Kings Avenue prefab bungalows very near to the Cross Keys, with her husband and daughter Maureen (now Mrs. Maureen Elliot of Bellwood, Pickwick). Yvonne informed her sister Isabella that the Small Pox House was empty and Pat Sythes, his wife Isabella and their son subsequently moved into the Small Pox house which became their home for over fifteen years.

When they moved in, the Small Pox House had gas lighting an outside privy with a wooden plank, no electric and no mains water; the garden well supplied all their needs! The house had a cellar that projected out under the ground towards the main road. In the winter, the cellar would regularly flood. The house consisted of two rooms downstairs, a kitchen to the west side and a living room to the east. A staircase led directly up from the kitchen into the two upstairs bedrooms. A small set of steps led from the east bedroom up into the small attic which was split into two and used mainly as a play room/den for their only child young Michael.

The house was so cold in the winter, that Michael's father covered young Michael with his RAF greatcoat to keep him warm in bed. The glass of water placed alongside, very often turned completely to ice by the morning! Isabella later became a seamstress and made dresses for Lady Methuen.

Here is a photo of a *cool* looking sixteen-year-old Michael with his pride and joy, a 150cc Lambretta scooter. In the background is the Small Pox house coal bucket sitting underneath a stone slabbed house porch that faced south towards Corsham. The front door lock had a huge cast iron key - most probably, still the original lock from when the house was built.

Most of the windows in the house had bench seats, as the rooms were too small to have any commodious furniture like the houses of today. As part of improvements to the Cross Keys junction, the house was designated to be knocked down to allow traffic lights to be installed and improve the safety of the crossroads.

To the west of the house, running alongside the main road, was a small nursery. This too, disappeared when the old Regis prefab estate bungalows were bulldozed to make way for the modern Council houses built in the late 60's.

Mr. Pat Sythes, his wife Isabella and their young son Michael moved across town in 1966 to 14 Prospect (Stowford), just before the Small Pox house was demolished. Mr. Pat Sythes and his wife Isabella are buried in St. Patrick's Catholic Church in Corsham. Young Michael, now 75, lives in the lovely village of Whitley on the edge of Corsham with his family.

There are very few photographs of the Small Pox house. In the next photo, you can just about see the north face of the building to the left of the lamppost.

SMALL POX IN CORSHAM: Smallpox is an extremely contagious and deadly virus for which there is no known cure. Due to worldwide vaccination this disease has been completely eradicated. There were two common and two rare forms of smallpox. The two common forms were known as variola minor and variola major. The two rare forms of smallpox were known as hemorrhagic and malignant, both of which carried a very high fatality rate. The virus is an airborne disease that spreads fast by coughing, sneezing, by direct contact with any bodily fluids or by sharing contaminated clothing or bedding. The smallpox vaccine created by Edward Jenner in 1758, was the first successful vaccine to be developed. He observed that milkmaids who had previously caught cowpox did not catch smallpox. He showed that inoculated vaccinia protected against the inoculated variola virus and went on to save millions of lives. It was one of the deadliest diseases known to humans. By 1853 smallpox vaccination was a legal requirement for newborns in England and Wales. In the commencement of his studies, Dr. Jenner was instrumental in forming the *Fleece Medical Society* which had for its object the improvement of medical science.

The following were among the members: ***Dr. Ludlow of Corsham*** **near Bath**, Dr. Parry of Bath, Dr. Hicks of Bristol, Dr. Mathews of Hereford, Mr. Paytherus and Dr. Jenner himself. The meetings (followed by dinner) were chiefly held at the Fleece Inn at Rodborough (in the district of Stroud, Gloucestershire) and occasionally in other parts of the country.

The idea at the time was to have isolation hospitals in every district, ready in the event of cases occurring, for reception and treatment of smallpox and other diseases.

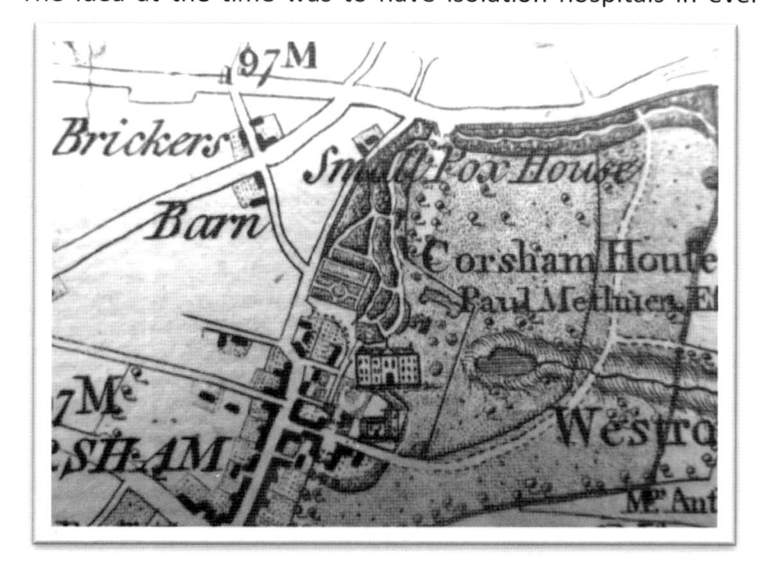

There was an Isolation Hospital in nearby Chippenham at Frogwell, Devizes and in Comb Down in Bath and this is where any isolated Corsham smallpox patients would have been taken. There was also a pest house for victims of infectious diseases, such as smallpox, on Bowden Hill which continued to be used throughout the 18th century.

There are no records to show why Corsham's No.5 Cross Keys cottage was called the *Small Pox* house, or if it was ever used for isolating patients suffering with smallpox. The house was probably just a small cottage with an outside toilet closet with a plank of wood for a seat!

The 'Small Pox House' name appears in the 1773 Andrews' & Dury's Map of Wiltshire.

In 1824 the Corsham Burial Records *(see below)* show how quickly smallpox can spread within a family unit. In the house of Mr. and Mrs. Bath who resided in Corshamside, six died of smallpox in less than three weeks of each other.

On 4 February 13-year-old Anne Bath dies of smallpox (SP). On 10 February, 35-year-old Mrs. Elizabeth Bath has a stillborn baby named John, a week later on 18 February, her 11-year-old twins Jane Bath and her sister Ann both pass away - all dying of the smallpox virus. Three days later on 21 February mother Mrs. Elizabeth Bath and her 2 year old son David pass away.

1824	Feb	4	BATH	Anne	13	d John,SP,Corsham Side
1824	Feb	10	MANLEY	John	61	Pickwick
1824	Feb	10	BATH	child	0	c John stillborn [sextons book
1824	Feb	12	WILTSHIRE	Elizabeth	47	
1824	Feb	13	NORRIS	Matthew	56	killed by falling stone in qua
1824	Feb	18	BATH	Jane	11	Corsham Side,s pox [Reg]
1824	Feb	18	BATH	Ann	11	Corsham Side,s pox [sextons bo
1824	Feb	21	MOODY	James	5m	s John, Gastard
1824	Feb	21	BATH	Elizabeth	35	wife of John,s pox
1824	Feb	21	BATH	David	2	s John,SP,Corsham Side

In 1829, a notice *(see photo below)* is posted around Chippenham asking the public not to expose themselves on the streets and highways if they had smallpox, otherwise they would be imprisoned!

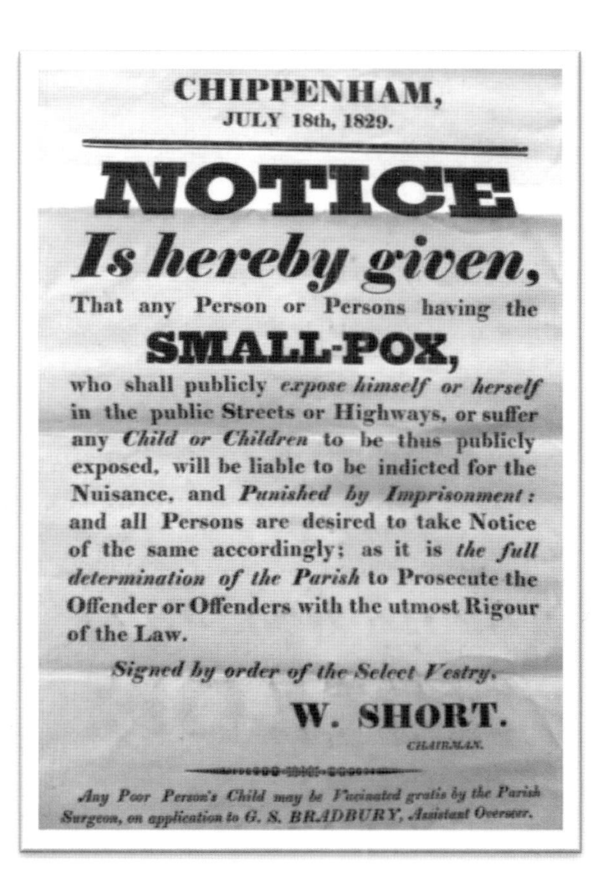

CHIPPENHAM,
JULY 18th, 1829.

NOTICE
Is hereby given,
That any Person or Persons having the
SMALL-POX,
who shall publicly *expose himself or herself* in the public Streets or Highways, or suffer any *Child or Children* to be thus publicly exposed, will be liable to be indicted for the Nuisance, and *Punished by Imprisonment:* and all Persons are desired to take Notice of the same accordingly; as it is *the full determination of the Parish* to Prosecute the Offender or Offenders with the utmost Rigour of the Law.

Signed by order of the Select Vestry.

W. SHORT.
CHAIRMAN.

Any Poor Person's Child may be Vaccinated gratis by the Parish Surgeon, on application to G. S. BRADBURY, Assistant Overseer.

In 1840 smallpox is raging in Corsham again. A railroad labourer who recently arrived in Corsham was seized with the malady and died a few days later. Only one friend attended him in his illness and it was not without difficulty that enough bearers could be procured from his railroad labourers.

It was a dreary aspect at the December evening graveside, with only one lantern available to light up the burial. The solitary person to attend the ceremony was he who kindly attended him in his short illness.

On 6 March 1888 a public meeting was held in the Corsham Town Hall to discuss the *Smallpox Vaccination Question*. The Registrar General showed that in 1881, 58 children had died from cow-pox or vaccination; in 1882, 65 in 1883, 55; 1884, 53; 1885, 59; and in 1886, 45.

Chairman Mr. J. Fuller who presided over the large audience, told them that this was purely a non-political subject. Speaker Mr. Philip Braham, F.C.S. said that the smallpox vaccination which had a powerful effect upon the organism should be performed within three months of the birth of a child.

He believed that the vaccination had an *injurious influence* upon the teeth of a child and that it was not conductive to the health of an infant, as proved by the disquietude of sufferers for at least 12 days. Mr. Philip Braham believed that all the Vaccination Acts that had been *smuggled though* Parliament was the means of increasing the death-rate from smallpox, syphilis and other diseases. He contended that vaccination was powerless to prevent smallpox and that the decline of the disease was due to improved sanitation - *little did they know! [Ed]*

The Rev. G. Newham replied that; '*Despite all that he had heard that evening, he believed the vaccination laws had been the means of an incredible amount of good and what women would like to have her face pitted all over with the marks of smallpox?*' He believed that very few children suffered from vaccination and that the suffering of the few where nothing compared to the advantages which the whole community derived from vaccination.

Since the passing of the law to make vaccination compulsory the terrible disease of smallpox had diminished. The Rev. G. Newham finished his speech by saying, *"He did not think it gracious on the part of anyone to turn around and find fault with Parliament for making those laws".* [Applause and groans from the audience!']

Mr. Edwin Hill and Mr. Harbuut of Bath who were seated in the Town Hall audience, strongly denounced the system of vaccination, and contended that the decline in the number of cases of smallpox was due more to the efforts of the sanitary engineers, than to the vaccination laws.

1899: In December, George Alex Gifford a farmer of Colerne and Isaac Aubrey Joyce of Ridge Farm Corsham, were summoned for neglecting to have their children vaccinated against smallpox. They were ordered to pay the court 17s.

In 1901 two men who attempted to sell anti-Vaccinators refused to pay their fines for non-compliance of the *Vaccination Laws*. A portion of their goods were retrieved and offered for sale in the presence of a large crowd outside the Corsham Town Hall. No bidders could be found and the goods were returned to their owners.

They were then put on a conveyance with a placard advertising 'Vaccinated Furniture' and paraded round the parish accompanied by a crowd of vociferous people headed by the Corsham Town band.

In October 1901 Lady Dickson Poynder of Hartham Park, who had been staying at her town house in Chesterfield Gardens, contracted smallpox from one of her footmen. It was hoped that the case would be a mild one. Her husband Sir John was away in America at the time. By early November, Lady Dickson Poynder and her footman were back home in Hartham Park.

There was some concern that the servant who had smallpox had left Hartham without the consent of the Medical Officer. Notices were put up warning visitors to the house.

In 1903 a stableman from Corsham was taken ill and on being examined, was found to have all the symptoms of smallpox. The patient was isolated by Dr. Briscoe.

In the spring of 1913 a young woman living at Green Hill in Neston, who lived in the local general shop with her grandmother, contracted smallpox. The source of infection was not discovered and the patient recovered well after the attack.

During a Corsham Parish Meeting, it was explained by Medical Officer Mr. Field that the cost incurred in dealing with a recent case of smallpox at Corsham was as follows. Expenses of the Nurse came to £17. 1s, compensation for damage to bedding etc. came to £6. 5s, making a total of £23. 6s (nearly £2,000 in today's money!).

The Inspector continued by saying, *"God save us from any number of smallpox cases if we have to pay all these expenses for one."*

The Parish Chairman replied, "*It is much cheaper than maintaining a hospital*".

Mr. Bolton said, *"Two guineas a week is a very small sum indeed for nursing a smallpox case."*

It was resolved to pay the whole costs, with Mr. Field being the only dissentient.

The Small Pox House location is registered as plot 1304 on the Corsham Tythe Map, and was demolished around 1966/67.

Note the old Bricker's Barn turnpike road ran <u>*behind*</u> *the Cross Keys Inn (see Chapter 53).*

A tythe (chiefly British spelling of the word tithe) is a tenth part of one's annual income contributed to support the clergy or a church.

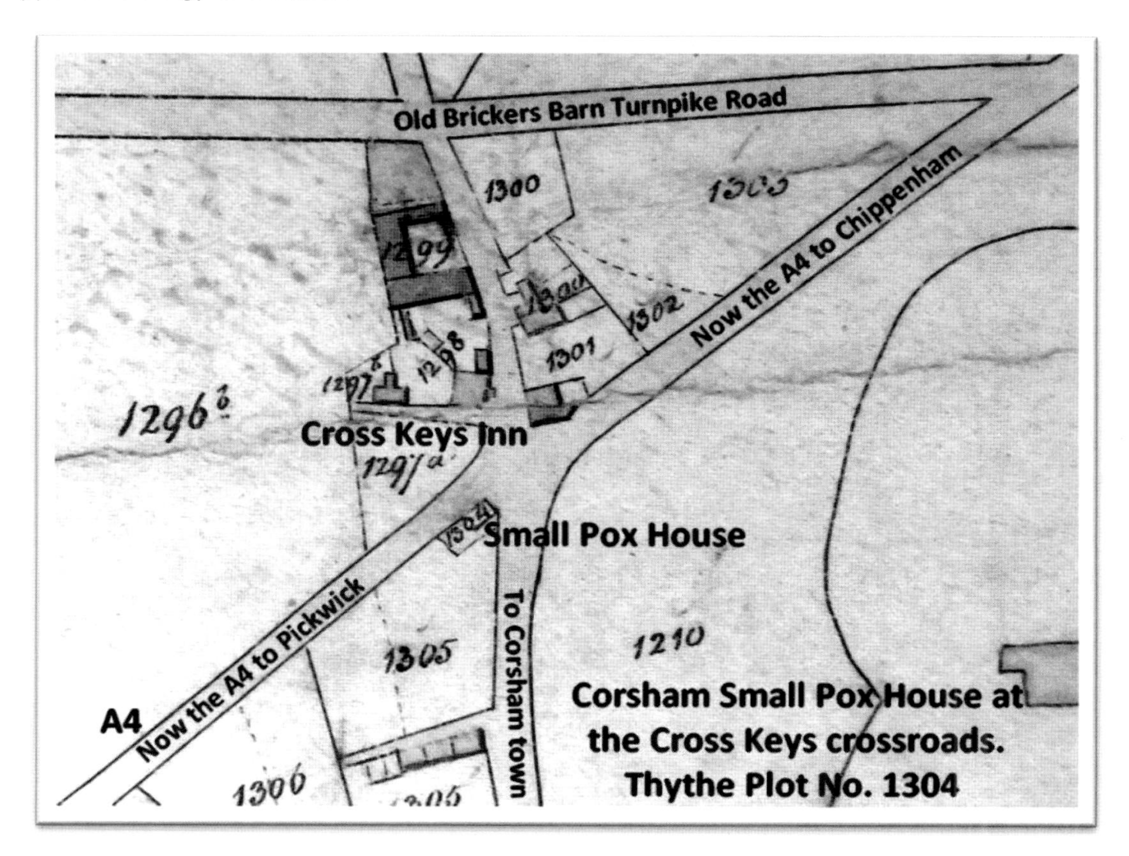

Many thanks go to Michael Sythes and Maureen Elliot for telling their story of the Small Pox House.

Chapter 45. Spackman - Sylvia's Story

Sylvia Hope Spackman once lived in Dill House (previously Rose Cottage) at the top of Priory Street alongside the flats, just as the road bears right. [Ed] I remember seeing Sylvia with her white hair looking out of the tiny attic window at the very top of Dill House as we walked down the footpath and across Priory Street on our way to the Regis Primary School in the 1950s, making us feel a little scared as children. I think we must have been doing this lonely old lady an injustice, as she was once a talented teacher who travelled the world, and was haunted by her own tragic love affair.

The sketch here shows *Miss Spackman,* pencil on paper, 1953, © Howard Hodgkin.

Below is Sylvia's story - but make sure you've got a supply of handkerchiefs *at the ready!* Sylvia Hope Spackman was the oldest of the renowned Corsham photographer Herbert Spackman's three daughters. Sylvia was born in New Zealand on 2nd February 1898. It was Sylvia's birth that prompted Herbert to seriously take up photography. Herbert (who had earlier emigrated to New Zealand) returned home to England in 1900 with his family. They later moved into Rose Cottage at the top of Priory Street on 30th August 1906.

When Sylvia was 4 years old, she started her education at Miss Laws' Dame School in Corsham, and remained under her tutelage until 1910. A Dame School is a small primary school run by elderly women, especially in their own homes. Sylvia was a talented student who was later awarded a scholarship to attend the Chippenham Secondary School; she travelled there by train each day. In 1912 Sylvia was awarded the French Prize and also passed her Oxford Junior Scholarship award. She then spent a year at the Melksham Lowbourne Elementary School as a pupil-teacher learning her trade. In 1917 Sylvia attended college in Reading studying French to become a qualified language teacher. *The sketch here, is the actual view of the attic where Sylvia used to sit and watch the world go by.*

She went on to teach at the Chippenham College and in France at a large school in Aurillac. In 1922 she became the French mistress at the Leamington Secondary School. In July of 1924 she was awarded a second class Honours Degree in English and French and in 1925 she studied shorthand, typing and business studies before moving to Belgium for work. In November 1925 she returned to London, working in an engineering firm and later in 1927 as a personal assistant to an American in London. In the meantime, she was learning German.

Photo shows Sylvia's father Herbert Spackman.

In 1927 Sylvia also worked for a while in an office with Nestles in Vevey, Switzerland. The next few years saw her return to England where she had several jobs including one in Jersey. In short, Sylvia was indeed, a very talented highly educated foreign language teacher, who had many jobs here in England and abroad.

In 1936 when working as a teacher in the School of Language in Stettin, East Germany, Sylvia became romantically attached to a German Spanish teacher called Otto Schwarz and they later became engaged. This was in the era when Hitler was in his ascendancy. One of Sylvia's teaching colleagues, referred to only as 'Mr. P., mysteriously disappeared in October 1937 without a trace. Sylvia's new found love Otto, was technically still married to his first wife who had recently deserted him. In an act of revenge (more likely jealousy), Otto's wife reported him to the Gestapo for consorting with Jews. When Otto was interrogated and asked if he knew any Jews, he coolly replied, *'Of course I know Jews, I am a language teacher and have a living to earn'.* Somehow, he got away with it!

Otto employed Mr Hanff, a Jewish Lawyer to undertake a divorce case against his wife for betraying him to the Gestapo. In the meantime, Sylvia and Otto, persuaded Mr Hanff's young son Dietrich to write to Sylvia's younger sister Heather and her husband Robin Tanner in England, to see if they could help raise £100 *(a substantial amount of money in those days, worth nearly £5,000 today)* as a guarantee to get young Dietrich safely over to England, as he was now in great danger from the Nazis. Luckily, in March his permit came through and Dietrich left Germany on 1st April 1939 in the *nick of time* to escape incarceration in one of the concentration camps. mThe Tanner's also desperately tried to get Dietrich's Jewish parents safely over to England as well, but the additional application form arrived too late and Dietrich's parents both sadly perished in the holocaust along with the rest of Dietrich's family in the gas chambers of the Piaski ghetto in southeast Poland; a ghetto that was plagued by disease and hunger. Due to the lack of space there, the poor ghetto residents had to sleep in turns. When Dietrich Hanff finally arrived in England, he was adopted by Sylvia's sister Heather (nee Spackman) and her husband Robin Tanner and lived with them just outside of Chippenham for the rest of his life, becoming a naturalised British citizen in 1947. Dietrich passed away at Chippenham on May 14th 1992. **R.I.P.**

The photo here, shows left to right, Heather Tanner, Dietrich and Robin Tanner.

As *War* threatened on the continent, Sylvia returned to England from Germany to escape the Nazis and to care for her ailing diabetic father Herbert, who later died in April 1949. Herbert was buried in the Ladbrook Lane cemetery along with his wife Daisy. **R.I.P.**

Sylvia was desperately hoping to eventually marry her love Otto Schwarz. A few months after Sylvia returned from East Germany to England, Otto visited her in the summer of 1939 and returned to Germany on 2nd August. Wondering when the two lovers would ever get to see each other again, they parted with great sorrow - this was sadly the last time Sylvia ever saw Otto.

A year later, the Red Cross, via the Bath Citizens' Advice Bureau told Sylvia that Otto was still teaching in Stettin and a message was received in January 1941 to her from Otto saying, *'I wait for you.....Heaps of love to all.'* In 1945 a final message was received from Sylvia's German employer, Madame Ley, saying that Otto was still in Stettin, but was *'complaining of starvation rations in the town'*. One can only imagine Sylvia's thoughts on a lost love and the brutality of war. And what sort of life Otto had had in post-WWII East Germany. Sylvia never married and because of the War she never returned to Germany. After her father's death, Sylvia continued to live in Rose Cottage, sub-letting out rooms to those who found it difficult to find accommodation in Corsham and to the Bath Academy of Art Students when they were based at Corsham Court.

The photo shows Sylvia on 27 September 1920 in a Persian costume.

Sylvia Hope Spackman passed away in 1965. R.I.P. Sylvia. Dill House, No. 69 Priory Street, was later owned by Jenny Davis in the 70's, a tutor at the Art College in Corsham Court with her husband, two children and the dog all sharing the rambling house with three students and their visitors.

If you want to know more about Sylvia and her family - you can find more details about her life in *'A Life Revealed'*. From the Diaries of Herbert Spackman, by Ernest Hird; first published in 2008.

Chapter 46. Speke Memorial.

The John Hanning Speke Memorial:

In the far corner of a large field on the edge of Corsham, near to the second *Fiveways* junction on the B3109 road to Bradford-on-Avon is a famous memorial dedicated to John Hanning Speke (4 May 1827 - 15 September 1864). Another much larger memorial to Speke was erected at Kensington Gardens in London in 1866 two years after his unexplained death in Corsham. Speke was associated with discovering the source of the Nile in 1862 and the discovery of Lake Victoria as part of Burton's expedition to Africa in 1858.

[Ed] As a teenager, I worked for a while for Mr Webb the local farmer at Atworth. As I was *tilling* the *'memorial'* field up and down in a tractor one day, I came across a strange looking memorial hidden in the undergrowth alongside the dry stone wall. This led me into reading Speke's story in an old dusty book found on the shelves of Corsham library. I became fascinated with this Victorian explorer. I'd never heard of **John Hanning Speke** before - and certainly not as being anyone famously linked with Corsham.

Captain Speke often stayed with his brother William at Monks Park and sometimes appeared at the local church with him. They also had another brother, a clergyman who created great excitement once, by disappearing the day before his wedding. As his hat and coat were found on the banks of a river, it was generally supposed that he had drowned himself, but no traces of the body could be found. He turned up in London six weeks later. He eventually did marry a few years after, but not to his old sweetheart, who naturally declined to have anything more to do with her erratic lover!

'Accidental death by explosion of a gun.'

The memorial marks the spot where John Hanning-Speke mysteriously died on 15 September in 1864. Thirty seven year old, unmarried Speke was visiting his Uncle Mr. J. Fuller at Neston Park and in the afternoon, went out *partridge shooting* at about half-past two with George Fuller and his gamekeeper Daniel Davis.

After about two hours of shooting, Speke mounted a two foot high, loose stone opening in a dry stone wall, with the gun held in his hand, which was unfortunately pointed towards himself. For some means never ascertained, the gun went off, lodging the whole contents of a *charge* in his abdomen. At the time of the accident, Speke's companions George Fuller and Daniel Davis were both about sixty yards away when they heard the gun fire.

George Fuller tried to hold the blood back with his hand and as he did so, Speke mumbled, *'Don't move me'*. Fuller left the gamekeeper Daniel Davis with Speke and quickly went for assistance.

Speke survived for fifteen minutes, but by the time Mr. Thomas Fitzherbert Snow the surgeon from Box had arrived, Speke had already died from the wound on his left side, near the breast and about an inch long. The wound's trajectory lead in an upward direction towards the spine and had passed through the lungs, dividing all the vessels near the heart, but not touching the heart itself.

After the accident, it was noted that the right-hand barrel of the gun was half-cocked and the left had been discharged. The gun was a Lancaster breech-loader without a safety guard, but generally quite a safe gun. Speke was thirty-seven when he died.

John Hanning Speke discovered the source of the Nile on August 3rd, 1858. When exploring Africa with Burton, both of them became ill. When Speke recovered, he set off in command of a small party without Burton (who remained behind, still ill in camp). Speke came upon what he later described as *'a vast expanse of the pale-blue waters'* of a northern lake. He named it Lake Victoria and believed, correctly, that it was the source of the Nile. Burton would not accept Speke's claim to have discovered the Nile's source, for which he felt there was no convincing evidence at that time.

Burton believed that the true source was more likely to be 'his' Lake Tanganyika. But Speke got back to England in May 1859 before Burton and announced that he had found the source of the Nile. Burton felt belittled and was infuriated by Speke's account of the expedition in Blackwood's Edinburgh Magazine. The breach between them was never healed.

Speke was due to give a speech the next day (after his death) at the British Association in Bath (Friday 16 September) and to have an encounter with Captain Burton in a public discussion as to the true source of the Nile, a very contentious subject at the time!

The two men, once the best of friends, were now completely at loggerheads and another debate between them was eagerly awaited for by the public. It was not until years later that Speke was proved to have been right and that Lake Victoria Nyanza is the source of the White Nile (though the lake has several feeder rivers).

An inquest was held in the residence of the deceased's brother Mr. W. Speke of Monks Park Corsham. The coroner from Corsham was Mr. Kemm and the jury was made up from the respectable inhabitants of Corsham.

After hearing all the evidence as to the cause of the accident, the jury unanimously recorded a verdict of, *'Accidental death by explosion of a gun.'* adding that, *'The deceased had died from the accidental discharge of his own gun, after living a quarter of an hour.'* But there remains some unfounded supposition that he could/may have committed suicide.

The body was removed on the Monday following the inquest, for internment in the family vault at Jordans, in Somersetshire.

'The breach between them was never healed.'

A Rankcolor theatrical film movie called Mountains of the Moon was made in 1990, depicting the 1857-1858 journey of Richard Francis Burton and John Hanning Speke on their expedition into Central Africa.

The Speke memorial in Corsham reads:

'THE DISTINGUISHED AND ENTERPRISING AFRICAN TRAVELLER CAPTAIN JOHN HANNING SPEKE LOST HIS LIFE BY THE ACCIDENTAL EXPLOSION OF HIS GUN SEPTEMBER 15TH 1864.'

A few years before his expedition to discover the source of the Nile, Speke had survived a harrowing ordeal and was very lucky to be alive. After a term of ten years service was completed, Captain Speke was appointed to an expedition organised by the Bombay Government for exploring the Somali countryside in 1854. The expedition was a failure, due to the mismanagement of the native officer who was placed at the head of the party. During the expedition, Speke had been taken prisoner by the treacherous Somali; how he managed to escape was little short of a miracle. Whilst his hands were bound, his jailer who held Speke tethered by a rope, coolly stabbed him with a spear, and then knocked him down with the spear almost cutting Speke's jugular artery. The spear was then jabbed towards Speke's heart but in raising his bound hands in defence, the spear gorged the flesh on one of his hands to the bone.

The villain then stepped back a pace and dashed his spear down the bone of Speke's thigh. Speke grabbed the spear with both hands but was then struck a violent blow. The Somali had withdrawn a shillelah *(a thick wooden cudgel)* from his girdle and cracked Speke's arm, making him fall to the floor in agony. The captor then dropped the rope that tethered Speke to him, walked back a dozed paces and rushed Speke with a savage fury, plunging his spear through the thick part of Speke's thigh and into the ground, passing it between the thigh bone and the large sinew below.

Speke, fearing for his life, sprang upon his legs and gave the miscreant such a backhander with his double-bound fists that the Somali lost his presence of mind. Taking the opportunity, Speke now almost naked, ran away as fast as he could over the shingle beach. The man quickly followed and threw his spear at Speke like a javelin but Speke *ducked* down at the last minute and the missile flew over him. Having the better of the savage, the man gave up, yet Speke still had forty more savages to pass through. Luckily, they were scattered a little distance away looking for what *spoils* they could pick up. These men seeing Speke, tried to cut off his escape but he managed to dodge them and their spears to reach the seashore having the satisfaction of seeing the last man give up the pursuit. Speke, now faint with the loss of blood, sat on a mound of sand and using his teeth, unpicked the knots which bound his hands. He was found there later by some members of his party who were looking for him and was taken back to camp in a sorrowful state.

Once he had recovered from his wounds, Speke returned to England and though still a cripple, applied and obtained employment fighting in the Crimean war as a Captain in a Turkish Regiment.

Where is the Speke Memorial in Corsham?

There are two ways that you can get to the Speke memorial; one via a public footpath that starts at Chapel Plaister on the B3109 Bradford Road between Corsham and Bradford-on-Avon, and secondly, via a shorter route commencing from the public footpath entry on the edge of the busy A365 Bath road, approximately 200 yards left from the Fiveways traffic lights, near Wormwood Farm towards Melksham (more details are below).

If you visit by car, the easiest way to the memorial is via the footpath entrance on the very edge of the A365. If you drive from Corsham towards Bradford-on-Avon on the B3109, when you get to the traffic lights at Fiveways, turn left towards Melksham and Atworth. About 200 yards from the traffic lights, you come to a right-hand bend at the top of the hill. Turn left up the small country road on the bend and park your car on the side of the verge.

Note: Don't try and drive back out the same way, as it is a very dangerous bend! When you make your return journey, instead, just head north up the lane, as it brings you out at Neston. The walk back through the lane to Neston is also very nice! After parking the car in the lane, make your way back to the main road, and a few metres back towards the Five-Ways traffic lights you will see a rambler's sign pointing into the field. Enter the field, and keep the dry-stone wall to your right. The monument is about 100 yards in. You can't miss it. The monument is up against the dry stone wall near to a tall electricity pole - you really can't miss it! Please be careful if you have children, as the main road here is fast and busy and very dangerous, and it's on a sharp bend! The alternative way there, is to park by Chapel Plaister and walk along the public footpath through the field. Depending on what time of the year you visit, you may have to skirt around the edge of the field if crops are growing.

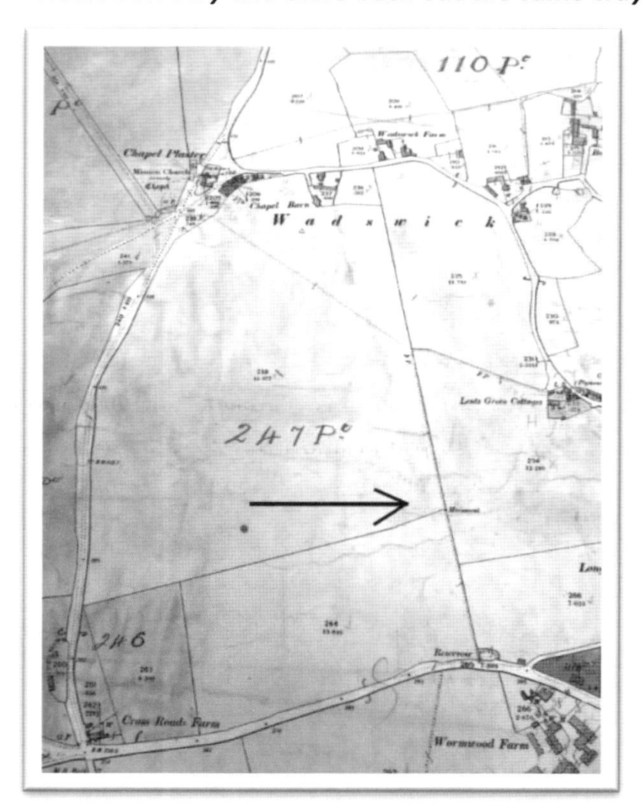

Chapter 47. Starwell (or Holy Well) Corsham.

If you were brought up in Corsham, you most probably would have visited this place sometime in your childhood.

WHERE IS IT? Heading west on the A4 towards Chippenham from the Cross Keys Inn traffic lights at Corsham, take the first left down the country lane. Pass Stowell Farm on your left, and just past the crossroads, as the road dips and turns sharp right, you'll see a field entrance on your left with a rusty old metal farm gate. Starwell is approximately to the front/right of the large pylon at the far end of the field. Wellington boots are essential, as to get to the well you will need to cross over to the far side of the stream (via - if you're lucky - some conveniently placed stepping stones).

Tread carefully, as it can get very boggy there in winter! The best time to visit is during the dryer seasons. Cattle have trodden down and *mashed up* the surrounding earth near to the well; in winter this becomes a quagmire, whereas in summer the deep hoof printed soil is baked into the consistency of a concrete minefield!

WHAT IS STAR WELL? It is a freshwater spring in the side of the hill that flows into the nearby stream which makes its way toward the River Avon at Lacock via the Pudding Brook near the Pheasant roundabout in Chippenham. Starwell has suffered from its popularity, as damaged and displaced blocks of masonry indicate that the well once had a stone surround and a drinking trough. The remnants of many of the displaced *shaped* blocks can still be seen scattered in the stream nearby.

WHAT CAN YOU FIND THERE? If you are lucky, you might find some tiny star shapes which give the spring one of its names. The stars are the tiny isolated stem parts (columnals) of crinoids, a plant-like sea-creature commonly known as a sea lily and related to starfish. To extract the fossils you have to sift the sand at the bottom of the stream near to the well, by filtering the icy cold water through your fingers until the stars appear - much like panning for gold. These fossils are carried to the surface and deposited in the silt bed of the spring after being freed from the underlying rock by the water. You may need to spend some time sifting about in the freezing cold icy water and will need good eyesight.

WHY IS IT SO SPECIAL? This most magical of Wiltshire wells has a mysterious atmosphere surrounding it, (hopefully not created by the large overhead buzzing electricity cables!) Local legend says that the stars are fossilised elderflowers.

The seventeenth-century, Wiltshire antiquarian John Aubrey noted; *"East of Bitteston, there is a spring - they call it a Holy Well, - where five-pointed stones doe bubble up (Astreites) which doe move in vinegar."* (Aubrey 1969).

If you place the stars in a bowl and place a drop of weak acid, such as vinegar over them, the liquid will bubble. This happens because a reaction causes a little bit of the calcite to break down, releasing the carbon dioxide gas bubbles. If you put the calcite stars in a bowl of vinegar, they will actually move around and bubble before they dissolve. It is also said that during a full moon, fairies and water nymphs appear in the Starwell hollow, dancing and singing to the whispering wind. The well was also a possible *stopping off* point on the pilgrimage route to Glastonbury which came westwards through Biddestone towards Corsham.

Heather and Robin Tanner make the following passing reference to the well, in their mystical book of 1967 called 'Wiltshire Village': *"Starwell is in the parish of Stanley Fitzurse, though it is nearer to Kington Borel. The field in which it lies has been nicknamed Starveall on account of the poverty of its soil, but the corruption has some justification, for in the water are found tiny fossilised starfish."* Note: Starveall Farm is nearby just to the north of the well along Chippenham Lane towards Biddestone.

IMPORTANT ACCESS INFORMATION: There is no right of way or public footpath across this marshy field. You should ask the nearby Stowell Farm owner's permission to enter his field before you visit. Do not walk to this location along the country lane, as it is very dangerous. If you need to park your car, do so safety at the crossroads down one of the side roads. If you have children, please be very careful, as cars using this lane seem to think that it is a Formula 1 racing circuit. Respect the countryside and do not leave litter or create any damage and be aware that this field is often inhabited by cows and sometimes man-cows!

Chapter 48. Stické Tennis Court at Hartham Park.

If you go to the end of Middlewick Lane in Pickwick and look north-west, across the valley to the left of Hartham House, you'll see the Grade II huge wooden listed Stické Tennis Court building on the skyline. The court was built in 1904 at Hartham Park for Sir John Dickson Poynder (later Lord Islington) and it is a rare building type of which only a few survive. Its architectural detailing and decoration is of a high quality design and craftsmanship.

The building of the court at Hartham Park coincided with late-C19 improvements to the gardens and it was built in a piece of woodland on the edge of the pleasure grounds. A decorative rustic style was adopted, built around a pre-fabricated timber-frame with decorative split log cladding (Larch). It has more then a hint of a Swiss chalet about it.

This is one of only three remaining Stické Tennis Courts, two of which are in England (i.e. at Hartham and Knightshayes Court in Tiverton, Devon); the third court is in Shimla, Himachal Pradesh (India). There were at least 39 courts originally built throughout the British Empire from 1875. The game started at almost exactly the same time as lawn tennis; sharing the same scoring system and rules, but, as is the case at Hartham Park, with a slightly deflated ball. The only difference is that Stické Tennis is effectively lawn tennis played inside a huge box with sloping walls around you and it is played indoors!

It is conjectured that Stické's origins lie in the Scientific School of Gunnery (est'd 1859) at Shoeburyness, Essex, somewhere around the early 1870's at almost exactly the same time as lawn tennis began. Reportedly, the game became known as 'Shoeburyness-Stické' – and later it became shortened to Stické! In the 1800s, the Souls' a social group of aristocrats, politicians and writers, embraced Stické because it was played by men and women and built on the principle of 'balance' – whereby no side gained advantage by following a particular tactical approach.

From the 1880s Stické tennis became a popular sport amongst the affluent and was played by both sexes. It is fairly easy to play and the rules are simple. The name stické comes from Sphairistike, which in ancient Greek means "to play with a ball". This was soon abbreviated either to sticky or to the mock-French stické. The ball is only allowed to hit the floor once, even after it has rolled along the sloping penthouse walls (which are about 9ft high), hit another wall, and come off the back wall behind you and onto the floor, making it extremely difficult as there are so many surfaces that the ball can roll off.

Following The Great War, the weakened economy brought the social whirl of English Country House parties to an abrupt end; the Second World War pretty much spelled the demise of Stické Tennis.

Corsham has a Stické tennis Club, details of which can be gained by contacting Hartham Park. The centenary of the court's building was celebrated in 2004, with a competition between players from Hartham Park, the other usable court in the UK, Knightshayes, and invited guests. Part of the building has recently been converted into a gymnasium for the staff who work in the offices at Hartham Park.

It's a beautiful building and yet another gem for us to be proud of here in Corsham.

Below is a photo of the inside of the Hartham Stické Tennis Court.

Many thanks to Allan Bosley for his help in producing some of this chapter.

Chapter 49. Telephone Exchange.

Goodness knows how someone in Swansea ended up with rare photos of one of the first telephone 'Call-Offices' in the back of Spackman's shop in the Corsham High Street in 1905 - but here it is, *folded* out of what looks like an old packing crate, and stored in amongst the Spackman grocery shelves and sacks of oats at the back of their High Street shop!

In March 1905 Corsham Parish Council were informed that the National Telephone Company had decided to open an exchange at Corsham and the district Manager Mr. Pike from Trowbridge, would be getting the necessary wayleaves and permits required etc.

The first telephone exchange for public use in Corsham was subsequently opened on 3rd October 1905, after the employees of the National Telephone Exchange Co Ltd (NTC) had been busy at work for many weeks installing Corsham's first Telephone Exchange, by scaling the poles and putting the telegraph wires in order.

The main exchange was *fitted up* in the converted front room of 8 Paul Street at Mr Townsend's house *(for annual rent of £16.10s)* and was manned by an operator. A *public* telephone was fitted near to the front door. The long expectant 17 Corsham subscribers, who first appeared in the NTC directory dated January 1906, were no doubt looking forward to using their new *'candlestick'* telephones. To call the operator, they had to turn the hand generator, hence the term – 'RING UP' the operator.

To supplement and link into the main exchange in Paul Street, several *'Call Offices'* were set up at convenient places in the town; one of those was at the rear of Spackman's grocery shop, where UltraWarm is today in the High Street. These *'Call Offices'* were used largely by the general public, with *Proprietors* offering their facility as a service - with the view of obtaining new customers!

The first telephone users in Corsham are listed below:

Public Call Offices: 1. J Barnes Stationer High Street. 2. National Tel. Co. 8 Paul Street. **Private Subscribers:** Barton W. Land Agent Corsham Estate Office: Beszant W.H. Butcher High Street: Brakspear H. Architect. High Street: Butt. Alf. Tailor/Breeches Maker: Carter F. Builder Stokes Road: Corsham Quarrying Co. Quarry owners: Fuller GP. JP. Neston Park: Fuller JMF. MP. The Jaggards: Gane PJ. Land agent Pickwick: Goldney Sir John T. Monks Park: Poynder Sir John Dickson Hartham Park: Poynder Sir John Dickson Estate Agents Office: Spackman Lewin High Street: Spackman & Son Drapers/Grocers High Street: Yockney & Co Quarry owners.

In 1915 the Telephone Exchange Manger at Paul Street was James Hancock.

On 3rd March 1922 there were 53 subscribers, with 60 telephone sets connected.

In 1928 the Parish Council discussed asking the Post Office to erect the first Public Telephone Kiosk in Corsham. The annual expense would be £15, of which the Council would be asked to guarantee a maximum of £8 for a period of seven years. No further action was taken at this stage.

In December of 1930 a communication from the R.A.C. sent in by Field-Marshal Lord Methuen was submitted to the Parish Council Meeting. It stated that a permanent point-duty man and a telephone box had been arranged to be installed at the Cross Keys crossroads.

In 1930 Mr. E. Borman, Head Postmaster, presented Mrs. Hancock with an eight-day clock with a brass plate engraved. 'Presented to Mrs. Hancock by the Post Office Staff, Chippenham, 18/8/30', accompanied by the following letter:

'Dear Mrs. Hancock, I am very pleased to hand you this clock as a small token of appreciation from the telephonists, engineering staff, assistant superintendent and myself, on the termination of your services as caretaker-operator at the Corsham Exchange. We trust it will be a pleasant reminder of your long association with the telephone staff over the last 20 years'.

In 1933 the Police Telephone Number was Corsham 7. The Ambulance Corsham 60; and the Labour Exchange Corsham 52.

On the 30th September 1936 the exchange became automatic with a Unit Automatic Exchange (UAX) fitted. At the same time, the exchange moved to the new purpose built building at the end of Alexander Terrace. By this time there were 277 subscribers and 335 telephone sets connected. By 1956 subscribers could dial directly, plus 999 for emergency services and the speaking clock were now both available.

Corsham has another historical telephone exchange in the 'Burlington Bunker'. It was built in a series of rooms contained within the worked-out chambers of a former Bath stone quarry. The exchange was adapted to be used in the underground environment at a government facility alongside Spring Quarry in the mid 1900s - the Central Government War Headquarters (CGWHQ). This exchange was built as part of a defence against the peril from the threat of nuclear strikes from Russia that Britain faced during the Cold War.

The rooms were fitted out to provide a telecommunications facility, *(known as Woodlands)* including two telephone exchange operator consoles and a supervisor desk in one area, and a number of rooms to the rear with plant and racking containing the associated equipment required for a telephone exchange.

This underground exchange is now designated as a Scheduled Monument and is the only known telephone exchange of its type. Some pieces of equipment, such as the Automatic Telegraph Exchange, are thought to be the only surviving examples of their type.

The Exchange system appears to have been operational and regularly tested until 1992. Thankfully, the CGWHQ underground complex was never needed or used for its intended function and was reduced in capacity over a number of phases during the late 1900s.

The underground site was de-commissioned in the early 1990s. It was de-classified in 2004.

Chapter 50. Temperance Hotel, Corsham.

The definition of temperance in English: Abstinence from alcoholic drink. *[The Oxford Dictionary meaning, including self-restraint, restraint, moderation, self-control, self-discipline, lack of indulgence, teetotalism, abstinence, abstention, sobriety etc.*

Where was the Temperance Hotel? *Corsham* was once home to a fairly prominent Temperance Hotel, situated immediately opposite the Flemish Weaver's Cottages at the end of the High Street. The hotel comprised of two adjoining buildings; Nos.75 *(built circa 1740)* and 77 High Street *(Caxton House, built probably late C1805 on an earlier core),* both are fine examples of Grade II listed buildings. The post code is SN13 0HA.

Temperance Hotels were mostly a nineteenth century phenomenon in the UK, encouraged by the temperance movement which professed to supply no alcoholic liquors for its customers. Even later from 1830 to the outbreak of the Second World War, the control, or even the total abolition of the liquor trade was a major political issue. The temperance movement has almost completely vanished from view now. The first temperance societies appeared in the USA in the 1820s. The idea soon crossed the Atlantic; societies were formed in Belfast, Dublin and Glasgow during 1829, and in February 1830 the first English Temperance Society was formed in Bradford.

Caxton House has belonged to several families over the years; Mr Harrison, Taylor, Bradbury, Lewin Spackman printer (see photo), Cockeram, and Emma & Stephen Heaney who are the current owners in 2018. It has had many uses over the years, including a livery supplier, stationer, printing (Caxton Printing Works) and a dry cleaning business (Kilmisters).

In 2004 Caxton House underwent an upgrade that allowed its original features to be restored and highlighted, which included renovating the wooden floorboards, exposing timber beams, stone walls and revamping the stunning cast iron windows. To the rear of the property, is a lovely high walled courtyard with raised flower beds, summerhouse and an old privy which is used for garden storage.

The building is now a charming fronted residential house which has been very tastefully restored in keeping with this picturesque part of Corsham. No. 79 High Street, the building to the right of Caxton House, is reputed to be the oldest house in Corsham, dating from before 1540.

Temperance was a trait revered in Victorian Society. If you look carefully between the right-hand (upstairs and downstairs) windows of the 75 High Street building, you can still see the faded letters, **'TEMPERANCE HOTEL'**. The lettering is gradually fading away each year, and it will not be long before another gem of our 'unknown' Corsham disappears completely.

[Saturday 25 June 1892 Wiltshire Times and Trowbridge Advertiser]: A Temperance Meeting was held in the Corsham Town Hall on Tuesday 25 June 1892. Addresses were given by Messrs. E. Spackman, C.W. Churchill and H.J. Lucas. A resolution declaring that all places licensed for the sale of intoxicating drink should be closed on Sundays, was carried with acclamation!

In 1906 on 9 October at the annual meeting of the Woman's Union of the Bristol Diocesan Branch of the C.E.T.S., held in the Mansion House, Lady Methuen said; *'The great evil of the present day was over excitement. Everything was being carried to excess, and the want of self-control, particularly amongst the young, was very noticeable. They wanted temperance in all things; not only in what they ate and drank, but in other things as well. If they were more temperate and made their children more temperate and the young ones who were always with them, they would help to create this spirit of self-control which was so very important and which ought to be one of the first duties they taught to the young.' [Applause].* "I'll drink to that!" [Ed].

Many thanks to Emma & Stephen Heaney for their contribution.

Chapter 51. Thingley Junction Rail Crash.

The 'Dart' No. 70 Engine overturned at Thingley Junction 16 January 1907

A collision took place between two trains on a clear night at 7:12 p.m. on 16th January 1907 at Thingley Junction near Easton, Corsham on the Great Western Railway.

Fifty-three year old Charles Powell, the driver of the 6:30p.m. (Engine 70) four-coach passenger train containing about 20 people, from Westbury to Paddington (via Chippenham and Swindon), failed to stop at the red *home* signal at Thingley Junction, resulting in a head-on collision with the 5:05p.m. down-line Swindon to Pymouth, a 43-wagon goods Engine 2448, driven by forty-nine year old Robert Butt.

The drivers and firemen of both trains were injured with bruises and burns, the worst cases being those of the goods train fireman James Kryan and driver Butt who sustained severe scalding of hands and injuries to his head and scalded legs. Thankfully, Driver Butt was able to resume duty on 26th Aug 1907. Three other servants of the Railway Company who were in the passenger train were bruised. Five passengers were injured, one seriously. A total of 12 people were hurt.

The engine of the goods train turned over onto its side, whist the passenger engine managed to stay upright on the line, along with three of its four coaches. The front five wagons of the goods train were derailed and piled up on each other; the next 11 remained on the rails but piled up in a remarkable fashion.

The junction at Thingley is an ordinary junction, with a slight curvature. The signals are all well placed and well elevated so as to be easily seen by engine drivers. The two trains approached Thingley at the same time about 7:12, with all the signals being at danger.

The signalman Frank Stokes, decided to give the goods train the preference. Whilst passing over the junction, it was run into by the passenger train, then travelling about 10 miles per hour. The goods train was travelling between 15 to 20 miles per hour.

The passenger train had failed to stop at the *up-line* home signal which was set at danger! Charles Powell, the engine driver of the passenger train could not explain how he had missed the clear danger signals, even after previously receiving a 'Warning' from the Melksham signalman, that the junction at Thingley was *blocked*.

The driver excused himself, by saying that he must have been attending to the *injectors* of his engine and failed to see the two signals. An *injector* is a simple, if unlikely sounding device that was invented by the Frenchman M. Giffard in the 1850s. It uses a jet of steam, from the boiler to force fresh water back into the boiler, heating it up in the process. It has virtually no moving parts and is thermally very efficient and widely used on steam locomotives.

At the enquiry, driver Powell stated that he had completely missed the distant signal and also the home signal until he was right on top of it. Even if he had seen the home signal, the passenger train (consisting of only four coaches) could easily have been brought to a stop along the slightly rising gradient as the junction is approached.

Although the Signalman Frank Stokes at Thingley Junction, acted in accordance with the current 'Warning Arrangement' regulations for Thingley Junction where the first train to present itself would be allowed to proceed, perhaps he could have acted with more prudence.

Maybe he should have waited for the passenger train to actually stop, before allowing the goods train to proceed; but he could hardly have anticipated that Powell, the passenger train driver would completely ignore and miss his two danger signals which clearly indicated that he should stop.

The primary cause was 'driver error' by the passenger train driver Charles Powell.

Previous to this, the only other serious accident to occur at the Thingley Junction, was on the 5th November in 1875 during a similar occurrence, when one train ran through a red signal and crashed into a passing train, causing the guard to be killed and 12 passengers injured.

Chapter 52. Toilets - at your convenience.

CORSHAM, CARRY ON AT YOUR CONVENIENCE!

The Corsham Parish Council was created in 1895.

During one of its first meetings of that year, Lord Methuen's agents were not very happy about a proposal to build a men's' urinal in Station Road near to the entrance of the cricket ground; as they felt that the local pubs already met the need! Nevertheless, an agreement was reached on 14 November to go ahead with the building, much to the 'relief' of the 'Sanitary Committee', and no doubt, to the male population of Corsham!

Originally, the building was not much more than a tiny *lean-to* with a flat roof and a simple gouged out trough at the bottom of the wall. It was not until forty years later in 1936, that a closet cubical was added onto the Station Road urinal - and even that was not a *big job*!

In September of 1901 the owners of the Carpenters Arms in Corshamside were asked to find a solution to block off their outside public urinal from being exposed to the viewing public passing by on the thoroughfare, i.e. to stop men relieving themselves in full view of onlookers!

In 1908 the Corsham Police had to deal with *improper* unspecified use of the Station Road toilets! It was agreed that a lamp should be made available near or over the new convenience, not only to deter any inappropriate use, but also to presumably aid direction and to minimise any splashing of the men's shoes! The walls were whitewashed twice a year and an automatic flushing tank was provided for use during the summer months to keep the dreadful *stink* of men's urine at bay!

For those of us who remember using the *'Station Road bogs'*, the permanent stink is forever etched into the linings of our nostrils! I swear that you can still smell that *pong* when you walk past there even now! [Ed]

Thankfully, the Station Road urinals have long since disappeared and were subsequently incorporated into part of the large new Cricket Club pavilion building.

In 1909 an enamelled sign costing 17s 6p was erected by the Parish Council stating:

CORSHAM PARISH COUNCIL -
One pound reward will be given for information leading to the conviction of any person using, writing or drawing on, or otherwise damaging any part of this public urinal -
BY ORDER.

I doubt if the Parish Council/Police ever caught anyone, as the lurid graffiti continued to appear.

In 1912 the urinals in the Great Western pub at the bottom of Pound Pill were exposed to public gaze and had to be redesigned! During WWII in 1940, the police were asked to prevent men urinating on the Town Hall sandbags as they were deteriorating fast and would be of no use at all in an air raid!

In 1942 there was a renewed hope for more public toilets to be built in the town. The site behind the Town Hall was rejected in favour of one of the Parish Council's preferred options; in the Mansion House garden, in Post Office Lane or in Church Street.

In 1944 there were more complaints about men urinating in the streets of Corsham. This is not surprising, as the only convenience for men was the *(now flushing)* tiny Station Road facility. The ladies did not fare much better, as they had to make do with a single *closet* in the Town Hall.

During the Saturday Dance Nights in the Town Hall, (where up to 250 people would turn up) the queues for the *single closet* were longer than the queue for tickets!

In 1945 inadequate facilities in Corsham for the relief of full bladders continued for yet another year. At Christmas, Miss Coats had agreed to allow the Council to lease one of her buildings in Post Office Lane which could be converted into a public convenience!

Seeking relief for full bladders continued until March 1946, when a tender was put out by Mr. H.B. Coats, Clerk to the Corsham Council, for the conversion of the Air Raid shelter at the bottom of the Recreation Ground to be converted into a Public Convenience for children, i.e. a B*oys and Girls loo* with a drinking fountain placed outside on the front (see following photo). And for those of us who can *'smellmember'* the stink inside those dark and narrow (and somewhat frightening) narrow corridors, it even surpassed the Station Road pong!

The Recreation Ground loos (see photo) used to give children the collywobbles, as they were very scary places. [Ed] As children, we would never venture into that maze of stink; rather, we boys *peed* around the side of the Girls entrance!

The only use we children made of that building was to clamber up onto the roof and then jump down like Superman (or Zorro) onto the grass! You only entered them if you were wetting yourself. The old loos along Post Office Lane were not much better! [Ed].

In 1948 pennies were getting stuck in the newly installed Ladies toilets in Post Office Lane, and *unmentionable objects* were blocking the WCs on the Recreation Ground! A caretaker was appointed to look after the renovated toilets in Station Road and the new *Gents* and *Ladies* loos in Post Office Lane. On Saturday's, the caretaker was *paid time and a third!* ;-)

The two photos above, show the old toilets in Post Office Lane.

In 1969 the children's conveniences at the bottom of the Recreation Ground were greatly damaged by vandalism and (thankfully!) had to be pulled down.

In 1967 the following three *replacement* sites for the Station Road loos were considered; behind the existing loos, by the Bowls Club or in the corner of Grove Field - all failing to materialise.

But provision was already planned to provide new toilets in the newly built shopping precinct; where today they stand ready to be used and sparkling clean in the corner of the Newlands Road car park.

Chapter 53. Turnpike Road to London - The Great Bath Road.

When the London to Bath turnpike road was established in the 1600's, it split into two when it reached Beckhampton *(which lies between Calne and Marlborough)* a little beyond the eighty-fourth milestone from London. One route went west via Calne, Chippenham, Corsham and Box, and the other south-west via Devizes, Melksham and Atworth. The Bath road was measured from Hyde Park Corner and is a hundred and five miles and six furlongs in length. The distance to the Cross Keys in Corsham is ninety-seven miles from London. In those days, Hyde Park Corner was on the very western fringe of London and in the early eighteenth century, Londoners would have considered this to be in the countryside! At that time, Bath was the most fashionable place in all of England. Crowds of invalid or mentally afflicted people would travel to Bath seeking a cure in its spa waters. The road to Bath must have seen quite a regular throng of Bath Spa visitors passing through Corsham.

When the south-west route reached Chippenham, the horse-drawn coaches were not able to traverse Chequers Hill *(now the long established A4 route)* as it was too steep and in those days was not much more than a short-cut muddy farm track to Corsham. Instead, a quarter of a mile to the south of the present A4 route, the turnpike road took the less tortuous route to Corsham from the Pheasant; i.e. roughly 200 yards along the B4528 Saltersford Lane *(by the side of the large blue Herman Millar building)* over the Pudding Brook at 'Salters Ford' and then right along Easton Lane *(past the Brunel Builders Yard)* and then parallel *(along what is now a footpath/bridle path)* a quarter of a mile south of the current A4 road to Chequers Hill. When you walk along this particular public stretch of the old turnpike road from Easton Lane to Chequers Hill, you can still see parts of the original road surface of crushed stone. It's like going back in time!

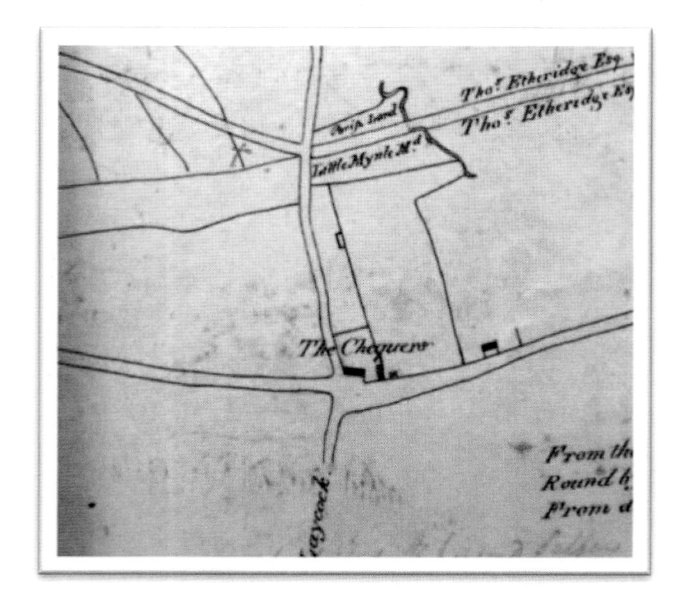

The road travelled past the isolated 'Old Road Cottages' to Mynte Lodge opposite the massive gated piers which were once the entrance to a Carriage Drive leading to Corsham Court. This is also where the original *Chequers Inn* used to be before it opened in another building lower down on the crossroads a quarter of a mile away. The Carriage Drive went west through Mynte Wood for about a quarter of a mile before veering left (south) to go past the Boat House on Corsham lake, and then sweeping *right* along the trajectory of the current footpath which skirts the southern Corsham Park boundary alongside the Lacock Road, and on to the park gate near St Bartholwmew's.

The old turnpike road skirted to the right of the gate piers and ran west, just outside the north boundary of Mynte Wood and then on to the Cross Keys. From the Cross Keys the turnpike road separated; the lesser branch passed through Pickwick village (on the A4 route), the other route went *behind* the Cross Keys Inn along a descent cutting across the Hartham Park fields, straight across to Hartham Church, past the end of Middlewick Lane in Pickwick, past the Hillsgreen Lodge cottages and alongside Pickwick Lodge Farm, and then out through what is now the disbanded RAF Rudloe Manor site at the top of Box Hill. From here at the top of Box Hill, the early turnpike road's route to Bath was not via the current A4 route down Box Hill into Box, but via Chapel Plaister and Kingsdown *(know as the Blue Vein route).*

Apart from two *private* sections of the old turnpike road between: (a) the Cross Keys/Hartham Church and to the end of Middlewick Lane, and (b) Pickwick Lodge Farm to the top of Box Hill, it is still possible to walk on *(or at least to be right alongside)* the old London to Bath turnpike road route from the Pheasant pub in Chippenham to the top of Box Hill near Rudloe. It's a fascinating walk that takes you all the way back to the 1600/1700s, as fragments of the original crushed-stone turnpike road still remains visible in the Easton Lane to Checkers Hill section. It's not difficult to imagine the mail coaches from London rattling along over the bumpy stone surface and throwing the passengers about as they hung on for dear life!

The responsibility for maintaining the turnpike roads lay with the parishes that they ran through. All parishioners were obliged to either perform a stint of labour or to provide horses and carts for use in repairing the roads. The large hidden open quarry *(known locally as Tin Pan Alley - see Chapter 38*) in the copse immediately behind the Cross Keys Inn *(an area previously know as Brickers Barn)* and the old quarry hidden in *Prestley* woods behind the Hillsgreen Lodge cottages would have been used to provide the crushed stone for the turnpike road surfaces in Corsham.

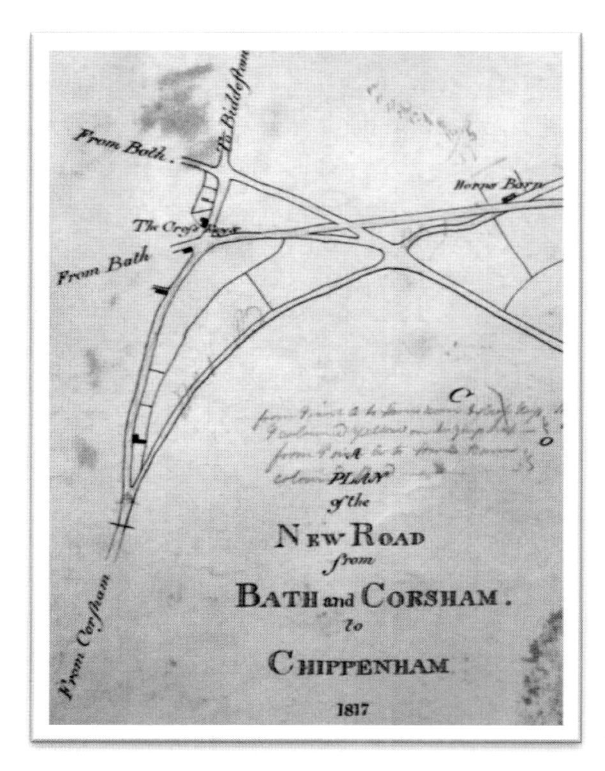

1657: The first stagecoach travelled the turnpike road from London to Bath. It took three days, commencing at 5 o'clock in the early morning! They were known as the *slow-coaches*. Passengers paid a fare of one Pound five Shillings each.

1713: The road to Bath past Chapel Plaister and Kingsdown, was trurnpiked and was now the main route into Bath.

1716: The first daily coach from London appeared.

1737: It took two days to get from London to Bath. The horses had to be changed every eight miles or so. Hence the Hare and Hounds in Corsham became a main staging point from Bath to London *(on the alternative route through Pickwick)*. The following advertisement appeared in the Daily Advertiser, in April 9, 1737*; 'For Bath. A good Coach and able Horses will set out from the "Black Swan" Inn, in Holborn, on Wednesday or Thursday'.*

1744: The road from Chippenham to Pickwick was *turnpiked* i.e. you had to pay to use it.

1756: After lengthy opposition from landowners and existing trusts, a new direct route from the Cross Keys, through Hartham Park, to Box and Batheaston Bridge was established by the Corsham Brickers Barn Trust *(along the current A4 route down Box Hill)*. Prior to this, the main route to Bath from Corsham, was via Chapel Plaister and over Kingsdown.

1778: Highwayman John Boulter, who hid with his gang in Chapel Plaister and robbed travellers if they went over Kingsdown, was caught and hanged on 19th August. He was nicknamed 'The Flying Highwayman', whose very appearance was terrifying; a tall, swarthy man with a thick scar on his cheek, the result of bullet which tore the skin off his forehead and burning his left eye during a thwarted robbery (see Chapter 18)**.**

1784: The price for sending a letter via the fast mail coach was two shillings. This was very expensive compared to the normal cost of sending a letter by *snailcoach* at four pence to places 80 to 100 miles away. It was Robert Palmer, the proprietor of the Bath Theatre who drew up a scheme two years previously, for a mail coach to carry four passengers inside, a coachman and a guard, and to be drawn by four horses at a rate of between eight and nine miles an hour. He argued that the journey from Bath to London could be accomplished in sixteen hours, including stoppages to change the horses at five inns along the way. Robert Palmer's idea came to fruition on 2 August, when for the first time, the Mail Coach travelled the whole distance all the way from London to Bristol in one day. To help achieve this, mail coaches were given an exemption from turnpike tolls, which enabled them to speed through the notorious and numerous *Toll House* bottlenecks.

1787: On 25 January Bath Chronicle: John Prichard, landlord of the (now destroyed) Red Lion (near to the Methuen Arms) *'begs leave to inform his friends and the public, that his house is commodiously fitted up for the reception of Gentlemen Travellers, and others; has laid in a choice assortment of Old Wines, and other liquors; and by rendering the accommodation as reasonable as in his power, and proper attention to the guests, he hopes to give general satisfaction to all those who shall be pleased to honour him with their commands. N.B. Corn and Seeds on the lowest terms'.*

1792: *Page 485 Wiltshire Archaeological Magazine Vol. L*: On December 24th, 1792, the Trustees of the 'Blue Vein' Turnpike Toll in the parish of Box met at the 'Red Lion Inn' Lacock and the Tolls of that Gate were sold by what was known as *'Auction by the minute glass'*, i.e., a sandglass like an egg-boiler that took only sixty seconds to pass its contents from one bulb to the other. The auctioneer proceeded on these lines. When he received his first bid, he placed the minute glass before him on the rostrum, and as the sand ran through, the prospective bidders watched it closely.

If, before it had exhausted itself, another bid was made, the glass was turned over and the operation repeated until no further bid was received during the fall of the sand. It will be realised with what keenness that last passage of the sand was watched, above all by the maker of the latest recorded bid. The lucky bidder had to keep the Tollgate and house in good order and repair. The lot included the tolls, fines, and forfeitures for evading tolls, with the free use of the tollhouse and gate for collecting the tolls. The agreement lasted for one year, and the price paid for the 'Blue Vein' lot, was £500. It was bought by Isaac Nichols of South Wraxall.

1796: Gunner John Baker was sent home to recover after narrowly escaping drowning when his frigate *Diomede* was wrecked off the coast of Trincomalee in Sri Lanka. On the final leg of his journey back home, he was killed when the Bath to London coach capsized at Reading

1800: It now only took one day to get from London to Bath.

1803: Just before his work had come to an end in Corsham in 1803 and as part of the Corsham Park development, architect Humphry Repton diverted the London to Bath turnpike road. A new road section *(now the Cross Keys Road)* from the Cross Keys into Corsham Town, amounted to 1091 yards. Mynte Wood was enlarged and new boundary dry-stone walls were laid to encompass what is now known as the Withy Bed wood opposite the Cross Keys pub and opposite the top of Bences Lane. Folly Farm and its land then became part of the park *(ref: Map of the Manor of Corsham, 1806; Corsham Parish Plan, 1820),* and a new park wall was built further north. Formerly, in the mid C18, Folly Farm then situated outside the park wall, was screened from the park by a plantation. The latter was removed by Humphry Repton, who made the farm into an *eye-catcher*.

1812: It cost nine pence to send a letter between London, Bath or Bristol.

1815: By now, the various coaches were competing on how quick they could travel the distance. The first coach to be named in this spirit was the 'York House' from the York House Hotel in Bath, then came the 'Beaufort Hunt' from the White Lion which managed a steady speed of 11 miles an hour, but their over-zealous drivers managed to overturn the coach twice in a fortnight!

1816: When outside passengers were introduced, they had to endure the perils of the road in winter and foul weather. When the road was one yard deep in snow, one traveller recalled that, *'Had it not been for the stiff doses of brandied coffee at each stage, I would never have been able for these words to have been written'.*

1821: Mail coaches were now reaching an average speed of eight and three-quarter-miles an hour, including stoppages, completing the distance from the General Post Office in London to Bristol in fourteen hours. This was the peak of the coaching era when there was fifteen or sixteen day and night coaches running between London and Bath.

1829: Mr Gurney's steam-car was the first automobile to travel along the bumpy turnpike road at a rate of sixteen miles an hour from London to Bath. They used the southerly Devizes route when it branched off at Beckhampton. Whilst passing though Melksham, they were stoned by an angry mob, loudly denouncing the unruly contraption! The high Kingsdown route was replaced with a lower-level new road *(now the A365)* from Blue Vein to Box, where it linked *(at the now Box traffic lights)* into the new (1761) A4 road into Bath.

1835: The original turnpike roads were only one lane wide, and disputes very often happened when coaches and wagons met head-on in a narrow part of the road! So to prevent disputes, a legal penalty was imposed for failure to keep to the left in the face of oncoming traffic. This still applies today.

1836: The Duke of Wellington had to be dug out by labourers on the Marlborough Downs when the great snowstorm resulted in fourteen to sixteen feet of snow falling on that exposed stretch of the turnpike road. In another incident, when one of the stage coaches reached Chippenham it was noted that three of the outside passengers had died of cold and many others suffered from frostbite.

1837: A conveyance document of this time, described the part of the route between 'Hartham Corner' *(at Hartham Estate Church in Hartham Lane)* and 'Rudloe Firs' as an 'ancient turnpike road or common highway' named the 'Hills Green Road'.

1838: On June 4, the Great Western Railway reached Slough, with the turnpike coaches completing the journey by road from there to Bath.

1840: The railway reaches Reading.

1841: On June 30 the railway reached Bristol and the turnpike roads became deserted. Traffic on the roads drastically reduced and the turnpikes quickly began losing money. Mail was now carried by train and the turnpike road mail coaches ceased.

1843: The last through-stagecoach from Bristol to London made its final journey.

1846: *Devizes and Wiltshire Gazette, 3rd September, 'NOTICE is hereby given, that the TOLLS of the Pickwick, Box, Blue Vein, and Lacock Gates and Side Bars hereto belonging, will be LET by AUCTION, to the best bidder, on Tuesday the 8th day of September next, at the METHUEN ARMS INN, in Corsham, between the hours of 12 and 2 o'clock, for one year, from the first of October. The Tolls will be put up in one lot, and at such sum, and subject to such conditions as the Trustees then present shall think proper. Whoever happens to be the best bidder, must pay down one month's rent, and give security with two sufficient sureties, for payment of the rest of the money monthly, in Advance. Robt. Hulbert, Clerk to the Trustees.'*

1849: In the late 1840s huge sales were held of the old turnpike road coach horses, coaches, post-chaises and pieces of harness. Many unwanted vehicles never found a buyer.

1853: A valuable freestone quarry in full and working condition situated at Pickwick adjoining the turnpike road and known as *'Woodsman's Quarry'*, together with the cottage and outbuildings standing on the same close, now occupied by Mrs. Mary Norris was put up for auction at the Methuen Arms on Wednesday 16 November.

The stone quarry is of excellent quality, easily worked at a small expense, and its proximity to the Turnpike Road offers great facilities in the Sale and transit of the stone. Mrs Mary NORRIS passed away at 92 years of age on 6 February 1871 and is buried in the Corsham Churchyard.

1864: On 1st July turnpike gates were abolished and responsibilities for road maintenance were handed over to the elected local councils, financed by the ratepayers.

1867: It seems even in those days, accidents did happen on the road from time to time, as shown in the Salisbury and Winchester Journal: *'The waggoner, according to the plaintiff's statement, was sitting in the head of the wagon, and had no reins so as to exercise proper control over the horses, but there was a little boy walking alongside the leader. The plaintiff called out to the waggoner to let him pass and after a little time the waggoner drew his vehicle a little to the proper side, but just as plaintiff was passing at the turn leading to Giddleton, the horses in the waggon, not being under proper control, dashed round the corner of the road at the junction with the Sodbury and (Corsham turnpike road) and coming into collision with the dog-cart, threw it violently over. The plaintiff and his wife were both thrown out, and both were very much injured. The plaintiff himself had one of his legs broken in two places, and the broken bones protruded threw the skin when he was taken up. One of the wheels of the waggon passed over Mrs. Leonard's shoulder, and it was so near passing over her head that a quantity of her hair was torn off by the wheel and ground into the mud on the road. The plaintiff was confined to his bed for seven weeks, and was unable to attend fully to his business for seven months afterwards. His wife was also much injured, and disabled for a very considerable time'.*

1870: The Corsham Trust, an amalgamation of the Brickers Barn Trust (i.e. Cross Keys) and the Blue Vein Trust (i.e. Kingsdown) was wound up. The Toll Houses at Pickwick and Kingstown were sold for £50. The Toll House in Box which was obstructing the main street was pulled down. The Bath Road began to revive with the growing popularity of the bicycle. In August, two cyclists (Gardener and Fisher) completed the journey of 107 miles both ways along the crushed stone road in five days.

1880: Wat Britten riding an *'ordinary' (better known as the penny-farthing)* cycled the whole length of the London to Bath road in 23 hours. This was an amazing feat at the time, considering the variable crushed-stone road surfaces and on a contraption that was nothing more than a simple tubular frame with hard rubber tires.

1887: Pneumatic bicycle tyres became available, and women's bicycles started to appear.

1891: On August 1, R.C. Nesbitt travelled the distance both ways in 15 hours, 40 mins. 34 seconds.

1897: On October 30, F.W. Barnes cycled the double journey in 11 hours, 48 minutes.

1900: The speed limit for cars was 12 m.p.h. and reduced to 8 when passing though towns.

1908: The spraying of tar on roads commenced, with the London to Bath Road being amongst the first to be treated. The old white roads turned to black!

1920s and 1930s: The current A4 from London to Bath and Bristol was finally built in total.

1936: The London to Bath road was classified as a trunk road, thereby losing its old historic name, (The Great Bath Road) and has since been known as the A4.

1958/59: When the town of Corsham was beginning to recover after demolition of the wartime prefabs by rebuilding a modern town, the Architects on behalf of the District Council put together proposals for the A4 to be diverted through Hartham, roughly in line with the original Turnpike road, bypassing Pickwick completely and joining up again at the top of Box Hill. This was the proposal to extend Corsham's inner built-up boundaries. Many liked the idea, but the *powers that be* thought it far too ambitious at the time!

1971: When the M4 was opened throughout its length in December, the A4 was no longer classified as a main route, and was de-trunked; although it is still a very busy road today.

2015: It now takes 90-120 minutes to get from London to Bath! It takes about 3+ hours to walk the old turnpike road from Chippenham to 'Rudloe Firs' at the top of Box Hill in Corsham! 'Our roads, in general, are so fine, and our speed has reached the Summit'. *John Byng, The Torrington Diaries, June 1791.*

2017: The section of the old Turnpike road that runs from the Hillsgreen Lodge Cottages at the top end of Middlewick Lane to Pickwick Lodge farm was resurfaced with builder's gravel. Albeit that this stretch of the road is now flat and much easier to walk along, it's a shame that the old turnpike road's crushed stone surface that has been visible for 400 years has now disappeared and been lost.

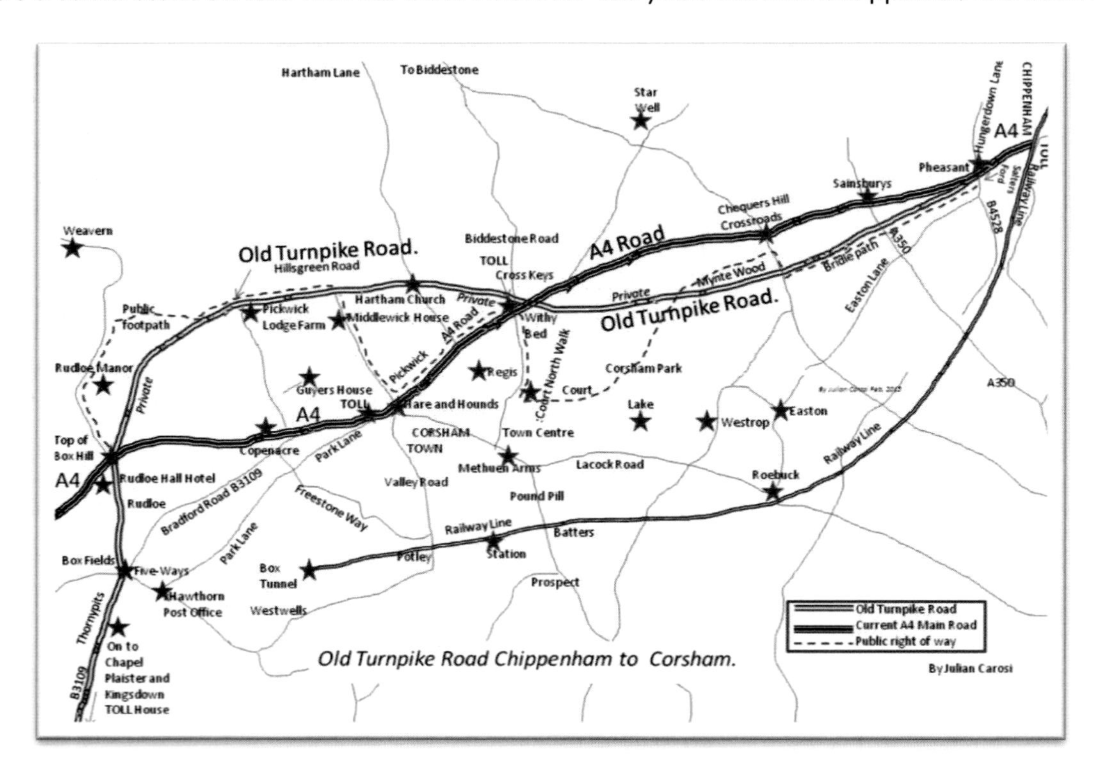

Old Turnpike Road Chippenham to Corsham.

Chapter 54. Weavern Farm.

Weavern Farm, deep in the bottom of Box Valley sits in the Corsham Parish on the boundary line of the *Bybrook* - also known as the *By Brook* stream (and locally known as *Box Brook* or the *Weavern* downstream of Weavern Farm). The brook is a tributary of the Bristol Avon and is some 12 miles (19 km) long. In its prime, there were twenty watermill sites along the Bybrook course but none now remain in use. In Roman times, the mills were exclusively used for grinding corn but by the end of the 12th century this part of Wiltshire became an important centre for the wool trade.

With the decline of the woollen industry in the 1600's, accelerated by Civil War and plague, many mills returned to grinding grain and *fulling* finally ceased when steam power shifted cloth making to the north in the Industrial Revolution. *Fulling,* also known as tucking or walking (spelt *waulking* in Scotland) is a step in the woollen cloth making process which involves the cleansing of cloth (particularly wool) to eliminate oils, dirt, and other impurities, and making it thicker. The worker who does the job is a fuller, tucker, or walker, all of which have become common surnames. *Fulling* involved beating the cloth with hammers to wash it using fuller's earth as a soap to thicken the material.

The rise in demand for paper for packaging from nearby Bristol led to many mills in the 18th and 19th centuries converting from grinding grain to paper making. Although some of these reverted back to local corn grinding. Paper producing was a feature of the Bybrook valley well into the 20th century. The existence of so many mills on such a small brook caused many inter-neighbour disputes about water level management and use of resources; some of these resurface today.

The photograph above, shows *Weavern Farm* probably sometime in the early 1900s with cultivated allotments to the side and cows grazing in the meadows. Although the farm and mill were closely associated for centuries, only the old derelict Weavern Farm buildings remain. The mill buildings have long since disappeared, with only the sluice gate opening in its original location to the left side of the farm, hinting of the lost era of the mills.

The name *Weavern* is a corruption of *Wavering*, by which the meandering Bybrook was known at this location, although the name could equally refer to the process of cloth-weaving. The stream runs in a south westerly direction through the shallower valley in front of Shockerwick House, before joining the Bristol River Avon at Bathford at a point adjacent to the main railway line from London and the A4 road.

It's very easy to see how the alluring beauty and isolation of Weavern has tempted so many failed ventures (as listed below), with initial attractions eventually being defeated so many times by the remoteness and inaccessibility that somehow seems to protect its beauty for the rest of us. One hopes that *'Mr Developer'* never gets his hands on Corsham's Weavern gem and that it's left in peace to mature and shine as an everlasting haven of beauty for all of us to enjoy.

1332: The farm was occupied by William De Vevere.

1536: The earliest mention of the mill in the *Wiltshire Historic Environment Records*, names it as *Weversmylle*.

1538: Occupied by John Smythe, father of Thomas 'Customer' Smythe.

1580: Robert Burgis, a clothier at Veverne (Weavern) Mill died there. In his will, he left his son John a bequest of 10 shillings.

1603: At the end of the Elizabethan era, three mills were said to be housed under a single roof at Weavern, an *ancient fulling* mill, one *recent corn* mill and one *recent fulling* mill; the last two were listed in 1608 when they were surrendered to the Baillife family. Being so close to Castle Combe it is possible that the Weavern mill was involved in making the famous red and white cloth of Castle Combe which was renowned in the markets of Bristol, Cirencester, London and abroad.

F*ulling* continued there for another century when John Browning married Alice Scott, daughter of Chippenham clothier Walter Scott, but the industry was in deep decline as the old trade moved north with the changes introduced in the industrial revolution.

1728: The Weavern mill was owned by the Dukes of Somerset, probably as part of their Trowbridge estates and let to tenants, who would have had to work hard to make a living there.

Fulling mills were established by Sir John Fastolf in Castle Combe along the Bybrook, in the thirteenth and fourteenth centuries, originally supporting a thriving woollen industry. With the continuing decline of the woollen industry in the 17th century, now accelerated by the Civil War and plague, many mills returned to producing grain once again. Fulling finally ceased when steam power shifted cloth-making to the north in the Industrial Revolution. The rise in demand for paper for packaging from nearby Bristol led to many mills converting to paper-making in the 18th and 19th centuries.

1742: John Browning *(who had married Alice, daughter of Chippenham clothier Walter Scott in 1711 at Heddington,)* together with Francis Child, leased Weavern Mill, from the Duke of Somerset.

1769: The mill is advertised for sale.

1793: Now a paper mill, a 'For Sale by Auction' advertisement appears in the *Kentish Gazette, 7 June 1793*, describing Weavern as an excellent two-vat paper-mill, occupied by John Butler. *'An excellent two vat paper mill with water wheel and outbuildings with orchard and grounds called Weavern Mill. Capable of making the finest paper. At present in the occupation of Mr John Butler. Is held for a term of eight years. The landlord repairs the property.'*

Paper-making was a very valuable industry in the Georgian period as literacy became more-widely available. The process was very similar to *fulling* with hammers beating wood pulp and rags to merge and stiffen the fibres. This required considerable power to break down the wood and it was vital that the stream's current should be strong, especially over summer months.

There are numerous references to the strength of the Bybrook at the site: *An unceasing water supply ... fit for manufacturing the finest writing paper (1831). A never-failing supply of spring and river water (1820).* The water power was not a natural occurrence and the leat *(excavated water course)* at the west (left) end of the buildings was strengthened to produce more water power.

1794: The paper-mill was equipped with two engines.

1802: The Deeds of Paper Mill, in the Wiltshire History Centre show that the Weavern paper mill was now owned by Charles William Wyndham when he was Member of Parliament for New Shoreham, Sussex. This was at the time when a peace treaty had just been signed after the French Revolutionary Wars and Charles Wyndham lost his seat in the ensuing general election. The lease of the mill changed hands to Henry Garner, papermaker, at a rent of 17s.4d, a heriot *(death duty)* of £5 and a goodwill cost on entry of £550. Henry Garner was the tenant of the mill for the next 20 years. He was 52 years old when he took over the mill and he was an important person, much respected.

1820: Henry Garner was 68 years old, his wife had died five years earlier and he wanted to retire from work. He offered to sub-lease the farm to anyone interested. The mill struggled to find anyone to lease or to buy. It was subsequently taken over by his son, also named Henry Garner.

1823: The Bath Chronicle and Weekly Gazette *(published on Thursday 01 January 1824)* noted the death of the much respected Weavern farmer Henry Garner of Weavern on 21st December 1823, aged 71 of the Weavern Paper Mills. Henry Garner was also a Deacon of Corsham Chapel.

1828: The 73 acres the riverside dairy farm known as Weavern Farm is up for sale via auction again on 13 July at the Angel Hotel in Chippenham.

1831: The mill was put up for sale in Lots by Henry Garner junior on 3 January. The farm and mill buildings, barn and three cottages together with 13 acres of pasture, arable, orchard and woodland were offered as one lot, with four pieces of arable land amounting to 25 acres as the other lots.

1834: The Excise Records show that Weavern mill had ceased work by 1834 and the leat *(the constructed millstream)* had become disused. Thereafter, milling activity was superseded by farming in the buildings.

1851: Twenty-two year old Thomas Henly was farming the 57 acres there, using three labourers to help him.

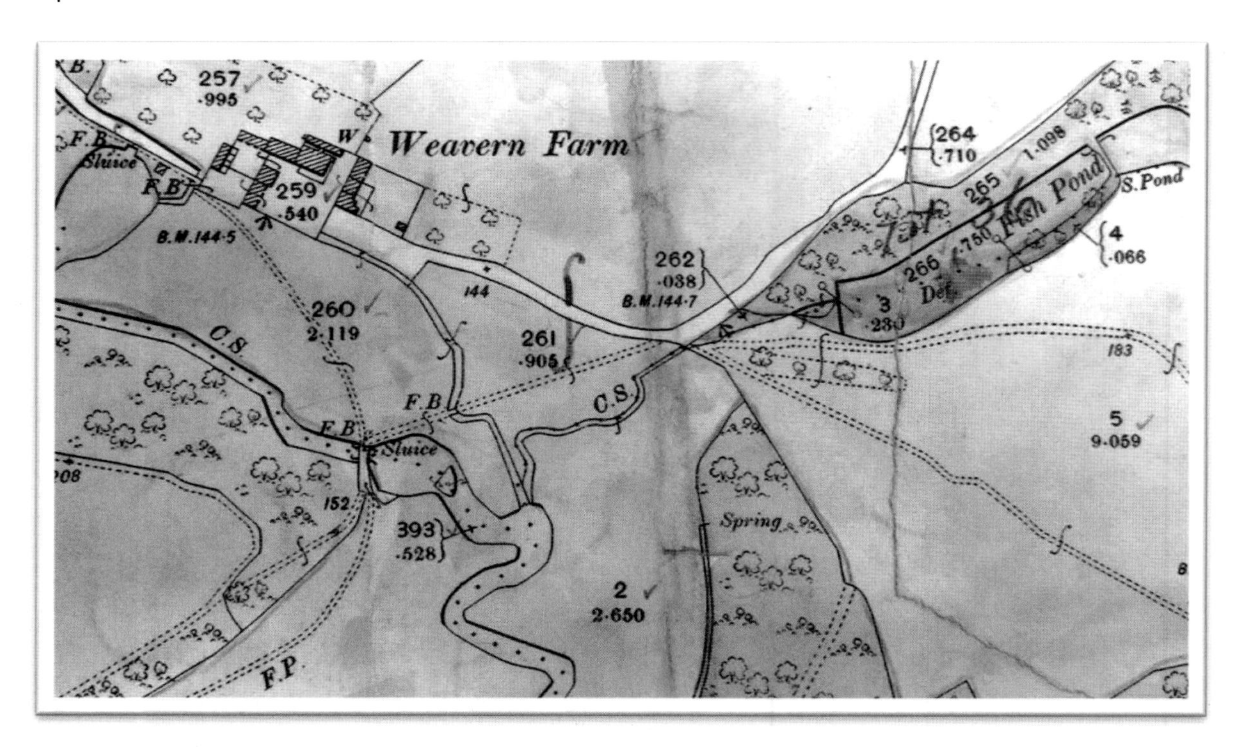

Above is an old map showing the original Fish Pond (top right) which is now completely overgrown.

1853: Thomas Henly's venture seems to have failed, as the mill was now advertised *To Let* along with Pickwick Lodge Farm.

1861: The property is listed as uninhabited in the 1861 census.

1871: The North Wiltshire Online Census Project 1871, shows the farmer to be 39 year old John Bence.

1878: James Wright had another go at farming there. Neither of the above two attempts worked, possibly because the land was waterlogged for much of the time.

1881: The Poulsom family moved into Weavern Farm and they ran it for the next thirty years. Joseph Poulsom, a butcher and farmer of 44 acres from Velly, Corsham, had married Jane and they had two sons, Henry and Charles William Green Poulsom. Henry was the elder and he took over Weavern in 1881 with his wife, Lucy Sophia, twelve years his senior.

When Joseph died in 1885 his widow, Jane, continued farming in her own right at Ridge Farm, Linleys, Corsham, looking after two of her children, daughter Mary and son Charles William, and her grandchild Percy James.

Charles William took over Ridge Farm on a tenancy from the Neston Estate and was running a dairy and arable business there in 1939 until his death in 1947 when his coffin was carried on a farm cart pulled by his favourite horse named *Duke*.

The 1881 Census of England and Wales show the occupants of Weavern Farm as:

Henry Poulsom, head, married, 26, farmer 72 acres, 2 men, born at Corsham.
Lucy Sophia Poulsom, wife, married, 38, farmer's wife, born at Chippenham, Wiltshire.
Percy James Poulsom, 3 months, born at Weavern in 1881 and who later married Laura Augusta Milson, daughter of the late Thomas Etwell Milson of Manor Farm, Hinton, Trowbridge.
Ellen Ann Sargent, servant, 10, general servant.
Stephen Jones, servant, unmarried, 26, a labourer indoors, born at Corsham.
James Baker, servant, unmarried, 16, a labourer indoors, born at Colerne.

1896: Henry Giles, a young man from of Hudswell, was fined for carrying a gun without a licence, and firing it at a rabbit on Mr Poulsom's farm in Weavern. He was fined 5s.

Sunset at Weavern, Near Corsham.

1898: A 1909 postcard depicting the *Weavern Fish Ponds* was sent to Miss Curtis, at The Hold, Mollington, Banbury. On the rear, was written the following comment. *'I have been visiting 2 weeks. This is a view of Hartham Fish Ponds & where the old clergyman drowned himself.'*

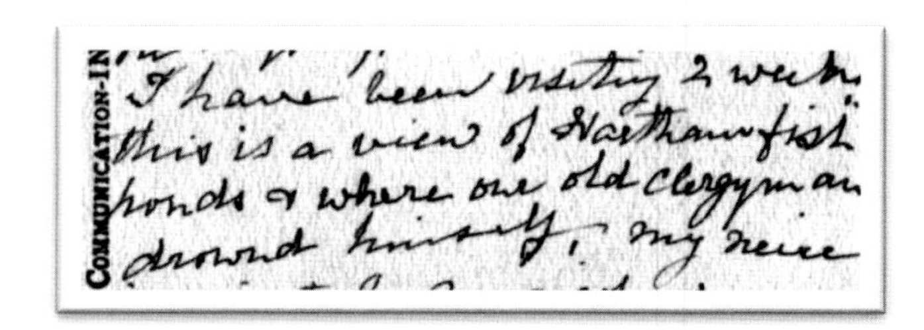
COMMUNICATION-IN

I have been visiting 2 weeks
this is a view of Hartham fish
ponds & where one old clergyman
drownd himself, my niece

Further investigation has revealed the following, as reported in the *Bristol Mercury Wednesday 26 January 1898 - 'THE RECTOR OF BIDDESTONE FOUND DROWNED. Considerable excitement was caused in the village of Biddestone and Slaughterford, near Chippenham (the Rev J.A. Johnstone), had been found in the fishing pond, in Weavern Wood, over a mile from his residence. It appears that the deceased gentlemen, who is about 65 years of age, has been about 16 years at Biddestone, is a single man, and left the rectory about 7:30 the previous evening, and about eight o'clock was discovered by a man in Sir John Dickenson Poynder's employ in what is known as Weavern Pond. The body was in an upright position. An alarm was raised, and the body was got out and taken to the Recotry, where an inquest will be held. Up to the present there is nothing to show how the deceased gentleman came in the pond.'*

On Wednesday 02 February 1898 the Newspaper: *Bath Chronicle and Weekly Gazette* reported the following:

'An inquest was held at Biddestone Vicarage on Thursday, by Mr. Coroner Browne, on the body of the Rev. J.A. Johnson, late vicar of Biddestone and Slaughterford, whose body was found in a pond on Tuesday morning last, Mr. J.C. Otway identified the body and said the deceased was aged 61. He last saw him about two months ago, and he was then in fairly good health.

Annie Griffin, a domestic in the deceased's employ, deposed that he left the house at about 7.30 on Monday night. Alfred Tylee, a labourer on the Hartham estate, proved finding the body in the pond between 8 and 9 o'clock on Tuesday morning, and with assistance got the deceased out. Dr. Wood, of Corsham, who had known the deceased for many years, said he last saw him about three weeks ago; he was then cheerful and bright. He had attended him professionally for attacks of suppressed gout. The Coroner, in summing up, said the case was a very painful one, and there being no evidence to show that the deceased intended to take his life, he suggested that the jury return an open verdict of "Found Drowned" Verdict accordingly'.

The Rev. J.A. Johnson who was unmarried, had been the Rector at Biddestone for 16 years and formerly a curate at Hempsted, Gloucester for many years. He was also a member of the local District Council.

1901: The state of Weavern Bridge was in a bad state of repair. The farmer, who leased Weavern from Sir J. Dickson-Poynder, was told that he was responsible for repairing it.

A letter from Mr Phillips, agent to Sir J. Dickson-Poynder, passed a letter to the Rural District Council stating that as the Weavern Bridge had been in existence sine 1780, there was no liability for Sir J.

Dickson-Poynder to pay for any repairs, as it had never been repaired by him, or any previous owners of Weavern Farm as it was a public right of way. It was resolved to refer the matter to the County Council.

The 1901 Census of England and Wales, show the occupants of Weavern Farm as:
Henry Poulsom, head, married, 46, farmer, employer, born at Corsham.
Lucy Poulsom, wife, married, 58, born at Sevington, Wiltshire.
William Poulsom, son, single, 18, farmer's son, worker, born at Biddestone, Wiltshire.
James Cornforth, lodger, married, 24, worker, born at Yorks.

1903: In May, the Rural Council refused to pay for repairs to Weavern Bridge, stating again that it was the farm owner's responsibility.

1911: The Poulsom family had given up farming at Weavern and Henry Poulsom was now boarding with William and Catherine at Rudloe Park Lodge.

The Biddestone census shows 48 year old William Bird *(Semington)* is the Weavern farmer along with 28 year old labourer John Norris *(Malmesbury)*. This was followed by a succession of different tenants and owners.

1914-15: Thomas Daniell was the occupier.

1918: The Hartham Estate puts the farm up for sale by auction.

1921: E.K. Symons sold the farm for £2,300.

1923: Jesse Mitchell was farming there.

1927: Miss Rosa S. Preston was a tenant there for a short period.

1928: The farm of 73 acres was once again for sale on 13 July with vacant possession.

A very rare 'Spackman' postcard taken at the approach to Weavern Farm.

1929: The farm was eventually bought by Miss Preston. By this time, the premises were gradually run down. The *Wiltshire Times of 28 December*, reported that the body of Mrs. Emily Charlotte Hazell of Ford, aged 55 was found by Frederick Ernest Gillard, employed at the Slaughterford Paper Mill. He had found his missing mother-in-Law in the water at the Luddsmead hatches in the Weavern river. She had gone to bed with her husband William Hazell at about 8 o'clock and he awoke to find her missing at 2:45a.m. She had disappeared after complaining of pains in her head. The previous evening, she told her husband that*, "She had such a bad headache, that she was inclined to jump in the brook!"* The coroner recorded a verdict that she had drowned herself.

1930: A new cowshed/barn is erected to the far left/west of the farm buildings. A plaque showing the date still remains visible on the side wall.

1955: On *January 5th the Wiltshire Times and Trowbridge Advertiser* reported that the *Avon Vale Hunt* killed a *tired* fox near to Weavern Farm by the river!

1956: On the 10th April some children entered into the uninhabited premises and lit a fire on the floor boards and set the barn alight! When the Fire Brigade arrived under Charlie Davis' supervision, it was burning *'well away'*, but it was soon under control. The new fire engine only just managed to get through the narrow lanes to the farm! The site today is in not much better condition, with a fine complex of buildings now derelict and in danger of collapse. And access just as bad, if not worse!

1950s: Prior to the opening of the eight-lane heated open air swimming pool in Monkton Park Chippenham, most of Corsham's residents learnt to swim in what was known as the *'Penny Pool'* next to the Weavern Bridge; where the most daring swimmers would jump straight off the bridge and into the icy cold water below! The pool was deep enough to swim in, and even these days, can have a fast moving current. It was also glorious place for children to paddle in and to play on the large sandy corners of the meandering stream! Weavern is such a beautiful place, that it was also once very popular for Corsham's Sunday afternoon picnickers, with whole families regularly feasting there at weekends.

1970s: The derelict farm buildings set deep in the valley alongside the murmuring stream, adds to the magical ambiance of the place. Weavern Farm and the stream were fenced off, prohibiting public access. The only *paddlers* these days are the herds of cows that have made a bit of a mess of the *(now)* muddy banks. A public footpath now takes you over the bridge and away from the farm.

Access to the site is either from Biddestone along the narrow Weavern Lane, or much better still, via the top of Box Hill on the A4 near Rudloe in Corsham, by walking down the lane into Box valley, past the *No Notion* cottages, and down the dirt track which meanders through the *Larches and 'Collet's Bottom' woods* to Weavern Farm. It's quite a steep descent and even steeper on the way back. If you take the latter route down and as you get to the end of the track, take a peep through the wood on your right, as you can still just about see the original old Stew Pond that once provided fish for the nearby Hartham Park Estate and where the Rector Johnstone drowned himself in 1898. You can still see this Stew pond on old Ordinance Survey maps. The old pond is now almost completely overgrown with trees and bushes, but if you look carefully, you can still see the walls that were built to retain the water at the lower end. A Stew pond or *Stew,* is a fish pond used to store live fish ready for eating. A new Stew pond has recently been built a little to the south/west in the privately owned *'Collet's Bottom'* woods.

Many thanks go to Verity Jeffery (Atworth) and to Boxpeopleandplaces.co.uk for their help in compiling some of this chapter and to the Chippenham & Swindon History Centre for some photos.

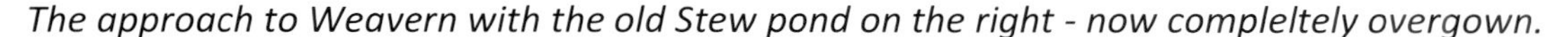

The approach to Weavern with the old Stew pond on the right - now compleltely overgown.

Chapter 55. Whores Pond.

If you walk up Monks Lane in Gastard and past Monks Chapel towards the Ridge, you will come to a sharp right-hand bend in the road. Nestled in the corner there, is the *Whores Pool*.

The pool was also once known as *'Green Emma's'* and the local name *'Whores Ground'* was once shown on a farm map. In recent years, children also called it the *'Witches Pond'*. A 1366 list of Corsham tenants includes the name *'Joan the Hore'*.

In 1594 several Corsham women of ill repute were taken to the pond and 'ducked' one-by-one. They were strapped into a 'ducking stool', consisting of a stool balanced on the end of two very long shafts with wheels at one end.

The *'ducking stool'* enabled the crowd of locals who had taken it upon themselves the task of executing punishment, to submerge the women down several times under the water, without getting wet themselves. The screams of the poor women who were ducked would have been frightful.

The victims were retrieved by pulling down on ropes that were attached to the upward ends of the two shafts. The *'cucking stool'* later became a chair for *'ducking'* the offender in a pond, but the old name was sometimes preserved. Repeated 'duckings' routinely proved fatal, with the victim dying of shock or drowning.

It certainly was not an experience that any perpetrator who survived would wish to repeat!

The *'ducking stool'* was previously known as a *'cucking stool'* which was essentially a *'stool of repentance'*; in most cases, a wheeled wooden commode seat or toilet, placed in public view, upon which the targeted person was forced to sit - usually by restraint, and often being paraded through the town.

The 'cucking stool' was used for women only: men suffered the pillory which in Corsham was sited at the left-hand corner of the Town Hall where the Town Hall bench is *nowadays (see the old drawing)*. Any Corsham landlord watering down his beer would have had a stint in the pillory here. In years gone by, the Whores Pool has been troublesome regarding overflowing of the road alongside.

In an 1882 report, it was recorded that *'clap'* stones (stepping stones) were placed along the road by the Whores Pond when it flooded and then staked to one side in the dry seasons.

As recently as 2011 the pool was drained to try to remove blockages that were stopping natural drainage and causing further flooding.

Now, it is a beautiful spot where it is almost impossible to think that such inhuman punishments may have once been performed there.

Chapter 56. Acknowledgements.

I wrote this book for you, so that I could share my love of how Corsham is what it is today. The detail has been gathered together from many sources over the last decade. Firstly, a big thank you to my proof reader Susan Duparcq who *dotted all the i's and crossed all the t's* for me (xjjx) and to Chris Perry of Corsham Printing, to Stephen Flavin for some nice old postcard photos and especially to all those at the *Chippenham and Swindon History Centre* for helping me delve deep into their comprehensive book, record and newspaper archives. And lastly to James Methuen-Campbell (the eighth generation of the Methuens to live at Corsham Court) for his sage advice and knowledge.

This is a self-publishing book and not a commercial enterprise. Below is a list of sources for which I am truly grateful. I have strived to be meticulous in my recording of detail - and can only apologise if anyone is missed out. The listing is roughly in alphabetical order! **Thank you, to all of you [Ed].**

100 Years in Corsham Parish by Peter Henderson. : A Life Revealed. From the Diaries of Herbert Spackman - By Ernest Hird. : Admiralty Records Division 25 - ADM/188/92/87260 National Archives. : Albion Gold Flake Cigarette card No.5 in the 'Cricketers' series. : Allan Bosley. : Almshouse - The Lady Margaret Huungerford Almshouse and Free School Corsham, 1668-1968, by Ernest Hird. : Ancientmonuments.info. : Architects at Corsham Court by Fredrick. J. Ladd. : Around Corsham and Box by Annette Wilson and Mike Wilson. : Around Corsham by the Corsham Civic Society. : B. Litt thesis. Unpublished (Oxford, 1950). Baacorsham.co.uk. : Bath Chronicle and Weekly Gazette. : Bath Chronicle. : Bath Freestone Workings by Liz Price 1984. : Bath Herald. : Bbc.co.uk/history/. : Beyond Bat & Ball' by David Foot. : Biodiversitylibrary.org. : Bluebell Railway Locomotive Dept News. : Boxpeopleandplaces.co.uk. : Brief Account of the Making and the Working of the Great Box Tunnel by Thomas Gale. : Bristol Mercury. : Bristol Mirror. : Britain from Above website www.britainfromabove.org.uk : British Listed Buildings. : British Newspaper Archive. : Burke's General Armoury Coat Of Arms. Encyclopedia of Heraldry, General Armory of England, Scotland, and Ireland - John Burke. Burke's General Armoury 1878 page 500. : Bystander magazine. : Castlefacts.inf. : Castlesandmanorhouses.com. : Cheltenham Chronicle. : Chippenham and Swindon History Centre. : Colwick Woods Nottingham City Local Nature Reserve. : Corsham - An Illustrated History parts 1 and 2 by C.J. Hall. : Corsham Born and Bred by Stephen Flavin. : Corsham Church by Harold Brakspear 1924. : Corsham Civic Society. : Corsham Commemorates WWI. : Corsham Court. : Corsham F.C.'s Southbank Review Program 26 Aug. 2017. : Corsham Facts & Folklore. : Corsham Parish Minutes. : Corsham Parish Plan, 1820. : Corsham Parish Registers Reference: PR/Corsham: St. Bartholomew/1157/1. : Corsham Spotlight Newsletters of the Corsham Civic Society. : Corsham Vestry Minutes dated 5 April 1877. : Corshamheritage.org.uk. : Corsham's Two Test Cricketers. By David Smith. : Country Life. : Cricketworld.com. : Dave Andrews. : David Haynes. : Deeds of Paper Mill, Wiltshire History Centre. : Defra.gov.uk. : Dennis Williams. : Department for Culture, Media and Sport. : Devizes and Wiltshire Gazette. : Devizes Gazette. : Devizes Museum. : Doomsday Book. : Dorset and Wiltshire Fire and Rescue. : Dr Marta Mirazon Lahr: (Director of the Duckworth Laboratory, Leverhulme Centre for Human Evolutionary Studies, Department of Archaeology & Anthropology, University of Cambridge. : Eighty Years of Cricket. A brief history of Corsham Sports Club 1848-1928' by H.S. Lakemam. : Eileen Cook. : Emptages of Thanet. : Encyclopedia of Heraldry, General Armory of England, Scotland, and Ireland - John Burke. : English Heritage's Record of Scheduled Monuments No. 19044. : Environment Agency - History of the By Brook by Ken Tatem. : FIFA. : Flying Highwayman of the West by Tinhead. : Flying Highwayman of Wiltshire. By Maureen Jolliffe, and updated by Jodi Fuller June 2014. : Frank Rowbotham Foster. : From Blackpool to Bungelows' by Julie Davis 2016. : Gazette and Herald. : Gentleman of the Road - Thomas Boulter Highwayman of Poulshot. Devizes Carnival 1976 booklet. : Ghosts & Legends of Wiltshire Coutrside by Kathleen Wiltshire. 1973. : Gleanings from Wiltshire Parish Registers. Wiltshire Records Society. Edited by Steven Hobbs. : Global Nonviolent Action Database. : Google Books. : Gov.uk. : Haunted Places of Wiltshire by Rupert Matthews. 2004. : Healthline.com. : Heaney - Emma and Stephen . : Historicengland.org.uk. : History and News website. : History Learning Site. : History Military and Municipal of

the Ancient Borough of The Devizes, by James Waylen, 1859. : History of Hazelbury Manor Box Library Ref: BOX333. : History-Magazine.com. : HistoryToday.com. : James Methuen-Campbell: (Corsham Court). : Jane Browning. : Joe James. R.I.P. : John Aubrey (1969). Aubrey's natural history of Wiltshire 1847 edited by John Britton. : John Bosley's memories. Box PC. : John Buonarotti Papworth. : John Cuthberstson - Corsham F.C. : John Gale - Corsham Cricket Club. : Journal of the Brewery History Society - Andrew Davison. : Journey of the Railway and Canal Historical Society No. 142. : Julie Bryan. : Kate Jones of Church Farm, Corsham. : Kate Tyte: (Natural History Museum in London). : Kathleen Crisp. : Keith Shacklford. : Kentish Gazette, 7 June 1793. : Kevin Gaskin. : Kieran Aust. : Kingswood Abbey and Wortley, Addenda et Corrigenda by E. S. Lindley 1958, Vol. 77 : Lansdowne MSS. (No. 827). : Leamington Tennis Court Club. : Lease Indenture 1728. : Library - Corsham. : Local Ghost Stories complied by Margaret Royal and Ian Girvan. 1976 : Louise King: (Archivist. Museums and Archives, The Royal College of Surgeons of England). : Map of the Manor of Corsham, 1806. : Maps.nls.uk. : Matilda Talbot - My Life and Lacock Abbey. : Maureen Elliot.: Megalithic.co.uk. : Michael Sythes.: Mick Walsh R.I.P. : Mike Lyons Editor - Box Parish Website. : Mike Slater. : Mills Archive. : MoD Corsham Wiltshire Values Study. : Monks Chapel History. : MonksChapel.com/. : Moonraker Firemen (of the past) Wiltshire, by Peter Thorpe. : Morning Chronicle London. : Mynte Farm map including field names. : National Botanical Gardens of Wales. : NationalArchives.gov.uk/. : New York Times Living History: World War II: The Axis Assault, 1939-1942. : Nicholas Keyworth - Former Osborne House owner and music composer. : Nick McCamley, Subterranean Britain. Second World War Secret Bunkers. : Norman Duckworth. : Norman Price. : Old-maps.co.uk. : Oswald Brakspear. : Owen Directory, 1878. : Paranormal Database. : Pastscape.org.uk. : Paul Richardson. : Peter Hayes. : Railways Archive. : Rev Colin Gordon-Farleig's online blog. : Revolvy. : Richard Morling. : Rob Kruszynski: (Curator, anthropology collections, Department of Earth Sciences, Natural History Museum in London). : Rudloescene.co.uk/ by Paul Turner. : Salisbury and Winchester Journal. : Scots Guards in the Great War 1914-1918 by F. Loraine Petre, Major-General Sir H. Cecil Lowther and Wilfred Ewart 1925. : Somerset Archaeological and Natural History Society. : St Patrick's online history page. : Steve Higgins of www.higgypop.com : Subterranea Britannica. : Subterranean Britain. Bath Stone Quarries. By Derek Hawkins. : Swindon Advertiser and North Wilts Chronicle. : Taking Stock - Catholic Churches in England and Wales. : Tanky Elms. Bath Stone Quarryman. Compiled by C.J. Hall. : The National Gallery. : The Wartime Memories Project - The Great War - Hospitals. : Thirty Years Afloat Abroad by Thomas Skuse. : Tim Unwin. : Times Newspaper. : Tony Wilkins. : Topographical Survey of the Great Road from London to Bath and Bristol, by Archibald Robertson. : The Bath Road by Charles G. Harper. : Trip Advisor. : Verity Jeffery - Atworth. : Visit Corsham. : Warminster & Westbury journal and Wilts County Advertiser.: Ways of Corsham by John Poulsom R.I.P. : West Gallery Music Association. : Western Daily Press. : Western Flying Post, Sherborne and Yeovil Mercury. : Wikipedia. : William, Henry Fox-Talbot - Correspondence of. December 1835. Doc. No. 04392. : Wilts and Gloucestershire Standard. : Wiltshire and Swindon Historic Environment Record. : Wiltshire Archaeological and Natural History magazines. : Wiltshire Community History. : Wiltshire Council. : Wiltshire Forefathers by June Badeni.: Wiltshire Gazette. : Wiltshire Independent. : Wiltshire Machine Breakers Volume I: The Riots & Trials. : Wiltshire Times and Trowbridge Advertiser. : Wiltshire Times. : Wiltshire Village published in 1987 by Heather and Robin Tanner. : Wiltshire.gov.uk. : WiltsUnitedChurches.og.uk. : Woods Hole Historical Museum in Woods Hole, Massachusetts. : Worcestershire Chronicle. : Workhouses.org.uk. : World Health Organisation (WHO). :

NWELYAMAID?

Chapter 57. The Author.

My name is Giuliano (Julian) Carosi; I was born in the Greenways Hospital Chippenham in 1952 and have lived in Corsham all my life. My father Francesco was an Italian prisoner of war who loved this country so much that he decided to stay here after WWII. He met and married my Italian mother Fiorenza (Enza) here in England and they set up their first home at 2 Wardle Road, in one of the old prefab bungalows just behind the Hare and Hounds. I have two brothers, Domenico Roberto, and Claudio Angelo and three lovely daughters, Melanie, Isabella Lucia and Sofia Francesca. And two lovely grandchildren George Dalibor and Ella Lucia.

I studied English at the Corsham School and later at Chippenham College. The old black library hut behind the Fire Station *(see Chapter 22)* was a favourite haunt of mine as a young child. This is where I became enchanted with a love of the written word. The *Famous Five* books by Enid Blyton were one of my favourites in those days and this is where my sense of adventure was kindled. Now, it is Charles Dickens and all of the other Classic novels of the Victorian era.

For a number of years, I was the Editor of the national Referees' Association magazine *'Refereeing'* and nowadays I run a local Facebook page called *'Mr. Corsham'* where I encourage discussion on Corsham's history with the members. I am now retired after a long career as a civil servant working in several Government departments in and around and *deep underneath* Corsham.

I live near the cricket field in Corsham with my dear partner Susan Elizabeth - and we have just finished renovating our lovely bungalow. Hence the dream we all have of writing a book is now here!

My interest in the history of Corsham began after winning the, *'Know Your Corsham'* history competition in 1979 *(see Preface for more details).* Since then, I have been gathering facts and stories for many years and discovering the many hidden places during my love of walking along the many public footpaths in and around Corsham. I feel as though I've covered just about every square inch of Corsham in my long years - above and below ground!

I once thought that Corsham was a sleepy little town with very little history of mention. How wrong I was. In this book, my aim is to share just some my findings with you. Hopefully there will be more?

I hope that it changes the way you perceive our little town. It did for me!

If you would like to contact me, I would love to hear from you.

Email me at: *juliancarosi@corshamref.org.uk*

Regards,
Giuliano (Julian) Carosi
2018